BY BERNARD BECKERMAN

Books

Shakespeare at The Globe (1962)
Dynamics of Drama: Theory and Method of Analysis (1970)
Theatrical Presentation (1990)

Shakespeare editions

Troilus and Cressida. Co-edited with Joseph Papp (1967)
Love's Labor's Lost. Co-edited with Joseph Papp (1968)

Other editions

On Stage: Selected Theatre Reviews from The New York Times, 1920–1970. Co-edited with Howard Siegman (1973)
Five Plays of the English Renaissance (1983)

Theatrical Presentation:
Performer, Audience and Act

Bernard Beckerman

Edited by Gloria Brim Beckerman and William Coco

ROUTLEDGE

New York and London

Theatrical Presentation is dedicated to Bernard Beckerman's students: those who knew him onstage, in the classroom or at the seminar table; those who knew him as Bernie, as Dr. B., as professor and as friend.

First published 1990
by Routledge;
a division of Routledge, Chapman and Hall, Inc.
29 West 35th Street, New York, NY 10001

Simultaneously published in Great Britain by Routledge
11 New Fetter Lane, London EC4P 4EE

© 1990 Gloria Brim Beckerman

Printed in England by Clays Ltd, St Ives plc

Library of Congress Cataloging-in-Publication Data
Beckerman, Bernard.
    Theatrical presentation: performer, audience and act /
Bernard Beckerman; edited by Gloria Brim Beckerman and William Coco.
    p. cm.
Includes bibliographical references.
1. Performing arts—Philosophy.   2. Theater.   3. Acting.
I. Beckerman, Gloria Brim.   II. Coco, William
III. Title.
PN1584.B4 1990
791'.01–dc20 89–24188 CIP

British Library Cataloguing in Publication Data
Beckerman, Bernard
Theatrical presentation: performer, audience and act.
1. Theatre
I. Title   II. Beckerman, Gloria Brim   III. Coco, William
792

ISBN 0–415–90280–0
ISBN 0–415–90281–9 (pbk)

Contents

Foreword

Gloria Brim Beckerman

Theatrical Presentation examines the intrinsic elements which appear in all shows, from vaudeville to *Nicholas Nickleby*; from fireworks, to parades, to dance. Expanding the views he introduced in *Dynamics of Drama*, Bernard Beckerman presents here a unified theory of dramatic performance. He reveals the nature of the theatrical event by considering all its constituent elements—actor, writer, director, designer, etc.—in relation to the audience.

The subject matter and observations in this book are the sum of a lifetime of thinking about and working in the theatre. Even before his ninth birthday, Bernard Beckerman was involved in theatrical activity. Although shy, he directed, wrote, and produced one-act plays in school, in his parents' Bronx apartment and during the summers in an anarchist community in New Jersey. When I, at 15, told him I admired Boleslavsky he, then 17, lent me his copy of the *master*'s work, *An Actor Prepares*.

He enriched his active participation in theatre by reading plays, books on dramatic theory and theatrical history (Artistotle, Barrett H. Clark, and everything written or edited by John Gassner), magazines like *Theatre Arts* and *Stage*, and biographical accounts of theatrical craftsmen like Meyerhold and Stanislavsky. And he saw plays as often as possible, fortunate to be growing up in New York in the 1930s–1940s, a time when Broadway offered a rich selection of traditional and experimental productions. The price of a ticket, albeit in the last rows of the balcony, was under a dollar. This meant skipping lunch for a few days, but watching the Lunts or the ensemble acting of the Group Theatre or, a decade later, dramas by Miller and Williams, made minor sacrifices worthwhile.

By age 22 when he received his MFA from Yale School of

Drama, he had written full-length plays and, at City College and at Yale, directed works by Capek, O'Neill, and Hellman.

His theatrical career was interrupted by World War Two. After basic training in the army, he was sent to Anzio, then on to Rome, and later Munich. His outfit captured Dachau, a place and an experience that haunted him for years . . . . At the war's end he returned to New York, directed summer stock and an off-Broadway production, and in 1947 started teaching at Hofstra College. In his eighteen years there he established a theatre department and a still-active Shakespeare festival, directed an historical pageant for all of Long Island plus four plays a year, and taught and directed scores of students, Francis Ford Coppola, Joel Oliansky, Charles Ludlam, Marilyn French, and Susan Sullivan, to name just a few.

Along with these activities, in the 1950s he worked on his PhD at Columbia University. His dissertation grew out of the strenuous and enlightening experience of directing Shakespeare's plays at Hofstra on a replica of the John Cranford Adams' model of the Globe Playhouse. Students, community residents, and theatre professionals like John Houseman made a yearly pilgrimage to Long Island to attend the festival. *Shakespeare at the Globe*, which won the 1962 book award from the American Shakespeare Festival Theatre and Academy, was based on the doctoral study. Subsequently—in *Dynamics of Drama*; in two volumes edited with Joseph Papp; in the collection *On Stage: Selected Theatre Reviews from the New York Times, 1920–1970* edited with his friend, Howard Siegman; and in some forty articles and lectures given around the world—he continued his careful analysis of drama and the theatrical event.

Familiarity with theatrical production, together with the ability to explore freshly the processes involved in the act of performance, became his strength and hallmark. Wherever he worked—at Columbia University as chairman of the Theatre Arts program and later the English Department, or as a Fulbright lecturer in Israel, or as a Mellon fellow at Tulane University, or as a distinguished lecturer in Kyoto, or as a leader of a seminar for Shakespeare scholars at the Folger Library—he happily shared ideas, enthusiasm, and love for the theatre.

In the last ten years of his life, he read and mastered current theoretical systems in art and literature, eager to find ways to view performance in light of these new perceptions. He was determined to clarify the nature of performance and to provide a working vocabulary for the theatrical event. Although his subject matter is complex, his writings are direct, forceful, and challenging. His is an unusual voice.

Theatrical Presentation then is rooted in this history and sphere of interest. It was started before 1980, the first draft completed by early 1985. By the summer of that year, some of the chapters were in final form. However, Bernard died that fall. Encouraged by Janice Price, who had contracted the book for Methuen (now Routledge), as well as by colleagues and friends, I began to edit the manuscript in 1986. Since I had read it and discussed the ideas as Bernard wrote, the text was familiar to me. Also, he made extensive notes for intended revisions. However, I found that editing the manuscript myself was difficult, and I asked William Coco to work with me. An experienced theatre editor, a dramaturg, an ex-student and later a colleague of Bernard's at Columbia University in both the Theatre Arts and English departments, he was a perfect choice. And we have worked well together.

Assistance came from friends like Professor Martin Meisel of Columbia University who read the original manuscript and offered valuable comments and strong encouragement, from Professor Maurice Charney of Rutgers University, and from family members: Nina, William Coco's sister and my son, Jonathan, both of whom helped with proofreading. Robert Greskovic, Howard Siegman and Diane Schacht advised in their specialties. Son Michael who, in his field of musicology, shared and delighted in his father's ideas, read the manuscript many times and made useful comments. Special appreciation is extended to Gita Voivodas for her careful preparation of the manuscript and to Sue Bilton for conscientiously seeing the book through the press.

Among Bernie's notes, I came across a passage that could serve as the start of another Prologue to this book. I include it because it vividly captures his personal feelings about the theatrical experience:

Presented Live

Wherever we are, heading along Shaftesbury Avenue toward a West End theatre, turning in from Broadway near Shubert Alley, hurrying out of the subway for the Taganka theatre in Moscow, searching out an attic of a fringe group at the Avignon festival, or strolling through the commodious lobbies of the National Kabuki theatre in Tokyo, we are filled with anticipation of something wonderful. We are not confused about where we are going. We know we are not about to visit a family or attend a lecture or confer on social problems. Our anticipation runs quite another way. As we linger outside the playhouse, wherever it may be, mingle in the vestibule, crowd through narrow doors into the auditorium, find our places, settle into the half-light of a half-awakened world, we are imperceptibly but voluntarily making ourselves receptive to an act of presentation.

Prologue

In a brief but suggestive passage from his *Ten Books on Architecture*, Leone Battista Alberti, the fifteenth-century Renaissance poet, philosopher, and architect, sets public performance into a frame of social exchange. His subject being architecture, he arrives in his eighth book at the point of discussing "Places for publick Shows." He feels compelled to justify his treatment of this matter, citing for his authority Moses. "Doubtless," Alberti writes, "[Moses] hoped the People, by . . . meeting frequently together at publick Feasts, might grow more humane, and be the closer linked in Friendship, one with another."[1]

To Moses' purpose, he adds other justifications before distinguishing between two kinds of presentation. "Of publick Shows, some are proper to Peace and Leisure, others to War and Business. Those proper to Leisure, belong to the Poets, Musicians and Actors: Those proper to War, are Wrestling, Boxing, Fencing, Shooting, Running, and every Thing else relating to the Exercise of Arms."[2] In our day this distinction between artistic display and athletic contest corresponds respectively to the Performing Arts and Sports.

In placing the Actor within the wider category of public shows, Alberti reminds us of the organic connections among all forms of performance. He is at the opposite pole from Aristotle who considered drama a branch of literary art. What Alberti identifies as Show, Aristotle catalogued as an inferior part of tragedy: spectacle. Alberti's practice coincided with and reinforced the practice of his contemporaries and successors. Until the Renaissance, most of these were rhetoricians. Their five parts of rhetoric—the number into which the subject was most frequently divided—included delivery. Here, it would seem, was an opportunity to discuss public performance since delivery concerned the manner of speaking. But quite the contrary. Writing on delivery illustrates the conventional and persistent subordination of the event of speaking to the composition of speech. So prevalent was this way of ordering the parts of rhetoric and poetics that rare indeed was the person who conceived of performance as an independent entity.

Aristotle's failure to pay more attention to the presentational features of drama is understandable, not only in light of his philosophical orientation, but also in consideration of performing conditions in his own day. A framework for public shows, sanctioned and supported by the Athenian state, had existed for nearly two centuries. The established festivals, celebrated at fixed times of the year, needed no justification. Alberti, on the other hand, grieves "that so excellent and so useful an Entertainment [as public shows] should have been so long disused," for, as he says, the Shows of Peace and Leisure serve "wonderfully to revive and keep up the Vigour and Fire of the Mind."[3]

We have neither the traditional stability of annual festivals, as Aristotle did, nor a lapsed memory of past performance, as did Alberti. Our Peace is bombarded by advertising for an enormous variety of shows: each neatly falling into a subcategory such as theatre, music, dance, popular entertainment, and so on. But today the division of these arts from one another is not absolute by any means. However independent dance may be of theatre and theatre of opera, they are all now grouped under the heading of Performing Arts. This umbrella designation reminds us of the links between various kinds of shows. It also encourages us to consider whether those links merely point to similarities of expression or whether they indeed represent a more profound communality of nature. As Alberti deduced the individual forms of presentation from his Shows of Peace and Leisure, we may in turn search for the core of public shows through reflection on the many types that entertain us.

Chapter 1

The idea of presentation

A show is a peculiar and wondrous invention. It springs from the imagination, but it is realized in actuality. However fantastic its conception, it must be expressed in corporeal terms. Pageant and dance, prestidigitation and play-making—different though they are from each other—share a common nature. As public displays, they alone of the arts involve the human being as producer and product.

A show is both a performance and a presentation. As a performance it is concerned with what people do and as a presentation with what is done. Show, performance, presentation —all three terms overlap each other, though each has a nuance that stresses a different aspect of a mutual act. A "show" connotes visual presentation, glamor, vitality of public exhibition. It encompasses performing media as well as painting and sculpture. Along with the word "presentation," show refers to what is offered to a public, rather than, as in the case of "performance," the rendition of what is shown. "Performance" alerts us to what the performer does; it contains the idea of process and hints at the changing nature of what is performed. In a simple sense, it stresses the *doing* of the show while "presentation" stresses the *giving* of it.

Of the three terms "presentation" suggests a multiplicity of meanings. It is rooted in the idea of offering a gift, in particular offering a gift by making it present, of the moment. Presentation thus not only incorporates the act of giving, but also the act of being—of the donor being in touch with the receiver of the gift. To this temporal connotation is also tied a kinesthetic one, of presence, of the donor not only existing in the now of the receiver but also existing in that now as a vibrant individual. Hence, presentation alludes to a thing offered, a double-natured thing, a thing that embraces the act of giving as well as the force of being. In that sense, while I shall use the terms show, performance, and presentation interchangeably and indifferently, I shall always intend them to convey that double quality of giving and being.

Presentation—the inner dynamic of a show—has its origin in the act of giving. There is someone giving, someone receiving, and some thing to be given. In medieval Latin *praesentia* signified a gift. And even now, in ceremonial gift-giving, we speak of someone making a presentation when the presentation is an actual object (a watch, a silver plate, or more symbolically, an Oscar). In such circumstances there may be a tension between the ceremonial and intrinsic values of the gift. But when we regard an object less for its material worth and more for its symbolic value, then a significant shift in the nature of the exchange occurs. The object becomes an "icon"—its semblance, in Susanne Langer's terms, emerges from its physical form.[1] "It's not the gift but the thought," is a colloquial expression of that shift in perception. *How* one gives something becomes more important than *what* one gives. It is not the exchange of an object as such—though an object may be involved—but of a mode, of a way of perceiving an act. Therefore, while giving is inherent in a show, it is giving as appearance. That does not cheapen the gift; it may indeed make it all the more precious. It does alter the nature of the gift, however, and because it alters it in performance, the gift-giving aspect of presentation may seem to disappear. That is unfortunate since the alliance of show and gift is vital. The ancient world recognized the connection: Athens gave plays to the populace as a social right of citizenship, and the Romans spoke regularly of giving shows and triumphs.

One feature of presentation-as-gift is particularly pertinent to our appreciation of shows. A gift, by its very nature, is gratuitous. It has a touch of divinity about it. While a gift in the guise of charity may occasionally satisfy a pressing need, say, for food or clothing, we usually think of it as a donation that overrides mere necessity. It is associated with holidays, and it is an unlooked-for blessing or richness that liberates us from customary restraints. A gift is superfluous in a double sense; it is both unnecessary and yet an overflowing benefit. It is the second sense that is more telling. A society produces shows not because they are necessary to life but because they express the ebullience of its pride, imagination, vanity, and human aspiration. A show is an apt instrument for a man or a city to celebrate a special event. Its glory is not in the doubtful claim that it fulfills one of our vital needs; in fact, it is a projection of our most daring and ambitious claims. Shows are superfluous because they are overflowings of our spirit.

Shows, as commonly understood, are usually associated with spectacles. But in the sense I am using the word—and indeed in the sense captured by the commercial notion of "show" business— shows can be any kind of public performance. They can be mass performances, such as processions and pageants, or solo turns, such as a performance by a stand-up comedian. They can be primarily visual, as are fireworks, or primarily aural, as is music. They can go on for days, as did the Corpus Christi cycle plays, or take a few minutes, as a song may. With all this variety, it may even be difficult to know what the term show applies to. Is a show an entire program, such as a play? Or is a show each number in a vaudeville bill? In Greek tragic performance do we have a show consisting of the three tragedies and a satyr play? Or do we have four shows comprising a show of shows?

Whatever our usage, a show, in the limited sense of a single item, seldom occurs in isolation. More usually, we can speak of a metatheatrical structure such as an annual festival, or a noted celebration, or a commercial system which provides a frame for individual performances. Thus, the Greek tragic festival provided the framework for tragic, satyric, dithyrambic, and even comic shows. In a similar way the great Renaissance celebrations such as the Medici weddings supplied the *raison d'être* within which a variety of dramatic, quasi-dramatic, and sports-like shows were given. On a smaller scale, the American musical is often the theatrical frame for dramatic sequences relieved by singing and dancing. Whatever the metatheatrical framework then, we can think of a show as both grand in its total conception and concentrated in its immediate expression.

Yet however grand or modest a show may be or whatever its medium of expression, it shares with other shows a common elemental structure. If we proceed from the root premise that a show is first of all an act of giving, then in its simplest form it has four elements. First, and obviously, a show relies on a donor, that is, a performer or performers. But who should be considered the performer? Only the one who actually transmits the gift or anyone engaged in its preparation? We shall return to this question. Next, and equally obvious, a show includes receivers of the performance: audiences, spectators, bystanders, members of congregations.

The third element is the gift itself. But since, as we have said, the gift lies not in an actual exchange but a virtual one, that is, in a symbolic gift, then the third element is the act that is performed. The act may be a conventional routine, such as a juggling trick, or a minutely choreographed piece of work, as in ballet. It has a format, and in that respect is part of a common collection of acts, but it is also freshly invented, and so individual. It inheres in the performer and is expressed through the performer, but may be best examined as distinct from the performer.

Last is an element whose importance varies considerably from show to show. That element is the spatio-temporal environment within which the show occurs. Because the physical context can encompass not only the immediate environs of the show but indeed an entire geographical region, it is useful to distinguish between the functional context of a show—that is, the context that is actively present in a show—and the larger space surrounding it. Instance: both a crowded arena and a city at large may be the context for a rock concert or show. But it would be the arena alone, acoustically, kinesthetically, and visually, that composes the functional milieu.

The four elements of a show are never entirely independent of each other. Yet each *can* act independently (performer, audience) or can be manipulated independently (act, context). As a result we have an interlocking system of unity and autonomy, the degree of which will vary from show to show. Comic routines presented by stand-up comedians fuse performer, act, and audience in a tightly bound exchange—indeed the performer and act may be virtually indistinguishable. By contrast, the precise rendition of a Noh role—whose inflections even are handed down from player to player—makes the act independent of the performer. To understand the esthetics and dynamics of a show, then, we should note in each case how the complex of elements is arranged and how each element relates to another.

By the performer of a show, we usually mean the live actor. But a more thorough treatment of the performer must include the concept of agency in Kenneth Burke's sense of the term.[2] The performer is generally and properly understood to be the one who renders the performing act and makes contact with the audience. But while the performer may be the agency through which the act is presented, the performer may not in fact be the effective force for doing so. Some agent—a director, for instance—may be the actual "hidden" performer. But once we expand our definition of performer to include an offstage agent, we are in danger of regarding any exchange as a show or a presentation. Yet there is one vital condition that distinguishes the show.

A show or presentation is a *unique* offering. By that I mean it is an offering in which the performing agency or figure cannot be replicated but must be in the presence of the audience for the presentational act to occur. From this point of view, the showing of a film is not "unique." The same work or its copy may appear in any number of places at different times or even simultaneously. It is not even possible to state which of the "movie showings" is the original. There is no original, only copies, all of which may be equally original. Since such a type of presentation involves considerations quite different from the esthetics of presentation as here described, I shall not treat "movie showings" as performance.

In presentation then we have a performer (an agent) whose presence makes a show unique. As we have seen in the case of the comedian, the performer may be completely identified with the act performed. The reactions or routines of Bert Lahr, Groucho Marx, or Charlie Chaplin were inimitable. Once the performer died, the routine disappeared. True, these routines were preserved on film, and their dissemination in many copies seems to belie their uniqueness. But most of these routines came from the theatre and retained much of their theatrical life. The initial films of the Marx Brothers all relied on routines the brothers had tested on the stage. After the first wave of popularity, they developed the next set of routines for films like *A Night at the Opera* and *A Day at the Races* in the presence of audiences before committing the material to film.[3] In that regard their comedy differed from Buster Keaton's which was filmic rather than theatric in conception and execution.

Though the performer may be closely identified with his act, he is not identical to it. We can see this in the way Groucho Marx has served as a model for parodists in recent musical comedies. In shows other than comic the identification of performer and act is less close. At quite the opposite pole, we have choral singers or dancers whose performances are literally interchangeable. One person can be removed and another substituted without any appreciable difference in quality or signification. In these cases, of course, it is the chorus as a whole that is the performing agent rather than any single individual within the chorus.

Most shows, however, utilize performers whose identification with the acts that they perform falls somewhere between the extremes. That is the case with most dramatic performers and illusionists. They have a playscript or a format, a pattern of an act which we may refer to as the *act-scheme*. It is this act-scheme which they present in a more or less individualized manner, yet which nevertheless retains autonomy as a presentational act. Separating performer and act-scheme makes it feasible to talk about performer and act as independent yet coordinate elements of a show.

Once we consider the performer as independent from the act, however, we face an anomaly. What is there in a performer besides the act that is performed? Is the performer not like the actress in Pirandello's *To Find Oneself* (*Trovarsi*) who discovers that she has no life except the life of her performance? Though there is something to this notion, there are other things we can say about performing in general before we consider the acts themselves. Recently, some writers, such as David Cole, have found it appealing to identify the performer with the shaman.[4] And there is a certain convenience in explaining the rhapsodic or libidinal energy of the performer as arising from an extra-material source. However, the extent to which we can regard the performer of most shows offered in urbanized settings as having origins in shamanism is doubtful. The shaman is better as metaphor than as source.

Yet there is no question that in the course of performance the performer projects an uncommon vitality—what Michael Goldman calls a "terrific" energy.[5] That vitality is projected through an appropriate channel: an acrobatic trick, a musical instrument, a hypothetical action. Or, the performer may project it directly at the audience, not so much at individual spectators but rather at the spectators at large. This is usually accomplished by scanning the audience rather than fixing attention on any one person. On the other hand, the performer may project energy at another performer or even upon an imaginary object. By means of such projection the performer can both concentrate energy and control it: intensifying and moderating impulses at will.

This capacity to channel and modulate one's vital force is not only central to performance of all sorts, it is the essential requirement for the autonomous actor. Whether freely improvising or going through a meticulously rehearsed routine, actors and actresses create the impression that what they are doing is spontaneous. In William Gillette's phrase, they create "the illusion of the first time."[6] That effect, so fundamental to performance, allows the performer to appear as his own inventor. We may speak of an actor making the author's lines his own. If the actor does not achieve that effect, his performance will appear mechanical and lifeless. To avoid that, the performer must appear to be *self-generative*. That is, the impulse that propels a gesture or a word must seem to arise from within the actor. Even in puppetry, the success of a performance depends in large measure on the puppet appearing to have an autonomous life. It is the principle of self-generation which gives spontaneity and uncertainty to an actor's personal performance, however well-planned it may be.

This common and widely recognized view of the performer is valid as long as the performer is individualized. But as the number of performers in an act proliferates, each performer becomes absorbed into the collective, and the self-generating force of the presentation no longer appears to spring from the individual. It may diminish or it may appear to be shared among the group of performers. Instead of the energy source arising from one individual, it becomes embedded in the whole and so appears to be *choreographed* rather than *enacted*. This does not necessarily lessen its power. A choreographed act has its own electricity, but it is different from the personal magnetism of a single performer.

In addition to choreographed performances, there are other kinds of shows in which the originating impulse is hidden. Both fireworks and theatricalized exhibitions of paintings mask the generating force that lies behind them. In both, human presence is hidden. As we watch fireworks, we are not conscious of the fireworks master or his assistants setting off the rockets and the flares. Instead, we are thrilled by the bursting patterns of light and their vivid brief designs against the night sky. An even more striking illustration of "masked" display was fashionable in the nineteenth century. Before the days of great public galleries such as the Metropolitan Museum of Art or the National Gallery, artist-entrepreneurs exhibited single paintings in theatrical settings for a small fee. One of the first paintings to tour halls in England and Ireland was Géricault's topical canvas of a shipwreck, *The Raft of the Medusa*.[7] In the United States, the touring canvas was even more successful. Frederick Church's exotic landscape *Heart of the Andes* had a long and profitable career touring major cities.[8] Church staged his painting, setting it in a hall with soft light and framing it with foliage to suggest that the viewer was seeing the mountains as if from a glade. A brochure advised the spectator to view the painting through opera glasses so that the eye could traverse the painted surface section by section. In short, to compensate for the static nature of the show, the exhibitor encouraged the spectator to be a kind of performer.

In presentation the propelling force of an act can run the gamut from self-generation, directly projected to an audience, to a socially complex action which is displayed before an audience. At what point the multiplication of performers in an act shifts focus from the individual to the group remains to be examined. As we shall see, this matter is a crucial one for the structure of drama.

But even if the performer does appear to be spontaneous—self-generating, cut loose from the normal constrictions that bind mankind—the act that is performed does remain, with very few exceptions, planned, communally produced, dependent on tradition, and comprehensible only as a social effort. Aside from those idiosyncratic acts that are peculiar to a single performer, a presentational act is normally part of a theatrical heritage. Many are the performers who offer the same act. Families of acrobats have performed the same feat for decades. Most magicians sooner or later have themselves bound in a box or trunk in order to show how they miraculously defy locks, ropes, and chains. Many are the actors who drink poison as Romeo, the women who stab themselves as Juliet. These acts, however individual the interpretation, come from a common source.

Yet to identify what I have called an act with a performance of it would be mistaken. Whether it is Houdini escaping from a trunk or Sir John Gielgud portraying Hamlet's death, the act has several planes of realization. The scene we witness on a particular day in a particular place is both a unique rendition that will never be repeated and an analogue of what is played on other days. To claim for a single performance a uniqueness that separates it from any other performance of the same material, as some writers do, distorts the understanding of the performing act. Each rendition of an act is part of a continuing rendition in a single production which, in turn, is part of a tradition of a presentational idea. For the moment we need to keep in mind the continuity of (a) the performance or single rendition, (b) the production (the sequence of separate performances), and (c) the scheme, that is, the fundamental idea on which the production is based. The act embraces all these phases of a presentation.

From performance to performance a production will vary. Yet each performance has something unique about it, something that cannot be repeated, something inimitable. In the 1960s and 1970s, theatre people reveled in this uniqueness, idealizing the goal of absolute transience. Yet even in more conventional theatre, circumstance, temperament, topical allusion, and chance might make one performance different from another. I recall a performance of George Bernard Shaw's *Caesar and Cleopatra* which featured Sir Laurence Olivier and Vivien Leigh. This was the widely heralded production paired with Shakespeare's *Antony and Cleopatra* during the Broadway 1951–1952 season. The evening I was to see the Shaw play, the curtain was late. After a fifteen-minute wait, Sir Laurence, dressed for his role of Caesar, came before the audience. He explained that Miss Leigh was indisposed. When the groans of disappointment subsided, he went on to explain that her understudy was a capable, young actress, and urged us to remain. Few people could resist his charming appeal. Nor were people disappointed. The understudy was good. But what was of even more consequence was Olivier's performance. As if to support his partner to the fullest of his abilities, he gave a stunning, brilliant rendition of Caesar. Nevertheless, I was sure that I had missed something. A few days later, after Vivien Leigh had returned to the cast, I went back to see another performance. Miss Leigh's version was very similar to her understudy's. That is natural enough. But Olivier, excellent as he was, did not have that extraordinary sharpness that I remembered—or fancied I remembered—from a few days earlier.

To some degree then, a performance is unique. Yet it is also only one dimension of a total act. It is an analogue of every performance of the same production. While one can distinguish variations between two performances of the same production, they nevertheless both belong to the same work. There is no mistaking that. Thus we can identify a second dimension of an act: a somewhat generalized pattern in a production to which each performance adheres. This pattern is the result of two contradictory processes. Initially, the pattern emerges from the preparatory and rehearsal period as a provisional plan for a show. Then, in the crucible of performance the pattern is modified or changed until it achieves a relative consistency, and so becomes the production.

Beyond production there is an even more abstract state that characterizes the presentational act. Let us consider one of the stock tricks among magicians: making an animal disappear, an elephant, for instance. Such a trick is one act in a magician's repertoire. It exists as performance each time he does the trick. It also exists as a sequence of performances placed within a production. From day to day the act may vary in small ways, but in all essentials it adheres to the same pattern. But this act is also performed by other magicians. It may be produced with some differences, in setting, in timing, in the pattern with which the magician builds to the climax. Yet the root idea of the act, showing an enormous creature and making it vanish before our eyes, does not change. Every version of the act is simultaneously different yet analogous.

Dramatic acts, while more complex, also contain the varying dimensions of performance, production, and scheme. A single production may be, and often is, associated with other productions, each of which has rendered an act in a different way. However different one actor's playing a role may be from another's, we recognize that they are playing the same role. We do not think it appropriate to compare Marlon Brando's Stanley in *A Streetcar Named Desire* to Lee J. Cobb's Willy in *Death of a Salesman* though we would, and can, compare Brando's Stanley to Anthony Quinn's Stanley. And we can make these comparisons because we recognize that there is something in the role of Stanley independent of Brando or Quinn.

So we see that there are separate degrees of specificity and concreteness that characterize an act of presentation. They go from the most ephemeral and, oddly enough, the most specific performance to the most stable and yet most abstract scheme of an act embedded in a tradition, in a text, or in musical notation. Can we say that only one dimension of an act is the true act? Hardly. To deny a performing dimension to a playscript is to have a very narrow notion of performance. What an actor presents to us one day cannot be divorced from what he presented the day before or from what he will present the day after. But then the minute we link one day's playing to another, we are abstracting it, creating a mental image of a possible act, an image that in turn has affinities to even more abstract states. As a result, the act of presentation may exist on several levels: the phenomenal, the schematic, and the conceptual. All these levels illuminate and reinforce each other so that it is possible to identify a structured pattern of activity as subsisting within each performance.

Given this variation from the phenomenal to the conceptual, what remains common to all the variant versions of an act? What changes? There is, of course, no fixed answer. From act to act and from performer to performer, both the type of variant and the degree of variation will differ. Some actors, for example, appear to give virtually identical performances from day to day. Other actors change considerably; but even so, the variations occur within boundaries. Usually the skeletal pattern of movements and gestures as well as the rehearsed dialogue remain fairly constant. Where there are variations, they tend to appear in timing, concentration, and energy level. These variations may in fact be slight, yet even slight differences in timing and concentration cumulatively can produce measurable changes in presentation.

When we compare productions rather than performances, however, we get beyond a matter of fine tuning. The same act may be realized in quite different ways. The greatest differences are usually apparent in the physical context of a show: dress, setting, theatrical space. Enormous differences may also occur between performers. Yet if the act is fundamentally the same, there is a set of structural relationships common to two productions of the same act. Indeed, the more communal the performing situation, the more likely is it that an audience will view one production of the same act in light of another. In Nigeria at Igbo Okumkpo performances the elders in the audience will heckle and drive off a masked performer who fails to live up to the standard expected in that show. They have an image of an act that the performer must match.[9]

What then is the relationship between a performance and the act as a whole? The act not only includes its separate manifestations but contains the essential idea in the presentation. That idea, if effective, is inherently provocative. It offers the performer the means for wonderfully concentrating energy in order to produce a powerfully reverberatory effect upon an audience. By speaking of an idea, I do not mean to suggest a discursive concept but a structural principle that makes an act potentially exciting. The avidity with which performing people search for an effective idea—vaudevillians called it "developing an act"—testifies to its importance. A good presentational idea juxtaposes performer and audience or performer and performer in circumstances that exploit the maximum potential for attention, excitement, and deep response. Often a performing idea, however good, only holds temporary interest. Early in this century, when theatrical producers presented Evelyn Nesbit to American audiences after Harry K. Thaw shot her lover, Stanford White, they were seizing on her notoriety for a quick box-office return.[10] It was an idea of the moment. But then there are ideas that are so rich, so provocative, that they are worked and reworked year after year, sometimes for centuries. Whoever first juggled objects discovered an act that has never lost its fascination.

In developing a performance out of an idea, the performer goes through a process of particularization and accommodation, both adding to the root idea and submitting to its guidance. In turn, when the performance arouses an intense response, the audience, while reacting to the particularity of the moment, also senses a more universalizing impact. In responding to a specific performance, it still shares in the more abstract principle that underlies the performance. As a matter of fact, because the specific behavior of the moment is governed by an overriding concept, it is possible for the immediacy of a show to stimulate a reaction that embraces all dimensions of a presentation.

The act, then, is a structured sequence with variant expressions that are at once unique and analogous. This description applies to all kinds of acts in whatever category they might fall. Determining categories of shows, however, is not much simpler than determining what an act is. In practice, we find two working categories that reflect historical and social conditions, and to the extent that these categories exist we cannot ignore them. One is a classification based on material considerations, the other on moral distinctions. Each category supports the other.

The first category of presentation—and the most widely used— relies on the material nature of the performing act. It divides acts according to their physical properties. There are primarily visual acts (dance, acrobatics, mime), primarily auditory acts (concerts), and mixed acts (opera, drama). Sometimes the last group is considered primarily visual, sometimes auditory. To a modern audience these categories may seem so natural that they are not even perceived as categories. Yet this manner of segregating shows is fairly new in the history of performance. As a distinct category, public presentation of music is not more than 300 years old. Traditional performance, whether in Africa, the Orient, or ancient Greece, did not separate vocal music, speech, dance, and instrumental music as rigidly as we do. Even the theatre of the eighteenth century combined music, dance, and drama on one bill. Only with the socialization of art according to class and its consequent specialization did performance become divided along the lines of physical nature. In the course of this division, certain arts—opera is a prime example—came to have a higher status than others. Along with the resulting specialization has come an increasing refinement in skill and esthetic finish. This has gone so far that in the case of music the virtuosity required of the performer is in danger of subordinating esthetic and imaginative power to physical dexterity. Recording and electronic composition are undermining the uniqueness of performance, and may eventually destroy musical performance altogether.

Along with a material category goes a moral one. Certain forms of presentation have a social distinction while others are dismissed as trivial. Bourgeois society throughout the nineteenth and twentieth centuries has distinguished between socially acceptable shows—music and opera notably—and socially insignificant shows—comic theatre, for instance. Associated with these social divisions is a moral emphasis upon serious presentation. Disregarding the very nature of performance as transitory, society has put a high estimate on performances of enduring significance. To elevate theatre as an art, critics and scholars had a penchant for treating the stage as a temple, a substitute for the dying church. All the better to hallow theatre, they sharply separated theatre art from popular shows. This inclination has flowered most recently in the holy theatre of Artaud, Grotowski, and Peter Brook. Though incorporating once-discarded elements of popular performance in their work—acrobatics and magic—they nonetheless have sought to sanctify presentation. Nowhere is the moral imperative more tyrannous than in its contempt for entertainment. Castelvetro, the Renaissance theorist, was one of the lone voices in theatrical criticism that insisted on entertainment as the main purpose of drama. And even where entertainment is accepted as a legitimate aim of theatre, it is regarded with suspicion.

The very divorce of theatre from popular shows is largely over the issue of entertainment. High art, truth, metaphysical speculation, social comment—these are presumed to be the proper ends of the drama. The popular show—circus, vaudeville, pageantry—is merely entertaining.

Yet entertainment is linked to what I have previously observed about superfluity. Entertainment marks the attainment of that first level of engagement which allows the play of fancy to hold sway. It opens the spirit to other possible exchanges between a show and its audience. It enables the spectator to take a leap beyond physical limitations into a realm of infinite possibilities. Because it does so, it can be deceptive and even trashy. But it also can stir transcendent responses.

To distinguish shows according to whether they entertain or not is futile, however. In a deep sense all shows seek to achieve that initial level of engagement called entertainment. They may do this by amazing us (fireworks, acrobatics), baffling us (illusionism), enthralling us (dramatic stories), or gripping us in other ways. But no single type of response is reserved to one kind of show and not another. Every show has the potentiality for stirring us in multiple ways.

But though material distinctions have a practical utility and moral distinctions a critical purpose, neither offers access to an understanding of presentation on its own terms. For that we must look to the kind of act at the center of any performance. Since so much ordinary behavior finds its way into shows, performance constantly is a process of transforming and sharpening non-performing acts. Dancing—to give one instance—is social as well as theatrical. More often than not, dance appears first as a community activity and only later may be adapted for public showing. But what happens when it passes from one sphere to the other? It is obvious that what was a coherent community becomes divided into two: the doers and the viewers. A dance that may have involved people kinesthetically now receives focal attention. In order to sustain and deepen that attention, the dancer develops variety, cultivates special facets of the dance, and tries to exceed expectation. In time the dancer becomes a virtuoso, and in that irresistible progress defines and widens the gap between an increasingly refined artistry and the similar but qualitatively different skills of the audience.

Although in every art such widening separation between ordinary and extraordinary abilities occurs, in the performing arts that separation takes on a strange and marvelous quality. It both divorces and yet connects performer and spectator. Because the performer is a human being—with all the frailty of a human being — a show is familiar, approachable, deceptively ordinary. Yet as performers transcend the limitations of human frailty, they create something alien, wonderful, and awesome before us. They defy limitation. They may *transform* their appearance through dress or self-display, or by sporting unusual garments, or by donning sacred objects such as masks. They may *do* something that astonishes others and through voice, or gesture, or physical prowess triumph over expectation. Lastly, they may *pretend* to do or be something they are not. In this case, they combine the being (the displaying) with the doing. By positing a hypothetical action or person, performers escape the normal rules of existence.

These ways of defying limitation correspond to three different kinds of shows which feed each other. The first sort of show involves *transforming* through display and celebration. It encompasses brilliant spectacles, perhaps utilizing rich dresses or pageant wagons. In that the richness is actual, the show is not illusionary. In that the pageant may have a symbolic significance, the show is somewhat illusionary. Such shows we can call *shows of glorification or celebration.*

Other shows present people *doing* something quite extraordinary, something quite beyond the abilities of the members of the audience. Juggling, fire-eating, gymnastics, and some forms of dancing and singing fall into this group. We can call these *shows of skill.*

Still other shows present people *pretending* to do something. Whatever they do is a representation of some other action. Such shows are *shows of illusion.*

Of the three types of show, the shows of skill and the shows of illusion are most distinct from one another. The drama belongs to the latter type of show.

Naturally, within dramatic performance there are many sub-divisions: plays, operas, ballets, and pageants. Some of these types of shows can exist only in the dramatic world: plays and operas, for example. By definition, a play is a show in which impersonation occurs. On the other hand, ballets and pageants can be dramatic, or non-dramatic, depending upon their formats. A ballet may be pure dance, at which time it is non-dramatic, or it may enact a story. In practice, of course, a form such as ballet exists on the line between the two types of show. Many ballets have a frame story within which a series of dances, some of them quite abstract, will be given.

Non-dramatic shows generally fall into one of two subdivisions: displays of skill or displays of glory. The former are essentially physical. Skills vary in popularity from age to age. For instance, the Elizabethan performer was not only an actor but also a tumbler (gymnast) and a dancer. His skills in the latter two arts overlapped each other. His "descendants," however, tended to specialize. The tumblers became acrobats and, though admired, did not gain the social status that dancers finally won. Yet we can see, even today, the vestiges of the acrobat in the dance. When dancers are included in variety programs on television, to cite one example, they usually perform numbers that stir easy admiration, that is, numbers that have a strong gymnastic element.

The point here is that, however much it is that time and convention have separated one type of performance from another, the essential structures do not necessarily reflect those conventions. There is an organic quality that links one show to another, and it is in periods such as ours, when social and esthetic forms are undergoing fundamental restructuring, that we become aware of links that have long been obscured.

But though shows of skill—acrobatics, dance, singing—overlap each other, there is a genuine difference between those performances that display skill alone and those that display skill—such as singing—in order to achieve an emotional response. In these cases, the "singer" tends to "dramatize" the performance, that is, to establish an imaginative relationship with some unseen component: God, a lover, a state of feeling. The singer may become a storyteller as in the Goethe–Schubert song, "The Elf King." In short, the display of vocal skill becomes fused with an imaginative purpose.

This distinction between the illusionary and the sensory realms is central to the nature of public shows. It helps us to understand the emphases that mark each category. The main distinction between the two categories, however, has to do with esthetic surface. What I call the sensory or non-fictive show throws its principal emphasis on the phenomenological surface of the presentational act. The acrobatic leap, the mass of brilliantly dressed marchers, the high notes of a trumpet—all are demonstrations of wonderful skills as skills. What I call the illusionary or fictive show includes the display of skill but shadows a second realm in the exercise of the perceptible skill. A corps de ballet is perceived not only as highly trained dancers on the stage but also as nymphs in a forest. The girl on the float in a parade is not only the homecoming queen but may represent Cleopatra. The magician is not only Blackstone working his tricks but an oriental wizard causing an elephant to disappear. It is such a double-imaged act that is the basis of drama.

Though in principle we can make a clear division between the dramatic and the sensory show, in practice there are fine shades of fictionalization. We have seen that ballet may combine a fictional frame with units of pure skill. There are even more tenuous examples of shows that hover between the two. In the 1950s and

1960s, rock singers tended to theatricalize their appearance—the Beatles wore their hair long and cut it in a distinctive and challenging fashion that came to be much imitated. The degree of fictionalization was slight, however. By comparison, rock groups such as Kiss in the 1970s dressed in outlandish costumes and assumed grotesque characterizations that were frequently at odds with their own persons. A gap opened between performer and role so that their shows became drama as much as music.

Similarly, in many of the great Renaissance pageants, a prince took a role, not so much as an actor but as an emblem. Among the festivities for the 1608 wedding of Cosimo II de' Medici in Florence was a splendid mock naval battle. A fleet of ships representing Jason's argosy in search of the Golden Fleece sailed up the Arno in stately order.[11] Most magnificent of the ships was Jason's, in which the bridegroom Cosimo sat—as Jason. Here the fiction was thinly disguised. Cosimo partook of the ancient aura of the mythic hero while he also endowed that hero with a contemporary glory derived from his person. Cosimo's role-playing enhanced the show just as Cosimo gained prestige from the magnificence and number of the ships.

In such a show as this, as indeed in all displays of skill and magnificence, we respond to the perceived surface. Brilliant costumes, patterns of physical movement, catch our eye: the music and the shouting strike our ear. If the richness and intricacy of design are well handled, we perceive the density of the display with relish. The entire work appears to be opaque. Life assumes a concentrated, glorified actuality.

This awareness of surface—this opacity—is unlike the response to a dramatic show. To the extent we see Jason in Cosimo, we see through the surface of Cosimo to the sign of Jason. In this instance, we have no wish to lose the sight of Cosimo in Jason. Quite the opposite. The show endows Cosimo with the aura of Jason. But onstage, where an actor represents a character, we do find a kind of transparency. We see the actor in his full presence, yet our gaze instantly fixes on the shadow figure that he represents. Even when our attention alternates between the actor and the character, it is the fictional ambience and action that claim our allegiance.

Along with the performer and the act, there is another feature of presentation. It is the environment that contains the first two and the audience. To what extent the environment, that is, the performing space and its scenery, plays a crucial role in performance varies from one type of show to another as well as from one historical period to another. By environment one can mean the immediate physical circumstance in which the show unfolds. Or one can mean the entire cultural climate in which it is embedded. Here I will comment only on the immediate context, what I shall call the functional milieu. In a later chapter I will deal with the broader climate.

The question of immediate context concerns the spatial setting of a show. While it is obvious that the locale of a performance is integral to its delivery, and that we have become increasingly sensitive in recent years to performance environment, we should not automatically assume that all shows are centrally dependent on their locale. In fact, the opposite is the case. While the trio of performer, audience, and act are central, the context, though vital, is complementary. The question has to do with the degree to which a presentation is dependent upon a specific space or exists relatively independent of it. At one pole we have examples of traveling mummers, Elizabethan plays, and comic sketches that can be given anywhere. They are almost totally independent of a specifically characterized space.

At quite the other pole are environmental shows such as *The Storming of the Winter Palace* in Leningrad (1920) that are tied to one particular locale and could be given nowhere else. Directed by Nikolai Evreinov, *Storming* re-enacted one of the decisive events of the Russian Revolution, the taking of the headquarters of the Kerensky government by the Bolshevists. It is reported that 8,000 people participated in the show.[12] This type of show constitutes a mass performance, and as a mass performance it has a characteristic relation to its space, for mass performances as a type usually utilize specific spaces: squares, streets, gardens, in effect, highly designed and particularized spaces. And this suggests an inverse link between the autonomy of the performer and the specificity of environment. The shows that are collectivized, that rely on a "hidden" intelligence, are also shows that are embedded in space. Shows that stem from self-generating performers tend to be shows in which the performer is loosely tied to a specific geographical space and creates a personal behavioral space in which to perform.

This independence of the performer from the tyranny of space is an important one. While there is a distinctive power that emanates from shows where crowds of players seem to obey a single plan, the responses we associate with dramatic and skillful performances arise from contact with autonomous, self-generative performers. That lift of freewheeling play seems to convey the essence of human freedom and audacity. However much we try to find the source of shows in social or cultural conditions, the creative action is a product of free choice. The very fact that there is *no* absolute need to walk a tightrope, juggle a ball, play a part, or pull a rabbit out of a hat liberates these acts from mere necessity. That is why they so excellently express the free play of the human spirit.

To dismiss the role of architecture and setting in performance would be ridiculous. No show can exist in a vacuum. But we have to guard against an inclination to give scenic space too much importance, an inclination fostered by modern and post-modern experience. From the end of the nineteenth century onward, directors and historians have adopted the principle that the performer and environment should be integrated. With the emergence of theatricalist and later environmentalist staging, the principle has become axiomatic, and runs something like this. The human being is an integral part of the world. Hence, the actor in portraying human existence should have an immediate, functional connection with the environment. The practical consequence of this principle has been that the theatrical habit of using a common pool of scenery for all plays was bitterly attacked, and the practice was introduced of devising a new setting for each play. The premise was, and is: the context of a play's action is so individual that no other scenery would do. Consequently, both on the practical as well as theoretical levels, scenery has come to have parity with performing.

Yet though the principle of an individualized playing space into which the performer can be integrated is valid for some shows, it does not have axiomatic force. Theatre and especially many forms of popular entertainment thrived in conditions in which the connection of performer to space has been of the loosest kind. Bearing his costumes in a bundle, packing the most essential apparatus in a cart, the performer has often played in an ill-defined, unlocalized clearing. In the early twentieth century Jacques Copeau recognized the value of generalizing scenery through a unit set, and in the last thirty years, with the reappearance of the open stage, actors are once again cut free from a specific space. What we have discovered as a result is that however admirable stage settings may be, they do not have the same primal power possessed by an actor or an acrobat or a dancer.

That power, as I have argued, is self-generative, yet it manifests itself through pre-planned acts. It is thus paradoxical, combining spontaneous assertion and predetermined sequences. It is the interpenetration of the sequence by the performer's spontaneous energy that gives artistic performance its tremendous fascination. But fundamental though this combination is, an even more paradoxical relationship serves as the foundation of presentation and gives it its explosive power.

What makes a show worth seeing? On the stage no human activity is inherently more compelling than another. All kinds of acts are potentially appealing. Yet to hold attention, an act has to be honed, that is, isolated—"defamiliarized," in Victor Shlovsky's term[13]—heightened, and shaped. Novelty and familiarity can equally fascinate an audience. Favorite songs, well-known tricks, and familiar plays are often quite popular. When these achieve polished form (polished not sophisticated), they can be presented over and over again without losing their luster. They seem to capture a central sentiment or fancy. Yet it is not easy to devise such an instrument of delight. It may even be that such recurrent acts cannot be planned but merely emerge.

More frequently, people are drawn to novelty and topicality. They constantly desire fresh diversion. In the 1960s, liberalizing influences led to the introduction of nudity onstage, but the novelty wore off very quickly. Within a few years nudity for its own sake disappeared.

Whether familiar or novel, a show embodies some quality of the extraordinary. That strange and wonderful quality may lie in the skill of the performer, the unusualness of the act (how often does one have a chance to see a parade?), the artistry of the player, or the significance of what is played. Acts that I described early in this chapter as dense or opaque, startle us with their color, texture, design, or variety; illuminations and processions produce strong sensory effects. Their unusualness makes them exciting. But the excitement is not merely the product of mere extravagance. To make a show extraordinary, the performers have to discover, invent, attempt something that exceeds expectation. In essence, they would do the impossible if they could. Failing that, they push themselves to the farthest edge of possibility, and, in so doing, transcend their own limitations.

This transcendence can be physical as well as illusionary. Acrobats fascinate us because before our very eyes they transcend normal human capacity. Always working at the frontier of their skills, they are forever seeking to extend the limits of the human physique. Even in dance we applaud the dancer who can defy the boundaries of the body. Mikhail Baryshnikov's attraction comes both from the actual leaps he makes and from the way he makes them: seeming to fling himself into space as though he expected to soar beyond gravity. By contrast, the performance of magic relies not on the magician actually transcending human limits but in *appearing* to defy them. We enjoy the magic of double-think. Despite knowing we are being tricked, we are amazed by the trickery.

A dramatic show relies on a parallel yet different kind of illusion. As Tennessee Williams tells us in *The Glass Menagerie* through his *alter ego* Tom Wingfield, "a stage magician . . . gives you illusion that has the appearance of truth. I give you truth in the pleasant disguise of illusion."[14] Through this disguise of illusion, the actor can directly show us life otherwise impossible for us to know.

Take the most obvious case where the performer does this: in the death scene. Shakespeare shows us this scene in both grim and playful versions. In *A Midsummer Night's Dream*, he shows us how Bottom, the eternal ham, imagines death to come as the climax of a fateful romance. In later plays Shakespeare no longer gives us a mock death but deaths that are images—hypothetical images, it is true, yet sober images—of the "real" thing. We see Hamlet die, Othello die, Antony and Cleopatra die. In many of his tragedies the finales almost border on the absurd, yet we are moved, for the act of dying onstage has an eternal fascination. It is the moment when the performer does the impossible. He employs common signs to denote the convention of dying, yet must give these signs a freshness in order to create a lifelike illusion of death. In performing this act, the player captures the absolute paradox of dramatic performance: defying human limitation at its most intransigent point. But even if the performer convinces us of his "death," we know this effect is momentary. We thus experience an event in which a mortal human being, someone like ourselves, appears to exceed mortal boundaries, *and*—this is most important—he takes us with him beyond those boundaries. This can happen only in theatrical presentation. Unlike the cinema, where the camera and not the human being exceeds life, in the theatre we are able to share the performer's leap into the impossible.

Ultimately, performance is central to drama not because it

supplies spectacle or gives three-dimensional form to linguistic clues but because the dialectic of the human and the superhuman can be found only in performance. The performer sets into motion a vibration between actual presence and the supposed (imagined) action. Since that action almost by definition is uncommon or wondrous, the performer transcends the ordinary. Even when an actor plays most naturalistically, the very ability to do the familiar thing publicly is wondrous in its own way, as we shall see more fully later on.

Pleasure of performance thus arises from the juxtaposition of mortal nature and immortal accomplishments. What gives dramatic performance its unique quality is the simultaneous linking of the earthly and the overreaching aspects of humanity. That overreaching may be physical, as in the dancing of Baryshnikov, or imaginative, as in the rendition of a role. But it is the *way* the performer's projective energy infuses and so takes on the appearance of a fictional energy (Prometheus defying Zeus, Stockmann defying the mob) that gives dramatic presentation its generating power. This projection of energy, lifting the players above themselves, is the field of force that binds the performers to the act they perform. When it is routine or mechanical, the presentational act loses its impact. When it is spontaneous and vigorous, it stimulates the sensation of transcendency.

Chapter 2

Imitation and presentation

Vaudeville is dead. Years ago the comedian Fred Allen officially pronounced its demise.[1] By now it is merely a faint memory of a bygone age. A crude and often naive mingling of shows, vaudeville lost out to the first media revolution: radio and movies. Yet while it thrived, it combined a rich mix of sketches, songs, dances, gymnastic feats, magic tricks, and appearances by the famous and notorious. On a single bill would be five to nine acts, each one, ten to thirty minutes long, taking shape from a series of short routines: a sequence of songs, a batch of tricks, a patter of jokes, or a playlet. Between them, act and turn composed a show, a show that was a microcosm of the possibilities open to theatrical presentation.

By the word "act," the vaudevillian meant a special routine offered by a performer or performers. Usually the players of each act were distinct from any others in the show. Occasionally, the same performer might play more than one act, but in general, because variety was essential, one type of act differed from another: a comic sketch might succeed a song or an acrobatic routine might precede a clog dance. Each act was a specialty of the performer, so much so, in fact, that frequently vaudeville bills only needed to list the names of players with the addition of the phrase "in their specialties."

But whatever the specialties, vaudeville acts divided into the kind of acts I mentioned in the first chapter, that is, acts of skill, illusion, or glorification. Acts of glorification were least common, but when offered, often proved to be the most notable, especially when a celebrity of the day, such as Jack Dempsey, the heavyweight champion, traveled the vaudeville circuit.

Acts of skill were far more common staples. Hardly a bill appeared that did not have a juggler, aerialist, or tumbler of some sort. It might include the wire acts of the Carmen Troupe or the comedy acrobatics of Rice & Prevost. The aerialists, most of whom came from the circus, offered such excitement as did Harry Thriller "who balanced on a chair and broom handle on the trapeze" or Lillian Leitzel who could do forty revolutions with one hand.[2]

Most widespread were acts of illusion, that is, magic acts or brief sketches that encapsulated a pathetic or comic situation. At times the sketch expanded into a full-fledged one-act play, frequently given as the final item of a bill.

Aside from the acts that clearly fall into one category of show or another are many acts that share elements of the three show types or shift into another category depending upon emphasis. Musical acts, for instance, might be shows of skill, glorification, or illusion, or a combination of these. Singers of romantic ballads, to the degree that they evoked a mood through their rendition, were illusionists, raising the audience to a heightened emotional state. On the other hand, an ordinary performer such as Frank Whitman gave a show of skill as a dancing violinist when he played the Palace in December 1913.[3] By combining what are often considered opposites, he gave not so much a display of musicianship as a glorification of contradictions. In this he exemplified a common tendency in vaudeville and in exhibitions generally to display the odd and unusual.

Richard D. Altick traces much of the English history of such exhibitions in his *The Shows of London*. These shows, as he writes, embrace scientific demonstrations, freaks, and prestidigitation.[4] They correspond respectively to shows of skill, glorification, and illusion. That displaying a freak can be thought a form of glorification might seem strange. But the impulse and the claim behind such a showing was to demonstrate the wonders of nature, even the monstrous wonders, as in the case of the renowned Elephant Man. This type of display constitutes negative glorification.

The mixture of categories appears vividly in animal acts. Dogs were favored and favorite performers. By putting them through their paces, the performer could show how well-trained they were: having them count, pick out objects, jump through hoops, or do a number of other tricks to show their—and the trainer's—virtuosity. But animal trainers usually went beyond these simple demonstrations of skill. If they did not, the audience soon would be bored. In addition, they often sought to create a relationship between themselves and their animals. In an act performed for many years, and later in *Sugar Babies*, Bob Williams devised the illusion that his dog, Rusty, would not obey him. By giving the animal instructions that the animal answered by doing quite the opposite, he induced the illusion that the dog had a mind of its own, entirely independent of his. That made for considerable comedy since the disparity between the command and the response was invariably ludicrous. In this the performer combined a show of great skill with the creation of an attractive illusion.

In speaking of an act, the vaudevillian meant more than a defined specialty. The term included the underlying idea that informed the specialty. That was a presentational idea, that is, an idea which could realize the potentialities of a particular kind of show, given the context of show business. In shows of skill it might be a way of doing an act that no one else had been able to do. Or it might be a way of glorifying someone or something in a fresh manner as Florenz Ziegfeld did for the "American Girl" beginning with his first revue, *The Follies of 1907*. Or it might be a kind of illusion or situation that is a variant of standard acts.

For the performer, the idea was a key to a good show. It had to make best use of the performer's natural talent. It had to appeal to the audience. It had to have staying power. Often it was extraordinarily simple. Skits, such as Smith and Dale's renowned Dr. Kronkite routine, might rely on an ordinary situation turned on its head. Though repeated for years, it was capable of being perfected in its minutest details, and because of that capacity for perfection, it was a good presentational idea. An act is thus not only the finished product but also the performing notion contained within it.

That product, being human in its expressive form, inevitably combines showing with showing off. All performers, no matter what they perform, show themselves off to some degree. They show off their skill, their charm, their feelings. They may do this directly as a football player does after he makes a touchdown, dancing out his triumph. Stage actors, however, often have to hide the fact that they are showing off. Currently, the ideal is for actors to submerge themselves in their characters; in other words, to show something rather than to show off. But the distinguishing mark of a major or star actor is his or her capability of showing off despite or through the character. Tallulah Bankhead showed herself off whether or not it suited her character. When it did, as in Regina in *The Little Foxes* or as Sabina in *The Skin of our Teeth*, the fusion was compelling. Sir Laurence Olivier, famed for his remarkable transformations of character, on the other hand, showed himself through his impersonations.

Showing something and showing off are two sides of the same act. When we show something, we ask people to look at the act itself—to weigh it, understand it, appreciate it. When we show off, we call attention to ourselves. We insist people notice us, admire us. Children start by showing off and only as their egos come under control do they begin to show something other than themselves. Temperamentally, performers retain the pristine delight of childlike showing off. Artistically, they develop the ability to show us a skillful feat, a wondrous object, or, entering a world of fancy, an image of experience. Any single act blends the impulses to show and to show off in a distinctive way.

Showing off, self-congratulatory display, an element implicit in the notion of presentation, is often conventionalized. Taking a bow is one of the simplest forms. That dance of victory by a football player is one of the purest examples of showing off. In the circus, it is common for a performer to initiate an acrobatic feat by boasting or, more acceptably and more effectively, having someone else boast (show off) about what will be done. The performer does the feat (shows it), and then takes a bow (shows off again). In this example the formalized frame of showing off celebrates the number offered to the public, a celebration based on the rare achievement of the performer. Within the frame of showing off, the performer concentrates on the task, showing us the feat. We can thus speak of the act as a core of showing within a frame of showing off.

To what degree showing or showing off prevails in any particular act depends on the nature of the act and the performer's attitude toward its presentation. By their very substance, shows of glorification are primarily devised for showing off. The self (a monarch, for instance) or a series of selves (pretty girls in the follies) present themselves or are framed to enhance their display. Not what they do but what they are is of first moment. By contrast, the core of most acrobatic feats involves showing something: a precise act that overcomes actual not fictional obstacles. Showing off, as we have seen, enhances and celebrates the core of doing. But only when the feat is perfunctory and does not demand full concentration do we find the performer substituting showing off for showing.

With these features of performing in mind, let us return to the nature of a presentational act and its underlying idea. Acts of skill are particularly instructive. They usually fall into fairly well-defined, traditional displays of dexterity, balance, and daring, each one of which requires certain specialized skills not demanded by other kinds of display. The dexterity of a juggler is far different from the concentrated balance of the wire-walker. Each type of performer functions within an established context of practice and performance.

Each act of skill is composed of a sequence of numbers that are successively more difficult. The novice working to become a full-fledged performer must master the rudimentary numbers before hoping to gain command over the demanding ones. The point at which the novice becomes or can become a performer is not absolute. Street jugglers of rude skill may attract a passing crowd with the most ordinary routines. But for the juggler to dazzle an audience, especially if the audience has seen other jugglers, requires skill of an extraordinary kind. But at whatever level jugglers are performing, they make use of a conventional pattern: the demonstration of a series of feats of mounting difficulty.

This general description covers the common heritage not only of jugglers but of most performers, as we shall see. It defines a climactic structure that is a primary imperative of theatrical presentation. Indeed, the quality of a performing idea is largely determined by its potentiality for building a highly imaginative climactic structure. To go back to our juggler, he or she must find a performing idea that can intrigue an audience. Commonly, the idea for a juggling act will center on the type of object to be juggled. Inherent in the juggling of plates, a highly favored choice, is the juxtaposition of the juggler's art and the object's frailty. Inherent in the juggling of knives is the projection of anxiety: skill against danger. Any object that communicates the message "I am not to be handled lightly," offers the potentiality for being juggled in interesting and exciting ways.

Different but equally effective could be an idea for juggling as a kind of illusion. Requiring immense skill but also demanding strong acting is a performance of an apparently inept juggler. In fact, the performer mocking his or her own art is a favorite way of extending the presentational appeal of shows of skill. By almost dropping plates, being overwhelmed by the number of objects in the air, losing track of the sequence: these are all ways in which the "clumsy" juggler produces comedy as well as amazement.

To realize the full effect of this performing idea, the "clumsy" juggler will elaborate secondary features. Dress is vitally important. It goes a long way toward defining the persona of the performer. The way the juggler relates to the audience also creates the appropriate setting for the act: Is the act distant? informal? apologetic? In fact, dress and behavior largely determine the degree to which an audience will be predisposed toward the show. Were our "clumsy" juggler garbed in clothes too large for him, wearing a hat that became entangled in the juggling, and at the same time behaving apologetically yet valiantly as he tries to carry on, the result could be endearing, with the double effect that we would sympathize with his apparent ineffectuality at the same time as we admired his enormous art.

Whatever the idea and however it is arranged, the act in a show of skill has a precise sequence. As we have seen, it has a general pattern of rising difficulty. The dynamic features of that pattern, such as timing or accent, might change from one performance to the next. But however much the basic sequence may change as a result of shifts in a performer's mood or an audience's composition, the primary pattern provides the structural core for the performance. In American vaudeville, with its continuous round of performers and its vast hinterland of theatres, acts repeated the same fundamental routine for years. But if vaudeville acts illustrate the clearest example of performing patterns, the principle of a structural core that is varied in performance applies to all kinds of shows.

Each act, whether of skill, glorification, or illusion, has a fundamental performing pattern or sequence which I call its *act-scheme*. In the case of acts of skill, the act–scheme is overt, easily recognized, very much on the surface. Where the performer is content to operate on the level of skill and doesn't move into illusionary play as the "clumsy" juggler does, the act-scheme is an accurate presentation of actuality. Depending upon the distinctive talents of the performer, the act-scheme achieves or exceeds professional expectations. Impelling its shape is the performer's effort to test the extreme limits of his or her skills within the framework of a given type of demonstration. As a result, each act-scheme in a show of skill shares with every other act-scheme a common structural arrangement.

In an analogous way, the act–scheme in shows of glorification has its own deep patterns. The one we have met in our discussion of vaudeville is a pattern of static display. This pattern appears with great frequency when freaks and strange creatures are shown. More widespread, however, is the processional act-scheme. One of the simplest forms of show, the parade, exists in every culture. Whether religious, political, or military in character, it follows a fairly basic pattern, relying upon the serial presentation of individual numbers to produce an effect.

The act-scheme for most parades in the United States alternates marchers and riders. Among the marchers are those in music bands and those who walk along, sometimes with banners and flags, sometimes with nothing in their hands. The riders usually occupy a float, that is, a barge on wheels upon which rides a fanciful emblem. In a parade such as the one sponsored by Macy's department store on Thanksgiving Day, interspersed among the marchers and floats are the giant balloons of famous cartoon or television creatures: Mickey Mouse, Snoopy, Kermit the Frog, and so on.

What distinguishes one parade act-scheme from others are the kinds of bands, floats, or balloons used and the sequence in which they are arranged. In the New Orleans Mardi Gras parade, the floats fit the chosen theme for the year, but the sequence of floats and how they are employed in the parade follows yearly custom. Each float is the work of a single social club or krewe. Members of a krewe, costumed and masked, ride the float. They are almost invariably men. As they pass along the prescribed route through the city, they throw out tokens, mostly plastic beads and stamped medals, to the crowd waiting along the way. Although essentially worthless, these tokens are eagerly sought by the onlookers, the triumph coming not only from accumulating the greatest amount but from establishing a momentary but intense glance with the masked figure on the float.

Much of the appeal in a show of glorification derives from tradition or from a special occasion. In traditional parades there are high points and more conventional numbers, but seldom is there a dominating climax. The giant balloons in the Macy's parade and the King of Mardi Gras provide some focus of interest, but not with the same intensity that we find in a special occasion. Parades devised for that purpose, such as a triumph for a Roman general, the welcome for a championship team, or the entry into a city of a Renaissance prince, build to a climax in celebration of the person or persons being honored. The act-scheme will differ to accommodate these distinct occasions, although, in fact, the distinctions in arrangement tend to be slight. Perhaps the single factor that separates one special occasion from another is the height of magnificence achieved in the numbers that make up the procession. Drawings of the individual carts in Renaissance entries illustrate the richness of design and marvelous fancy that went into their construction. Then and now, such carts and floats were the work of civic organizations or neighborhoods. They thus expressed communal consensus in honoring the day or person.

Like shows of skill, shows of glorification present act-schemes where appearance prevails. What we see is what exists. The returning hero, magnified though he may be, is a hero, nevertheless. The Rose Bowl Queen, while taking on the aura of royalty, is queen of no other realm except the festival. Not that forms of illusion do not appear in parades. They certainly do, and I shall discuss these forms later. But the prime power of a show of glorification is derived not from creating the fancy of another world but through transforming the actual world into a world of fancy. Such a show, by possessing what is invariably the civic heartland (the main route through a city, a square in the village), lays claim to its transforming power. It is not coincidental that most parades in New York march down Fifth Avenue, the street that best combines prime residential with prime commercial elegance. By commanding so distinguished a route and by overpowering it through hordes of marchers, the show of glorification celebrates the civic conquest of reality.

Where the show of glorification differs from the show of skill is in its juxtaposition of people and reality. The show of skill displays a human being actually overcoming obstacles, actually conquering human limitation. The show of glorification attempts to overwhelm actuality. It works by substitution, seeking to put in the place of actual space and behavior a magnified presentment of space. It transforms the heavens in fireworks and the earth in dazzling processions.

The act of skill, thus, has a single order of reality. In its essential form, it is an act that exists only for the purpose of presentation. The mastering of acrobatic feats may satisfy a person aside from the pleasure of performing them, but seldom are the most demanding stunts practiced by anyone except a performer. Most numbers require such extraordinary perseverance that the gymnast or acrobat must specialize for years in order to accomplish a feat that is worth being shown. While we may think of such a feat as symbolic of human capability, rarely does it have true symbolic power. We enjoy the act of skill for its own sake, not because it conjures up a wider image of experience. That is why acts of skill have something abstract and elegant about them.

By no means can we speak of this type of act as a reflection of life. It is life itself, a public defiance of human limit, and that makes it worth watching. Shows of illusion are quite another thing. Like shows of skill and of glorification, they have act-schemes that define the sequence of performance. But since these act-schemes allude to another dimension of experience, the secret of a magic trick or the fiction of a play, they work in tandem with what I will call the *act-image*. As a double display, a show of illusion provides interaction between the actuality of presentation, planned and structured by the act-scheme, and the virtuality of an implied or underlying event, the act-image.

As we move from shows whose content has only presentational existence, we increasingly become engaged in metaphoric activity. An act of glorification is an example. It does seek to impose itself upon reality in a massive physical way. But in doing so, it makes use of emblems that carry impressive associations of public assent. Cultural visions are brought to earth and domesticated. By mediating between god and man, the ideal and the real, the glorifying act metaphorizes actuality without departing from it.

It is when we look at illusionary shows, however, that we see the complex workings of metaphoric action. Let us consider an archetypical trick of illusion: sawing a woman in half. Initially devised, probably by P. T. Selbit in London,[5] it was later modified by Horace Goldin in New York, and became a star attraction, entering the repertory of many magicians. Possibly basing his idea on an act by Robert-Houdin, Selbit conceived the idea of placing a woman in an oblong box with her head and feet protruding at either end. He then cut her in half by "sawing" through the box. Initially Goldin did the same trick. Then in 1927 he thought of dispensing with the box by placing a woman on a bare board over which hung an electric buzz saw with which he cut through her. In a 1980 version of this trick at the Majestic Theatre, New York, performed by Harry Blackstone, Jr., the stage curtain opens on a large table surmounted by a frame holding a motor to which is attached an enormous gleaming blade that we might see nowhere else but in a lumber mill. The magician stands on stage. Next to him is an attractive young woman, scantily clad. He throws a switch. The saw roars and whines. An assistant sets a wooden plank on the table. The magician pushes the spinning saw toward us and through the plank. He turns off the motor. The assistant shows us the two halves of the newly cut wood. The preliminary demonstration is complete.

The magician then offers his hand to the young woman so that she can climb upon the table. She lies down in the exact position just occupied by the wooden plank. Once again the magician flips the switch. The saw whines. Slowly the magician pushes the revolving blade through the young woman's body, and she rises— unharmed. What makes this act and all its variants so compelling that it has become standard in the repertory of many illusionists?

As with so many tricks, the action is impossible. Yet it is being accomplished before our eyes. But what is significant is the peculiar image of impossibility. The instrument is not only dangerous, but the jagged teeth of the saw stimulate a special shiver in us. When the magician activates its destructiveness by turning on the saw, then the frightening aspects of the instrument are radically augmented. Against this monstrous horror he poses a "delicate" human being.

The fact that the person to be sawn in half is invariably a woman, and a scantily clad one at that, undoubtedly has sexual overtones. When he first performed this trick with a box, Horace Goldin used a man.[6] The performance failed. Success came to him only after he worked with a woman. It is the juxtaposition of the vulnerable and desirable female with imminent danger that arouses our pleasurable concern and with which this kind of act plays.

What makes it possible for us to witness a frightening act like this without flinching? Are we sadists? Hardly, for if we were, we would not recoil if anything suggested real danger. In fact, to induce belief that the danger was real, Goldin would park an ambulance outside the theatre where he showed this trick.[7] One reason we are content to watch the trick is that it is part of a show. All the features of performance: entering a theatre, applauding successive numbers, being pleased by the exotic dress of the illusionist, supply signals that reinforce the presentational and hence privileged character of the event. But then what makes it clear to us that the illusionist's event is "virtual"—that it is not "real"—while the acrobat's event is "actual"? For the naive this distinction may not be evident. Only repeated exposure to theatrical conventions enables one to separate the "actual" from the "virtual" and thus appreciate the sign character in the various parts of an act. The answer also lies in the nature of the acts themselves. A feasible but extremely hazardous act occupies a different realm of reality than does a hazardous but impossible act. We read each act as a different kind of theatrical sign, and this difference serves as a frame for the act.

As we watch the act, we also read each part as a signifying force. We have a signifying apparatus and a dramatistic confrontation. The saw, as we have noted, signifies a terrifying tool. Few members of an audience would be likely to have any familiarity with its cutting power and fewer still would have ever seen anyone injured by such a saw. Yet it has the capacity to excite a lively reaction from people, a result of an imaginative projection of its potential danger. This "real" prop is matched by another "prop," the lady. The magician makes no effort to individualize her. She is deliberately presented as a sign of beauty and delicacy, essentially an abstract figure. It is with these two props that the magician plays his game.

In the first phase of his trick, the magician demonstrates the "actuality" of the saw. Just in case we might doubt that the saw has true cutting power, he runs it through a piece of wood. He thus transforms the saw from a sign of a stage prop to a sign of an actual saw. But since the saw cannot be what it appears to be, the magician is already performing an illusion.

Next he takes the woman who, as I have said, is a sign of beauty and delicacy, and juxtaposes her against the saw. Yet the woman is more than the sign I mentioned. She is an actual person capable of being injured. She is thus a sign and something more than a sign. She stands for something but she also stands for herself.

The nub of the trick is reached. No matter how lethal the saw may appear to be, we know it must be rigged. Yet the magician works in the face of our disbelief. He creates so convincing an illusion of actuality that our eyes accept what our minds hold in abeyance. It is this conflict between eyes and minds that produces the sense of wonder in us.

A trick of illusion such as sawing a woman in half provides a simple but concrete illustration of how we "read" one event in light of another. We see before our eyes the blade of a saw pass through a woman's body. But none of the consequences of that act follow. There is no blood, no severed torso, none of the ghastly horror that logic tells us such an act would produce. We know that the act we have witnessed could not have happened and that therefore the act was not "actual," but "virtual," a perceptual not an existential event. Yet our memory of the "actual" experience persists along with our awareness of the "virtual" event. Appearance and logic set off sparks in our minds, sparks of amazement and delight. Though the trick as trick is over, the image of the trick, because of the continuing tension between appearance and logic, produces that reverberating sense of wonder.

What happens is that we undergo an imaginative transformation. The magic act first claims to operate on a plane of actuality. Sawing a board in half stakes that claim. But at the moment the saw passes through the woman, we discover that the act is, in fact, merely one of appearance, that it is a "virtual" action. We never do find out what actually happens. That is a secret carefully guarded by the magician. Yet since we know there is a secret even though we cannot fathom it, we continue to be mystified.

Dramatic illusion works in an analogous manner. Although it may not always depend upon transformation as tricks of illusion do, transformation is deeply rooted in drama, sometimes explicitly, always implicitly. The actor invariably bridges the gap between what we see and what lies hidden. In some numbers, a dramatic transformation is no different from a magic act. One show with recurrent appeal is the performance by a quick-change artist. In what appears to be an instant, a performer can change from one dress to another or from one character to another. In the 1981 musical, *Dreamgirls*, three aspiring singers dashed through the stage curtain, only to have it rise immediately to reveal them transformed in costume and hair style, presenting themselves as a star trio.

Though this magic-like transformation is one way to exploit dramatic illusion, more fundamental is the metamorphosis of the performer. In 1906, for example, a Dutch actor named Henri DeVries toured the American vaudeville circuit with a sketch in which he played seven characters. They included a cigar manufacturer, his half-witted brother, his father-in-law, a police sergeant, an innkeeper, a grocer, and a house painter.[8] The obvious attraction of the piece was in the way DeVries artfully put on one character after another, thereby inviting the audience to marvel at his protean powers.

Similarly, the Royal Shakespeare Company's renowned production of *The Life and Adventures of Nicholas Nickleby* also employed doubling, but so discreetly that it did not call attention to the actor's shift from one character to another. Rather it sought to hide that transformation by having actors play strong contrasts and allowing sufficient time for character changes to be made. This *sub rosa* transformation is, of course, standard in drama, for most actors do not explore the manner or degree by which they adapt themselves to the roles they play. Only occasionally does the theatre exploit that potentiality for allowing the audience to see the process of alteration.

Unlike a magician, actors or actresses do not pretend to perform an "actual" act which turns out to be mere appearance. They do not hide their real business in order to mystify the spectator. Instead, the actors or actresses perform actual business, say specific lines, engage in perceptible acts of all sorts designed for our satisfaction. These acts are "actual" insofar as they indeed are what the player does. They constitute his or her activity, and make up what I call an act-scheme.

At the same time this act-scheme is full of signs. They signify not a meaning so much as a purported level and sequence of existence: feelings, events, thoughts. These feelings, events, and thoughts belong to hypothetical figures engaged in hypothetical activity that we usually term the action of the play.

In certain shows the actor, like the magician, will present an act-scheme that reveals an action logically impossible but nevertheless psychologically compelling. The portrayal of a death scene, as I have discussed, is just such a show. In a different way though with equally startling results, Zero Mostel, the great American comic actor, achieved one of the classic transformations of the modern theatre in Eugene Ionesco's *Rhinoceros*. In this allegory of the contemporary condition, Ionesco depicts man, with one exception, succumbing to the pressure of the herd. In a dizzying orgy of conformity, people everywhere become thick-skinned, mindless beasts: rhinoceroses. Only Ionesco's modest hero, Berenger, resists the pervasive hardening of sensibility that possesses everyone else. Ionesco conveys the process of change that occurs throughout the city by the use of offstage sounds and onstage reports. Only once does he permit us to see the change for ourselves.

In the middle of the play (Act II, Scene ii), Berenger visits his friend Jean who has failed to appear at work. He is worried about Jean and apologetic about a dispute they have had. In the course of the visit, Jean, angry and stubborn, gradually turns into a rhinoceros. To help the actor portray this metamorphosis, Ionesco provides brief exits so that the actor playing Jean can, if he wishes, alter his appearance in order to create a convincing illusion of "man disappearing into the beast," as John Beaufort reported in *The Christian Science Monitor*.[9] Mostel, however, dispensed with such aid, using neither costume nor make-up changes. Instead, as observed by Walter Kerr in his *New York Herald Tribune* review, Mostel became a rhinoceros before the audience's very eyes: "The shoulders lift, the head juts forward, one foot begins to beat the earth, with such native majesty that dust—real dust—begins to rise like the after-veil that seems to accompany a safari."[10] As more than one reviewer testified, "his grunting and growling and primitive pugnacity [were] photographically vivid."[11]

But of course the reviewer does not mean that literally. Mostel did not transform himself into a "photographically" convincing image of a wild animal. What he did do was put together a pattern of discrete motions (snorts, pawing, wriggling rump, etc.) that could create an acceptable portrayal of what people could assume was rhinoceros behavior. But on what could they base their comparison? Doubtless, only on the most limited and generalized information, thereby leaving Mostel considerable room to maneuver. The electrifying effect—uniformly remarked upon by reviewers —came from the coherent way in which Mostel devised what Walter Kerr in his Sunday column called his "fantastic passage."[12] That fantastic passage was an impossible passage, and Mostel's magnificence lay in his ability to show us the shape of that impossibility. We did not in the least believe that he had changed his nature. Even while generating the image of the beast, he remained the performer. As with other forms of illusion, this transformation was double-faced: it consisted of a sequence of clever motions by Mostel the performer (the act-scheme) that induced an image of a beast (the act-image) which gradually overwhelmed Jean.

A number such as this highlights the relationship between the act-scheme and the act-image. Transformations, like magic acts, manipulate the connection between the two to arouse wonder and play with belief. Tennessee Williams sees the connection in terms of opposites. In Tom Wingfield's address to the audience, quoted in Chapter 1, he states that rather than truth, the playwright offers an image of truth, or to state the condition more accurately, an image of experience critical to the apprehending if not of truth, then at least of human power and limitation.

As a rule, the magician works upon surfaces—objects and people—and he does this through demonstration. By proposing the impossible to us, he defies us to see how he accomplishes it. Taking great pains to explain what he is about to do, he ostensibly creates conditions that should prevent him from achieving his objective. In that way the precision of the act-scheme is an essential part of the subsequent mystification. The more explicit the magician is about the gestures and sequence of the act-scheme, the more thoroughly he imprints an image on our minds that the actual act-scheme will confirm.

Unlike the magician, Mostel does not offer his number to us directly. The impulses that transformed Jean seem to arise spontaneously within the character and situation. Yet Ionesco lays out the plan for this number in his script, and Mostel structures Jean's mounting disgruntlement in a sequence as precise as Blackstone's for sawing a woman in half. Through that controlled structure, he makes the metamorphosis convincing. But conviction here has little or nothing to do with credibility. Again, whatever notion an audience may have about rhinoceros behavior is rudimentary at best and probably non-existent. Conviction must then come from the twin business of introducing a few signs that fit a conventional idea of rhinoceros and then building those signs into an internally consistent system of activity. Each part of the act validates every other part so that presentational rather than mimetic logic prevails. While mimesis may play a part to the extent that such a motion as pawing may serve as a sign for animal fury, the dominant quality of the act-scheme is metaphoric.

Another type of transformation, unlike that of Jean's, offers a further and somewhat different kind of metaphor. Rather than demonstrating an impossibility, it posits one. The situation is mundane: it shows a "woman" going through successive stages of pregnancy, delivery, and child rearing. The unusual thing about the act, however, is that the show is Italian *commedia dell'arte* and the "woman" is the trickster-servant Arlecchino or Harlequin.

A Dutch scenario of the eighteenth century presents "the illness, pregnancy, and marvellous [sic] confinement of Harlequin as well as the education of his young son."[13] Accompanying illustrations depict the key stages of Harlequin's strange experience. What is marvelous about Harlequin's confinement and subsequent trials is not the strangeness, however, but the very ordinariness. Harlequin goes through all the steps that any mother undergoes.

The humor and dramatic appeal arise merely from the fact that a man is the "mother," and moreover that man is the scamp Harlequin: the victimizer-as-victim. Behind the act-scheme of the actor playing Harlequin going through these routine steps are two act-images: that of Harlequin-as-mother and that of mothering in general. Because Harlequin is a stock character, however, and the identification between actor and role is intimate (as was the case with Charlie Chaplin and Groucho Marx), we do not perceive the act-scheme and first act-image as disparate. The dramatic interest lies in the discrepancy between the generic image of motherhood, familiar to the audience in a way rhinoceros behavior could not be, and the bizarre act-scheme the scenario provides. Interaction between that generic image and the act-scheme functions as an expanded comic metaphor.

Each of the three illusionary performances that I have described relies on double display. Each has a performer go through a number or series of numbers that we can see and hear. Each has another face that we can sense but not perceive. The play between what is evident and what is hidden provides the source of dramatic power. To what extent the doubleness of double display comes to the forefront of audience awareness depends on the type of illusion as well as its style. Almost all prestidigitation tantalizes us, challenging us to close the gap between the perceived act and the true act.

Theatrical styles, on the other hand, differ greatly in the extent to which they stress the distinction between performances and enactment. When there is obvious disconnection between the act-scheme, that is, the performative acts generated by the players, and the act-image, the fictional event it is supposed to signify, we tend to call that style *theatricalism* or *presentationalism*. In contrast, when the act-scheme approximates the appearance of the act-image, we call that *realism* or *representationalism*. But as will become clear, correspondence between scheme and image is never, can never be exact. Just as the idea for an act was central to acts of skill, so the idea of correspondence between dramatic schemes and images is critical. Each act-scheme is a complex of signs that stimulate both images of experience and ideas about images. In Peter Brook's production of *Marat/Sade*,[14] he has the Herald call for the execution of the aristocrats during the French Revolution. As their bloody deaths are enacted, one of the four singers pours red paint from one bucket to another. Later in the scene blood is poured again, but this time it's blue. The visual pun combined with the recital of the executions evokes a half-humorous, half-grim image of the stories we've heard and the movies we've seen of the reign of terror under the sign of Madame Guillotine.

Thinking of a dramatic show as a double display clarifies its continuity with other shows, illusionary or otherwise. Even more, it allows us to recognize the various ways in which components of this display can relate to each other. The act-scheme consists of the movements and sounds made by the performers as well as the way they manipulate objects. It embraces all perceptible features of a show: costumes, lights, theatrical space. Both the presentation and its context follow established conventions—are coded—and these conventions provide a foundation for a particular expression of the code: the individual act-scheme.

The act-image, in turn, may allude to any kind of possible, probable, or hypothetical action, human or otherwise. It may embrace a mode of action that cannot be realized literally but only figuratively. To dramatize Nicholas Nickleby climbing Sir Mulberry Hawk's coach in order to strike him, the director could have brought a coach onstage. That would have made one kind of act-scheme likely. But this act, as realized in the RSC production, resulted from actors transforming themselves into an idea of a coach, and thus produced quite another—and far more figurative —act-scheme. The literal coach, had it been used, and the figurative one both allude to the same general image, though the chosen act-scheme, by resorting to the unexpected transformation of people-into-object, wrapped the physical encounter between Nicholas and Sir Mulberry in an air of wonder.

The act-scheme and the act-image are thus complementary aspects of presentational double display. In one sense they have the unity that Saussure attributed to the signifier and the signified, and it is tempting to see the relation between scheme and image as similarly connected. But the tie between scheme and image is much looser, capable of being detached and reconstructed. While each presentation is a compound of these types of acts, the relationship between them is continually changing.

At the simplest level we can distinguish shows that embody contrast of scheme and image from those that treat scheme and image congruently. The scene of Jean's transformation, Harlequin's motherhood, the pouring out of blue blood, and Nicholas' leap upon Sir Mulberry's coach are all instances of contrast between scheme and image. The connection between the two is patently symbolic. Like a magician, the performer transforms the played sequence into an instrument by means of which we can cradle the ostensible image. Part of the theatrical excitement, furthermore, comes not merely from our fascination with the transformation on the mimetic level, but from our recognition of the virtuosity with which the performer makes the transformation. We thus entertain in our minds both the artistry of the player and the simulated image of the act.

Many cases of scheme-image contrast can be found in traditional theatre. The pantomimic sword fights of the Peking Opera or the assertive stance (*mie*) of the Kabuki are conventionalized schemes for conveying narrative images. A notable instance in which performers attempted to fuse new presentational schemes with new images occurred in the People's Republic of China during the Cultural Revolution. The forms of classical ballet were adapted in order to dramatize a new revolutionary heroism, as in the exemplary piece, *The Red Detachment of Women*. In contemporary theatre—especially that of the avant-garde—we can find many examples of contrast in double display. The many experiments in mechanizing or abstracting human action require just such contrast between scheme and image. In his production of *Ubu Roi*, Peter Brook stimulates a brilliant, disturbing image when he has certain of his characters hurl themselves against a brick wall at the back of the stage. For a moment they hold a pose, as though they were splattered against the wall, and then break away. But in that brief moment they give concrete vision to the idea of the wanton horror of political execution, the metaphoric concreteness of the act-scheme producing enduring reverberations in the audience's memory.

The interplay of scheme and image appears to operate differently in the naturalistic theatre. I say "appears" because the difference between naturalistic and non-naturalistic performance is more apparent than real. Differences there are, but they are differences of degree rather than of kind. In theory naturalism seeks to create the illusion that act-schemes and act-images are congruent. But absolute congruency is impossible to achieve, as we can readily see in scenes which depict a person dying. In the 1947 film *A Double Life* Ronald Colman plays a Shakespearean actor who in turn plays Othello. Unfortunately, the actor cannot divorce his own jealousies from that of the Moor, and so he seeks to strangle the woman whom he believes is betraying him and who, incidentally, is also playing Desdemona. Such fancies are intriguing, of course, but they are the stuff of film. However far a performer may go, he or she cannot produce complete congruence between what he or she acts onstage and what that act is intended to represent. Rehearsal and repetition make that impossible. Nevertheless, though absolute congruence is not possible, the illusion of congruence is well within the artistic capacity of the theatre.

By choice of subject as well as techniques of playing, the performer submerges the act-scheme. The principal means are proportionality and consistency. Instead of revelling in sudden changes or contrasts, the performer endeavors to keep all the elements in proper scale with one another, whether at the level of vocal delivery, scenic scale, or actor-audience relationship. Immediately, one can recognize that this type of unity of effect need not be confined to naturalism. The symbolism of Maurice Maeterlinck, as realized in Meyerhold's productions, treats the scheme-image link in the same manner. Both naturalism and symbolism have affinities to Richard Wagner's *Gesamtkunstwerk* in their tendency toward harmony, and Bertolt Brecht's insistence on breaking the harmony of performance is applicable to both styles. While Brecht proclaimed an anti-illusionistic aim in promoting disunity, he was actually demanding recognition once again of the value of scheme/image contrast rather than scheme/image congruence. Either relationship is illusionistic. The difference between them is artistic not mimetic.

Contrast of scheme and image, as we saw, enhances the marvels of performance and sharpens performing ideas. What then is the purpose of seeking congruence? Since presentation affords us the opportunity to exceed ourselves, congruence in illusionary shows seems to contradict the very nature of presentation. That is why it attempts to obscure evidence of performing. If the images of action are going to limit performing capabilities, then neither the scheme nor the image can go beyond what humans actually can do. Figurative action must be sacrificed.

But if the cost of naturalism was the reduction of human scale, the gain was the presentation of extraordinary environments. Instead of the wonder of action, the theatre offered the wonder of place. Sometimes that wonder was literal: houses appeared to burn onstage, chariots seemed to race through a colosseum, gods appeared to descend from the heavens. But even where the most depressing hovel was displayed, the audience had the chance to visit it—free of any risk to itself. In effect, the greater the exactitude with which a replica was put onstage, the more miraculous it seemed. Rather than finding the contrast between scheme and image, audiences found theatrical contrast between their presence in comfortable seats and the ostensibly literal rendition of a quite different place before them. The theatricality of naturalism was thereby in no way inferior to the theatricality of theatricalism. David Belasco knew that, and prepared the ground so well that the Moscow Art Theatre met great hospitality and eager imitation when it first played in New York in 1923.

A show then, of whatever kind, consists of performers who present acts capable of generating various kinds of images. Because the acts themselves fall into fairly distinct categories of skill, glorification, and illusion, the images too reveal distinct characteristics, depending on the kind of act. Scheme and image are volatile; they interact subtly with one another. But for the performer and anyone who works through a performer, control lies only through the scheme. Every scheme is performative. One is not more representational than another, for the moment performers rehearse or practice with the intention of performing, they modify otherwise normative behavior to meet performing conditions. This is manifest in so simple a matter as how they walk onstage. Whatever their act, they infuse the plan of it with a purpose that ideates it. They endeavor to create a scheme that will most richly evoke the sensations potential in the motivating idea. Thus, even in its most mimetic form, the act-scheme serves as a metaphor for the image it generates.

Chapter 3

Iconic presentation

Holidays mean celebration, and few holidays pass without shows of glorification. Parades and fireworks, sports contests and pageants sprout at these special seasons. The parade, as I've shown, is a type of celebratory show that is recurrent throughout history. Whether David dances his triumph in the streets or the Romans bring home their spoils of victory, whether Renaissance princes assert their authority in magnificent entries or modern states vaunt their patriotism on revolutionary anniversaries, parades and processions are communal demonstrations of universal appeal. As shows, they are also a key to an entire aspect of performance that is insufficiently recognized.

This aspect may be examined in a modest illustration. The Memorial Day parade in a small American town is one of the simplest and most unassuming forms of show. Local elementary and secondary schools bring out their bands in school uniform. Volunteer firemen march with their squads, following brightly polished fire trucks. Aged veterans, kepis on heads, sport medals as they shuffle along. And following this line of alternating bands, firemen, trucks, and veterans, will be an open car filled with Gold Star Mothers who lost their sons in military action. The simple movement of this line from one part of the town to another constitutes the show with the added spice of drum majorettes showing their skill in twirling.

Among the kinds of shows I have discussed, this type of parade is clearly a show of celebration. It celebrates the past and the present, the past glory, suffering, and achievements of the people, together with their present unity and idealism. In that sense the show confirms established values, and it does so by mere demonstration.

The Gold Star Mothers do not have to do anything. They merely need to sit as symbols of sacrifice. The parade displays them to the crowd that lines the streets and through the display links spectator and participant. Nor does the action of the parade in itself have any necessary meaning. Unlike the Stations of the Cross, the parade route does not normally symbolize any progressive action. In fact, it is absolutely imperative that the route *not* have significance because every section along the way, every street in which people stand to watch the procession, must have equal validity.

Despite the fact that a parade moves from one point to another and thus passes through time, it is primarily a spatial show. The parade successively demonstrates itself—its "Mothers," for example—to the crowd, but each demonstration is as important as any other. The exception is when there is a reviewing stand of notables. But even then, heightened though the excitement may be, the significance of each element of the procession is the same at every stage of the route. That significance is in pure display, a display that may have a touch of magic to the extent that temporarily people such as the Gold Star Mothers seem to have an aura about them. A more limited, yet essentially identical, type of parade-show occurs when heroes are welcomed to a city. Again, the mere display of the heroes—whether astronauts or world champions—is sufficient to constitute a show. They wave their hands, they smile, but essentially they do nothing. They are.

The display of being is central to shows of celebration. Behind the being may reside known skills, military power, or some historical event. But in the form that the show assumes, the key figures do not need to exercise any of these powers. They must only conform to the symbolic image invested in them by the spectators. And the extent of adulation heaped upon them is determined quantitatively. The numbers of those marching in a parade, the amount of paper floating from windows, and the size of the crowd lining the route decide the success of the show.

In the parades that I have described, despite the symbolization of the heroes, little effort is made to extend the symbol into the imaginative realm, which is perhaps a reflection of the democratic ethos. The royal entry of the Renaissance, by comparison, moved the procession toward an illusionary realm. Still, in essence these celebratory processions are alike. It is only in the detail and in the symbolic amplitude that there is a difference.

The ruler is the hero in the entry, and the procession takes him

through the main parts of the city. For the entry of King James into
London in 1604, sumptuous arches and obelisks were erected along
the way. As James and his entourage wended their way through the
streets, he was greeted at each stop, sometimes by speeches,
sometimes by song. The arches themselves, however, were
emblems of key ideas such as Britain as a Garden of Plenty and
Fortune standing above all. Figures in the guise of goddesses and
virtues addressed the monarch.[1]

The nature of this show is somewhat mixed because the ruler is
both performer and audience. He displays himself to the populace
in order to be honored. At the same time the populace, in their
devices as well as in their persons lining the processional route,
show themselves as good and loyal subjects. Each as performer and
spectator confirms the stability of the realm. Such an interaction is
possible only when the performer and the spectator are participating
in a shared value system. Indeed, the procession as a type of show is
celebratory because it celebrates a common bond. By uniting
morality, antiquity, and majesty, the procession embraces all
possible states of being.

In this instance, no attempt is made to transform the king into
another figure, though he is shown to have intercourse with
strange and wonderful creatures. But we have seen that not
infrequently, as in the case of Cosimo de' Medici, the "hero" on
display is endowed with additional grandeur as a mythic or
legendary hero. He assumes the mantle of the additional hero
without losing his own majesty. It is merely another way of
intensifying the being that is celebrated.

We can see that an essential feature of this kind of celebratory
show is a glorified stasis that exists solely for admiration. It is the
accumulated marchers, costumes, street decorations, music, and
professed honor that serve as a setting for the jewel of the
procession. Indeed, an inferior setting is a sign of disloyalty, an
insult, for a celebratory show has or seeks a focus which it aims to
endow with all the glorification that a community is capable of
bestowing. It may glorify power or it may glorify achievement,
but whichever it celebrates, it does so by blending massed
performers with a rich context of spectacle.

As I have pointed out, display is static and spatial. While the
admiration may increase in the course of the show, that increase is
less important than the widespread sharing that the show produces.
The dynamics of celebration operate in shows of skill and illusion,

too, though they do not appear in so pure a form, nor are they
always so prominent. Nevertheless, they do occur in all types of
presentation, for the qualities of the celebratory show embody one
potentiality of the art of presentation. While we usually think of a
show as being transitory, ephemeral, no sooner offered than over,
there is something in the nature of the show process that seeks to
concretize itself, to resist change, to make itself into a permanent
emblem. While in the show of celebration this tendency seeks its
fullest expression, it operates in all other forms of show as a
counter-action to the unravelling qualities of show.

One way in which the concretizing impulse works is by stressing
the act as illustration or example. Even in shows of skill, which
intrinsically are contingent rather than exemplary, some performers
treat their acts as demonstrations. The easiest way to do this is by
framing the focal action within a celebratory structure. "Ladies and
gentlemen," the master of ceremonies will say, "Mr. X will now
perform the feat for which he is known throughout the world. He
will complete a triple somersault without a net." Often the act will
be described graphically, thereby giving the spectators vivid
images of what they will see. A feature act of this sort can, of
course, be treated in a more "dramatic" way. The master of
ceremonies may stress the difficulty of accomplishing the feat, and
thereby raise fear that the performer may fail. This latter approach
is non-illustrative, for it heightens uncertainty while the illustrative
approach celebrates mastery.

The framing of shows of skill is abetted by other means of
stressing displays as display. The manner in which the performer
makes an entrance, the relationship with assistants, and the use
made of preliminary, rather simple, routines all contribute to the
exemplary nature of the performance. Often as a sequence of
numbers unfolds, the performer will momentarily pose as though
to say, "See how effortlessly I do this marvelous thing." All these
supporting means cannot change the fundamental nature of an act
of skill. It cannot be truly illustrative as long as genuine skill and
therefore genuine failure exist. In essence, however much it may
exemplify the performer's powers, the act of skill is only
tangentially a celebration.

Shows of illusion, on the other hand, are another matter. They
allow the performer greater latitude in presenting an act. We have
seen that the act of sawing a woman in half could be presented as a
demonstration of the magician's powers or as a daring attempt that

may not succeed. Unlike an act of skill, this act of illusion is essentially demonstrative. Though we are thrilled by the horror of seeing a buzz saw pass through a woman, we "know" that she will not be harmed. The magician is actually showing us his power to convince us despite ourselves, and to that extent is celebrating his command over us.

Certain great tricks—levitation, climbing a rope, sawing a woman in half, effecting the disappearance of tigers and elephants —in effect come to be ritualized. Since they contain peculiarly paradoxical metaphors—a man climbing something so absolutely limp as a rope, for instance—they assume a miraculous quality. Because we do not penetrate the mystery of their accomplishment and yet are repeatedly astonished by their achievement, we accord them a special status. They become exemplary of the magician's art and power. In the past particularly, the great illusionists such as Houdini, Thurston, Goldin, and Blackstone adopted an aura of majesty, and wove about themselves the illusion that the feats they performed did indeed defy nature. Their acts, as a result, no longer were intense efforts to achieve conviction but rather condescending demonstrations of their infinite powers. In effect, they sought to sustain the illusion that illusion was actuality.

As we see, the illustrative quality inheres in the very act of illusion as well as in the way a performer chooses to present it. The same is true of dramatic illusion, though drama permits a greater range of style. A fictional action is in itself neither didactic nor singular. It can be seen as an illustration of analogous actions or of abstract ideas. On the other hand, it can be regarded anecdotally, that is, as a particular case of more or less interest. Whether the illustrative or non-illustrative aspect of the action is emphasized depends on its treatment: its inherent structure and the way the performer utilizes that structure.

Drama as demonstration appears widely in the history of the theatre, but the demonstrative element is not normally perceived as one of the options in the art of presentation. The schematic and skeletal character of play texts allows us to project contemporary styles into the dialogue. And since post-Renaissance dramatic criticism has stressed drama as imitation rather than as demonstration, we are not attuned to noticing the exemplary nature of so much of our drama.

Our earliest proto-drama in medieval times provides us with a case. The Winchester Troper contains the histrionic-like trope known as the *Quem quaeritis*. We can read it as the dramatized experience of the three Marys learning that the Christ has risen. But in the context of the time and the biblical source, the little playlet is first of all a demonstration. This is made evident by the fact that it apparently was repeated at Easter matins. Its very structure reveals its exemplary character. After the angel tells the Marys that Christ has risen, the text directs the person playing the angel to reveal the place where Christ lay and to show the clergy and then all the congregation the cloths with which the cross was wrapped.[2] The display is thus a confirmation of a tenet of the faith and a demonstration of the power of the Lord. The action depicted is historical in one sense but is manifested in its symbolic vesture. In that sense the act is not only illusionary but also celebratory.

The demonstrative character is further reinforced by the depth to which the *Quem quaeritis* is embedded in the imaginative and liturgical context. It does not exist as an isolated piece of work but serves as part of the confirmatory process of the entire Easter service. Hence it is a special case. Yet throughout the medieval and early Renaissance periods, plays were regularly presented as exemplary. In such a piece as *Everyman*, for instance, the subject and organization serve an instructional purpose. But the exemplary form did not necessarily depend on simple didactic ends. It was so strongly established as a way of looking at human action in certain cultures that the most secular performances adopted a demonstrative structure. This is especially true of the English Renaissance where the double plot and copious action required this type of show.

The final scenes of Shakespeare's romances and problem plays provide a number of actions that are fundamentally exemplary. At the end of *Measure for Measure* Duke Vincentio gives a demonstration of his knowledge and power. We do not discover anything new; we merely witness a preordained action. In performance the scene has the effect of an unfolding ritual, every step of which is not unexpected. We are satisfied by the working of expectation. In *The Winter's Tale* there is surprise. We do not know that Hermione still lives. Yet the curious thing is that even when we do know the story, the finale loses none of its power. The surprise itself is not intrinsic, for we focus upon a demonstration of person vs. time. Its agent is Paulina, who stages it, and what is demonstrated is the conquest of time. One of the reasons that the temporal logic of events gives way in this persuasion scene of reconciliation is because the act we see is a demonstration. To effect reconciliation the lost child, who was divorced by space, has to be restored to the presence of father and mother. When this space is closed, time no longer matters. That is why the punitive separation of Leontes and Hermione for sixteen years has little meaning. Their actions occur in a moral and spiritual universe where time does not hold sway. It is futile to think about what Hermione did for sixteen years or what she and Leontes will now do, for the scene shows the wonder of rebirth as though it were a magician's illusion.

In terms of the dynamic structure of a demonstrative scene, the characters appear subordinated to the ritual-like activity that they choose or is chosen for them. Their course is laid out, very much like a magician's act, and their function is to display the event. The Duke in *Measure for Measure* and Paulina in *The Winter's Tale* move the action, but they move it according to a plan. They do not struggle against odds fraught with suspense. Instead, they proceed inevitably along a prescribed path. This exhibition of power and mystery is quite different in quality from the kind of uncertain parrying in which Hamlet engages in the duel with Laertes; by pursuing the set course the characters confirm a kind of moral faith. That faith is not so easily articulated as the faith implicit in the liturgical and moral plays of an earlier period, but it is a kind of faith, a faith in the mastery of spirit over event.

Perhaps the most significant aspect of scenic demonstration has to do with the treatment of time. Because of its unfolding nature, presentation is a temporal art as much if not more than a spatial art. "What next," is the implicit question we all ask as we watch a show. Therefore, any effort to retard time, or to mute it, works against the nature of presentation. But, as in every art, the artist often finds the greatest challenge in defying the inherent nature of that art. The painter seeks to create expression in the face of a subject; the sculptor to suggest movement in immobile blocks; the musician space in a narrow flow of time. So too does the performer seek to suggest permanence in the flux of action, and we have seen in a preliminary way how that might be done.

Reinforcing this esthetic impulse is a sociological one. The treatment of time in presentation reflects not only the imperatives of performance but also the conceptions of an historical period. In Western tradition there has long been a conflict in the image of time. Plato envisaged time as cyclical, or rather as a sequence of events that unfolded or turned in upon themselves. His notion has affinities with the Christian ideas of sempiternity and eternity. Yet the dominant Hebraic and Christian image was of an unfolding time, a time moving toward an ultimate union of man and God. This division, it should be obvious, is not so simple. There never was a distinctly Greek and a distinctly Hebraic notion of time that excluded its opposite. Nevertheless, there did prevail in certain periods conceptions of time that were different from each other. One conception tended to see life as recurrent and the unfolding of events as various yet fundamentally unchanging. Action was repetitious, and no matter how seemingly new a moment might be, it was merely an example of a continuity governed not by time but by idea, such as the idea of God or the idea of culture.

A contrasting conception, in fact the one that has dominated post-Renaissance thinking, sees time as irreversible. Whatever event occurs occurs only once; it may have analogous successors, but in essence it is a creature of time, of the past first of all. By moving through the present an event produces the future. To command events, then, people must struggle to use and master time. They are always engaged in a tussle with the future, and, therefore, are always aware of a disparity between where they are and where they wish to be.

In presentation the first conception of time finds its expression through the demonstrative form. Since events transcend time, as in *The Winter's Tale*, the performer can show the superiority of a moral, spiritual, or cultural ideal by exercising pure display. Not that time disappears. It merely becomes subordinate to other powers: spatial relationships and design in particular. But the full workings of demonstrative action have one drawback, because this type of action is effective only when there is common agreement between performer and spectator. The purpose of demonstration is to confirm established states, not challenge them. This is readily evident in agit-prop drama and its derivatives. Anyone who has seen plays that demonstrate the evil of capitalism, for instance, or the rapacity of imperialism, knows that the plays' effectiveness remains contingent upon one's accepting the principles being illustrated. The power of such a play as *The Trial of the Catonsville Nine* rested mainly on the fact that it was seen for the most part by believers whose strong beliefs were finally articulated publicly. The relief and sense of power that an audience feels when this occurs outweighs any questions of the presentation itself, for the presentation merely proves what the audience believes.

It is particularly in the turmoil and experimentalism of the twentieth century that the demonstrative character of drama has once again become important. Influential in opening drama to this style is the increasing respect with which non-western drama has come to be regarded. Traditional societies, as one might expect, would be more likely to have plays that are demonstrative in form since these plays would reflect established values.

The re-emergence of iconic presentation with its emphasis on demonstration and exemplary forms of action, may have its roots in the Marxian ideal of communistic time. Accompanying the image of the withering of the state is the expectation that class conflict, hence human conflict, will cease. No longer will there be need of competition or ceaseless striving, and once that stage is achieved the urge to *do* something, to pursue some goal, will give way to self-fulfillment, to contentment with being. Instead of time acting as a spur, it will exist as a seamless continuity affording cyclical renewal to human beings. Herbert Marcuse explicitly distinguishes between this image of communal time and the stress upon historical time characteristic of capitalism. For him the fierce struggles that have dominated industrial society reflect a concept of irreversible time.

Marcuse's division between a capitalistic, progressive time sense and a communistic, cyclical time scheme is another version of the distinction between poetry and history, first evident in Aristotle and which became a major concern of the Renaissance. Against Sir Philip Sidney's argument for the superiority of poetry, we need to set Thomas Carlyle's elevation of history. For Sidney, the universalizing capacity of poetry gives it its great power over the human imagination. But we need to recognize that the universalization of poetry is also a means of making poetry timeless. To the degree that a specific poetic work captures a universal sentiment or depicts a universal event, it is not subject to the ravages of time. In this idea lies the notable triumph of art. Shakespeare's argument to his friend in the sonnets, that his rhyme will outlast time, is an expression of that attitude.

Carlyle, by elevating history above all other endeavors, sacralizes the specific case. He arrives at this estimate just as industry and science are beginning to transform man's sense of himself in time. The possibility that humans can conquer time by manipulating nature is intimately bound to the sway of history. Karl Marx's work exemplifies in another way the belief that a command over historical process leads to a command over the future. To the doyens of history, events follow a linear sequence that may appear at times to repeat itself. In its essential character, however, the sequence of historical events moves inevitably through cause and effect to a series of crises. Within such a frame of reference time is an unfolding expression of economic, cultural, and political forces.

It is against this conception of time that Marcuse argues. It is also against this conception that theatrical experimentation has struggled in one form or another throughout the twentieth century. That struggle is expressed in many different ways: as an assertion of the theatrical nature of presentation, as a search for the exposition of the unconscious, as a means of revolting against the time-bound architecture of realistic drama.

Jean Genet, in his essay "The Strange Word *Urb* . . .," gives the clearest utterance to the root difference that has prevailed when he distinguishes between drama as history and drama as theology.[3] By theological time he clearly means a symbolic image of time that is not bound by natural causation. The source of the theology is conceptual, that is, the theatrical events move in a time sequence which obeys intellectual rather than astral powers. What a person displays in time, therefore, is tied not to a past or future but to the person's symbolic being. An action is thus an expression of that being, actually a demonstration of that person's being.

This view of a person in time is quite different from that of a person in historical time. It affects not only the way character is related to action but also the way the performer relates to his or her presentation. It is this difference that lies behind Bertolt Brecht's view of alienation or estrangement. The terms are unfortunate, however. Demonstrative performers are not necessarily alienated although their sense of their involvement in dramatic time is distanced. The techniques that Brecht cultivated among his actors encouraged them to "show" their action. By use of motion pictures during rehearsal, by storytelling exercises, and by concentrating on the events as events, he sought to enhance the illustrative purposes of his plays.

One of the great scenes of twentieth-century drama exemplifies drama as illustration or icon. It is that spectacular, almost miraculous transformation in *Galileo* when the former Cardinal Barberini is dressed in his papal robes as Pope Urban VIII. The scene deals with the question of whether or not to torture Galileo in order to secure a confession. At first the pope is against torturing Galileo. As the discussion proceeds, he is being dressed in his papal garments in preparation for a conclave. One garment after another is draped upon him, and with each garment his resistance to the torture lessens. By the time he is fully robed, he permits the Inquisition to show Galileo the instruments of torture.

The action here is quite obviously not psychological. The pope does not interact with the garments put upon him. Instead, there is a ritual determinism in the robing. The garments act as an external force that subsumes the man. Brecht is, of course, demonstrating one of his recurrent themes: the transformation of the human being by outside forces. Within the frame of his demonstrative purpose, the action does not have that simplified form of display which we saw in the *Quem quaeritis* trope. The effort of the inquisitor to persuade the pope to allow the torture conforms to a conventional linear time progression. The power of the scene does not arise from this rather simplified persuasion activity, but instead from the fact that this activity is framed within the broader, more startling iconic action of the transformation.

Indeed, the emphasis on transformation which we have seen in the avant-garde theatre of the last generation is a particular expression of the iconic form. The works of Meyerhold, Peter Brook, and particularly Joseph Chaikin grapple with the shaping of theatrical action into icons. Meyerhold's experiments in bio-mechanics sought to devise physical means that would give literal form to emotive and attitudinal states. By externalizing behavior and refining its artistic shape, he in effect turned the action from a transitory event passing through time into a nearly tangible embodiment of an idea about the event. More recently, Joseph Chaikin mythologized behavior by building a show about a theme. Perhaps his most thoroughgoing achievement along this line was his production of *The Serpent*. Around the theme of murder—its alienating nature to be combated only by communal unity—he arranged a variety of associated but not sequential actions. Each of the actions—the human Tree of Life or the repetitive replaying of the Kennedy assasination—was refined into a symbolic form. Most of these "numbers" lacked the dialectical interaction that we expect in Ibsenian drama. Instead, they functioned as highly imaginative projections of an informing image. As such, they were illustrative of that image. We did not see the performers presenting characters struggling through historicized events, such as the Kennedy murder. Rather they acted out a comment about that murder.

The strength of this iconic approach is evident in many shows. The musical theatre has always retained a touch of it, especially in the production numbers. It is also apparent in the struggle going on in various countries where traditional theatre is vying with western influences. Wole Soyinka dramatizes that struggle in his play *Death and the King's Horseman*. The play revolves about the determination of a British colonial official to prevent the enactment of a native ritual in which the horseman of the chief follows his master into death. In the first part of the play we have a glimpse of the people's ceremony; in the second half, the struggle to thwart the ceremony. Each half not only emphasizes the opposite sides in the struggle, the native people and the colonial society, but its form follows contrary theatrical examples. The ceremony combines two elements: recited praise of the act and a demonstrative dance revealing the joy with which the horseman goes to meet death. In this section the horseman's act transcends time by challenging death. It contrasts strongly with the second half, in which we are aware throughout of the pressure of time on every aspect of colonial action.

The few examples I have given of iconic presentation do not and cannot embrace all the variations that we find throughout the history of presentation. Often, drama mixes the demonstrative and the contingent. This occurs with considerable frequency in so-called episodic drama. When a dramatist employs a loose narrative, the choice of each scene is somewhat arbitrary. If narrative flow does not demand a particular sequence in any absolute sense—in other words, if the obligatory scene is not so firmly obligated— then the decision as to what will follow what is less tied to the organic flow of events and responds to other impulses. When Shakespeare places Henry VI on a hill to witness the contrasting actions of a father who slays his son and a son who slays his father, the purpose is not narrative cohesion (*III Henry VI*, II.ii). These contrasting actions instead serve as a moral demonstration of the horror of war. Like the famous robing scene in *Galileo*, the substance of the activity may depict conflicts of will but the setting of the activity treats it iconically.

Similar choices are evident throughout Shakespeare's work and indeed throughout English Renaissance drama. But, in a certain sense, the demonstrative form is characteristic of all drama. After all, the performer's choice of material is for display no matter how secretive that display may be. Even for the most unified of dramatic works, the play as a whole is an illustration of a view of human action. Yet even though in the most fundamental sense every presentation is a demonstration of some sort, it is useful and indeed necessary to distinguish those esthetic structures which are cast in the form of open demonstration and those that make the demonstration as oblique as possible.

The distinction is important for our understanding of how the act of presentation is structured and how the performers relate to that act. To sum up, the distinguishing marks of the iconic presentation are three. First, the performer stresses being rather than becoming. The performer's battle with time is less important than the fulfillment of it. The action has a greater spatial significance than a temporal one. Second, the action that is performed involves less the overcoming of temporal resistance and more the ritual enactment of prescribed movements. Indeed, the activity of speech and gesture is precise and critical. And one is conscious of an unfolding display rather than the relief of suspense. Third, the effect produced by the demonstrative event is illumination more than catharsis. We have a sense of an act falling into place (a puzzle solved, a miracle wrought). Not that the demonstration will lack emotional power. It is merely that the emotion is a by-product of the completion of the demonstration. Such iconic demonstration, as we have seen, moves us toward awe, wonder, and ultimately insight into mystery.

Chapter 4

Dialectic presentation

In contrast to iconic presentation, in which the performers reveal mastery over their acts, there is another mode of presentation. Here the performers engage in activity over which they do not have total control: this I call *dialectic presentation*. In shows of skill, that margin of incomplete control is actual. The acrobat or the juggler needs to exert unremitting attention on every phase of an act to assure its proper enactment. While such performers may have preliminary tricks that do not involve much risk, in order to excite an audience they frequently carry their shows to the limit where the risk is genuine and the control can slip away from them.

This showing of a risky act involves a significant shift of focus from what we found in iconic presentation. There the temporal dimension gave precedence to the spatial unfolding of an event. However, when the future is uncertain, as in a dialectic presentation, our attention becomes fixed on the moment-to-moment progression of the act. Whereas iconic presentation is absolute, dialectic display is provisional, and time supersedes space as the main ingredient of a show's structure. We watch the performer move toward the critical points of the act, figuratively or literally holding our breath. The performer's success in the act releases the mounting tension among the spectators and so produces applause.

In this type of act the dangers to the performer are actual. Gymnasts and acrobats have real problems of balance, timing, and inner uncertainty. Depending on the specific nature of the trick, timing may be the most crucial element, as it is among aerial gymnasts, or it may be balance, as among wire-walkers. Tension is an enemy and concentration a necessity. In sum, we have performers projecting an act and concentrating their energies to master those features that they know from experience hinder its effective completion. We can call these features collectively the *resistance* in the act.

Resistance is a key element in a dialectic act as well. It is the factor that the performer needs to overcome in order to realize a performance. It is the focus of the risk that resides in the act, and overcoming it produces an elemental pleasure for the spectators. In dialectic presentation, if there is a real question of control, the resistance has the distinct potentiality of defeating the performer. The tension between the will to do the act and the obstacle to its fulfillment is thus neatly calibrated so that when the performer prevails, there is not so much awe but release—that is, catharsis.

In certain shows of skill, such as gymnastics, the clear-cut completion of the trick is of prime importance. Yet there is a subtle connection between the doing and the way the doing appears. The ability to do a trick depends to a degree upon grace and form, especially if the trick requires niceness of timing and balance. In that respect, esthetics enter into the success of the show. But to this sort of functional esthetics is sometimes added another dimension. In ice skating shows, as in other contests or shows involving physical feats, athletes are rated not only on completing the required maneuvers but also on performing them with style. This is the element of demonstration that we have considered before and that the dialectic presentation shares with the iconic. The two modes of presentation thus are not absolutely distinct but reflect different emphases.

The balance between esthetics and skill is more neatly struck in the arts that have esthetic objectives but require superb skillfulness. Here dance and music are preeminent. The dance performer does not quite face the acrobat's risk or rather the risk is often shifted to the esthetic level. The problem may not be whether the performer will make the leap or the pirouette that is called for, but whether he or she will do it in the way that has been projected and the spectators have come to expect. The dancer too faces resistance, but it is artistic as well as physical. Even more, the dancer seeks to make that resistance apparent while in the process of overcoming it. Moving through space, the dancer makes that space tangible, shaping it by cutting through it, using time to defeat space.

As we have found before, when we turn to a consideration of shows of illusion, all the elements become extremely complicated. Take, for instance, the matter of resistance. In shows of skill, we saw that resistance derives from the actual impediments to doing a trick, those inherent in the form of the trick itself and those churning in the performer. In shows of illusion, resistance is multiplied. The resistance to completing the illusion (speaking a type of verse, for example, or making certain gestures) is similar to that which we found in shows of skill. There is also the internal resistance building within the performer: tension, lack of confidence, distraction, and so on. This parallels the obstacles that the acrobat faces. But in addition to these actual forms of internal resistance, the performer has to create an illusion that embodies illusory resistance.

Performers who present mental acts, constantly project the illusion that telepathic resistances interfere with their perception of an object or a message. These resistances are, of course, illusions employed to create the effect of the performer triumphing over odds. Instead, the real resistance lies in the danger that someone in the audience will perceive the hidden mode of communication by which the assistant conveys necessary information to the performer.

This double form of resistance characterizes all dialectic displays in shows of illusion. But naturally the kind of risk the performer encounters changes. Wherever a show stresses perceptual rather than physical skill, the resistance to be overcome changes too. The performer concentrates more on matching expected behavior, on manipulating experiences, on sustaining energy, and on controlling the shape of time. Moreover, in overcoming these resistances, the performer must largely convey the illusion that they do not exist.

To better see how the actual and virtual resistances relate to each other, let us consider the performance of a sword fight onstage, the kind of fight we find between Romeo and Tybalt in *Romeo and Juliet* or between Cyrano and Valvert in *Cyrano de Bergerac*. Were such fights to occur in life situations, the antagonists, presumably skilled swordsmen, would draw upon their repertoire of skills in a genuine duel. Neither fighter would be in control, but each would have to improvise the basic vocabulary of dueling. This is the approximate impression that the actors seek to create with the additional provision that the duel mounts in excitement.

Yet the way the actors create this impression is by doing precisely the opposite of what the characters do. Between themselves the actors figure out every move in the duel. They dare leave nothing to chance lest they actually hurt each other. Not only do they work in the set motions but they include, if they so desire, movements that indicate lapses, errors, improvisations. To carry out the duel with ease and spontaneity, the movements must be rehearsed over and over again so that they are exactly right and are so familiar that the performers can concentrate on the illusion of spontaneity. Where then does the risk lie, where the resistance? On the actual level, the risk lies in any lapse, any forgetfulness, any mistiming. One of these can result either in poor performance, or even worse, physical damage. The actors do work with blunted points, and thus they allow a margin of safety. Nevertheless, the risk is there. The resistance is the kind found in all physical tricks: balance, timing, and so forth.

Still, the fight conveys the illusion of conflict between the two characters. Thrust and parry are perceived as signs of actual thrusts and parries. Yet, it is not merely the actual motions that produce the effect, but the ancillary glances, snarls, and heavy breathing; in short, the apparent involvement of the total personality in the struggle. To duelist signs are added struggle signs, in order to provide a convincing show. In a later chapter we shall look more closely at the patterns of such a conflict. It is sufficient here to recognize that the illusion of actual resistance is created by modulation of several different kinds of physical relationships: *A* appears to be winning and *B* is on the defensive, and then a moment later *B* has the lead and *A* is on the defensive; from time to time, *A* and *B* seem locked in an evenly balanced grip, often with swords crossed and each actor straining to overcome the other. By running variations on these three relationships, the actors create a convincing duel.

What is particularly interesting about such a stage fight is the delicacy that is required to make it convincing. By some extrasensory sensitivity, an audience can tell when the stage fight becomes too real. An actor may be carried away by the heat of the performance or, in order to impart maximum reality to the fight, the actors may reduce the margin of safety and come very close to doing actual harm to each other. When the audience picks up these signals, it no longer enjoys the fight, but finds it painful and distasteful. Shows of illusion demand that the acts remain illusory and in dialectic presentation that the resistance be virtual and not actual.

In the stage fight, as we have seen, the resistance against which each character strives is lodged in the antagonist. The resistance there stands for physical struggle. But physical struggle onstage, though popular and periodically included in shows, occurs infrequently. For the most part the characters play in terms of social or psychological resistances. As in the fight, the actor creates the illusion that he faces opposition or hesitates to do what he wishes to do. It is obvious that the locus of his resistance is usually in another performer. But while this is frequent, it is not invariable. The locus may be in the audience, for instance.

A striking example of a performer's work on audience resistance involves the medicine show. In 1977 at a conference sponsored by the American Society for Theatre Research, the daughter of an old-line medicine showman gave a demonstration of her father's patter.[1] Among the sophisticated auditors, there was widespread skepticism and condescension. After all, we knew that the medicine show was rather shady, able to make easy marks of the country bumpkins to which it played, but too obvious for the rest of us. Yet as the daughter went through the routine, something happened. The art with which that routine was assembled made it totally convincing. We in the audience could sense our resistance melting away. Clearly, if she had had a bottle of patent medicine, most of us would have been ready to buy it.

A stand-up comic does something similar. In delivering his jokes to an audience, he has to overcome its inertia, skepticism, even dislike, in order to evoke a response. One of the skills a comic learns as he develops is how to spot the degree of resistance in a crowd and how to work through it. As with the medicine man, the comic is playing upon actual antagonism, neutrality, or aloofness. In both cases we are not necessarily dealing with illusion; at best we are on the edge between skill and illusion. But then we look at a play such as John Osborne's *The Entertainer*. The play alternates scenes in the life of the entertainer, Archie Rice, with comic routines that he plays to the actual audience. Archie is old-fashioned, not very funny, unwilling to give up. Essential to the performance is that Archie is playing to an unsympathetic audience, even though the actual audience may be quite sympathetic. The actor has a nice problem. As actor, he has to win a hearing for his rendition of Archie. But as Archie, he has to make the audience's indifference palpable. Since in all likelihood the actual audience will not take an active role in responding either to the actor or to Archie, the performer has to create the illusion of the audience's indifference through the way he has Archie address and respond to them.

These two examples, the stage fight and the entertainer, illustrate

the different loci of illusory resistance. In the first case, each actor
sets in motion an act of will. Since the two acts of will have been
choreographed to clash in an interesting fashion, we see the give
and take of thrust and parry. In the second case, the resistance is
located in the audience, but since the audience is unlikely to play the
role of resister in exactly the way the play requires, the actor has to
project upon the audience the attitude of resistance that the
character of Archie requires. The substance of both performances is
to answer the question as to who wins and, more important, show
what the characters go through as they struggle to win.

This kind of dialectic performance, as I have said, works through
time. While undoubtedly there are spatial relationships that are vital
to a scene, even compelling, as in the stage fight, it is the action
nevertheless that directs our attention to an outcome. Whether that
outcome resolves the play as a whole or settles provisionally one
phase of a continuing narrative, its insistent presence forces us to
anticipate what will immediately follow the moment we are
perceiving. In *Feeling and Form*, Susanne K. Langer has called
drama the art of the virtual future,[2] and to the degree that we speak
of the dialectic side of presentation, she is correct. Iconic
presentation, in its purest form, endeavors to create an illusion of
stasis, of endless continuity, and to the degree that it presents an
awesome act, of eternity. Dialectic presentation stresses flux. Each
act onstage is in the course of becoming something else. As a result,
the performer is never totally at rest but is always in the process of
moving toward an objective or moving away from another force.
For the performer each moment is provisional, and the time being
worked in is historical.

The kind of time that Genet rejects for the theatre, historical
time, as it appears in performance, is a highly concentrated
expression of the conception of time that has dominated post-
Renaissance thinking. Richard Quinones begins his study, *The
Renaissance Discovery of Time*, with the statement, "For the men of
the Renaissance, time is a great discovery."[3] The time they
discovered was the time of change, of progress, of forward
movement. It is also the time of the merchant, the industrialist, and
the social engineer. It is the time of nineteenth-century history, of
the novel, and of realistic and naturalistic drama. In its most
extreme expression it is irreversible.

In the transition toward a conception of time that still is more
iconic than historical, a transition that occurs during Shakespeare's

lifetime, even Edmund the arch-villain of *King Lear* can have a change of heart. Evil may be pervasive but it is not irremediable. Man can redeem the time, as Paul admonished. But once he moves fully into the conceptual realm of historical time, man cannot redeem the time. He is bound by evolution, by consequences. It is this image that prevails so extensively on the stage from the seventeenth to the twentieth centuries. How fitting that Sartre should present to us, in the midst of yet a new weighing of the nature of time, the ultimate image of the irreversibility of time in *No Exit*. Dialectic presentation is a direct product of this view of time. It is because of this pervasive image of historical time throughout the development of modern drama that the actor is called upon to depict the subtle changes of persona with time, focusing on contrasts between past and present, present and future. Ibsen too, in plays like *Hedda Gabler*, trades upon such contrasts, showing how people act when caught in the flux.

This contrast in time is paralleled by other contrasts, for dialectic performance tends toward the comparative. We have seen how it relies on the basic contrast in forces (the actor and the actor's own resistance), and on the temporal contrast of what is with what has been and will be. These two central forms of contrast are amplified by contrasts in characters, contrasts between characters and environment, contrasts in stage space and audience space, and so on. Indeed, so widespread is this pattern of contrasts that in the history of dramatic criticism it appears to be almost the only way of conceiving theatrical presentation.

There is reason for this prevailing view. Although I traced the beginnings of the historical conception of time to the Renaissance, it should be said that the Renaissance did not introduce this notion but merely concentrated on it and articulated it. Scholars trace the initial idea of linear time to the Hebrews and their eschatological bias, a bias that Christianity adopted. They compare this to the cyclical view of time that appears in Greek thought, most notably in Plato's work. Yet they admit that the distinction between the two cultures on this question is not so precise. In its conception of God, Christianity contained the conception of eternity while the search for truth that characterized Greek philosophy presupposed progressive discovery. Moreover, in tragedy the Greeks expressed an image of time that was more nearly linear than cyclical. The Greek propensity for rhetoric and the openness to the search for truth encouraged a form of presentation in which opposites dominated. Indeed, through the working of protagonist against deuteragonist, the idea of opposition was given concrete expression. That is why the protagonist so often achieves the opposite of what is intended. Oedipus strives for truth and gets more truth than he bargained for; Clytemnestra welcomes the news of Orestes' death into her home only to bring in her executioner. Each episode in the tragedy is one step along an often irresistible course.

Mindful of the extended legends of which each play is a part, we see the characters as caught within a rush of time which they have little power to deflect. Yet there is a balance in the form that reflects the Greek genius for reconciliation. Most, if not all, of the choruses are songs and dances through which the chorus seeks to bring the particular events of the episodes into harmony with some larger vision of events. Often they are celebrations of eternal cosmic movements, and to the extent that they are, they are iconic presentations that contrast and balance the dialectic interchanges of the episodes. Together episode and ode express both the cyclical and the historical image of time.

This reconciliation is neither so systematized nor so inevitable after the Renaissance. Instead, the various ways in which the drama of the seventeenth century sought to retain vestiges of iconic performance come under attack and in the eighteenth century are replaced by plays that emphasize contingent, transitory experience rather than eternal principles. The controversy over *Le Cid*[4] was a struggle against the historicity of time. By imposing the rule of the unities, critics sought to accommodate the pressure toward a linear time scheme (harnessing time as science does) by isolating and enshrining time in a supposedly logical scheme. The very argument that this scheme was to achieve verisimilitude indicates how perverse the reasoning was. In effect, the realistically based notion of the unity of time actually enabled the French dramatists to deal with eternal verities that would iconize the court of Louis XIV.

It is in these contexts—of the episodic-odic reconciliation of the Greeks, the artificial time schemes of the French, and the emphatic causality of the nineteenth-century drama—that dialectic presentation developed. Though rooted in the nature of presentation itself and refined by the changing notion of time, it came increasingly under the sway of literary theorists. Its growth was divorced from other forms of presentation so that it came to be seen almost solely in terms of mimetic structure. Concurrently, the iconic forms of performance, as embodied in the great Renaissance entertainments, began to disappear while the more popular expression of this form went underground, into spectacle or into forms of drama, such as melodrama, that did not win respect. I don't intend to trace the history of both kinds of presentation but only to set the stage for recovering the presentational character of the dialectic form which came to dominate modern theatre.

Unlike most types of show, dialectic presentation tends to hide its showlike nature. This fact is often associated with the mimetic character of drama. But that is only a partial and not entirely correct explanation. Even in the acrobatic trick, the showlike qualities are muted during the course of the trick. As I have remarked before, the trick may be framed by celebratory action, but the heart of the event is located elsewhere. The reason for this anti- or non-showlike form of display lies in the very structure of the presentation itself. Because the trick concentrates on the way the performer will transform the moments to come, and because it requires working precisely through the resistance inherent in the type of action, the performer necessarily works in terms of an objective and not in terms of the audience. For the duration of the trick the performer permits the audience to oversee the act, but the performer's attention is actually on the appropriate point in the resistance.

Dramatic acts share this kind of structure and reveal similar characteristics. In any individual "number" or "scene" one actor takes the lead, focusing on the fellow actor, on the audience, or on the abstract force which must be transformed in order to play the action. When the actor focuses on the audience, the audience is in effect given a role, albeit a passive one, upon which the actor works. But wherever the attention of the actor is directed, the actor works to make the transformation called for by the scene, demonstrating to us the shifts within and between the characters that bring about the fictional event. Though we might suppose that the actor does this in relation to some notion of actual experience, that is not necessarily so. A performer can and often does work with a life model in mind. But that model is not a necessary feature of the presentation itself. The event the actor shows us is lifelike to the extent that we can conceive a human being engaged in it. But insofar as the root structure of a dramatic show is concerned, its plausibility is incidental. What is essential, however, is that the actor go through a hypothetical action involving some aspect of transformation: narrative, emotive, rational.

The arbitrary nature of what the actor does is confirmed by the way he handles time, time which is so central to dialectic presentation. No matter how the passage of time appears to us during the show, the actor is usually speeding up events or slowing them down. Events move with speed, and we are hurtled forward. Or events are deliberately retarded so that we are given an excruciating sensation of how slowly a moment elapses. In this very manipulation of time, we find one of the prime means by which the performer controls the display of events. Marlon Brando's speech pattern as well as his slow movements in *A Streetcar Named Desire* clearly illustrate this.

In other ways too, the actor continues to control the showlike qualities of his performance, though he appears to be immersed in the interplay with others. It is, of course, an indirect form of control, and depends on the way the actor calibrates his performance. There is, moreover, another aspect of this hidden show that is vital to this kind of presentation. It is an aspect inherent in the root structure of the dialectic.

As we have seen, a dialectic performance proceeds with the actor working in terms of a resistance of some sort, often a counterforce. The appeal and effect of the show are therefore determined by how actor and counterforce relate to each other. For a dramatic act to be compelling, it is not sufficient for actor and counterforce to be brute opposites. While a stage fight can be fascinating, it is hardly the prime example of dramatic interest, which is more likely to derive from balancing the provocative forces.

One of the most frequent and fruitful juxtapositions of such forces comes in the form of good and evil. This is the basis of melodrama. Each age evolves its own image of good and evil, using the contrasts in often repeated ways. In the revenge play the contrast is often between a noble or abused hero and either a devil-like intriguer or a tyrant. The conventional melodrama of the nineteenth century pitted the chaste and warm-hearted heroine, often surrounded by poor but pure-hearted parents, against an established figure such as a landlord. There is apparently something attractive in placing a vulnerable but good person against a powerful but evil individual. Variations on this pattern can be found throughout dramatic history.

For such melodramas to advance, either the good person seeks to remedy a previous wrong done by the villain or the villain seeks advantage over the good person. In either case, action is possible only when there is a rough balance of forces. The good person hides his knowledge (Hamlet) or the villain has to accomplish the seemingly impossible (Richard III wooing Anne). However, since the allegiance between audience and characters is set from the very beginning, the outcome is predetermined, and the performer or dramatist has to devise a thrilling way for the good person to overcome the evil.

This clear-cut application of morality to presentational structure has socio-political as well as esthetic functions. On an esthetic plane, the impending danger posed by villainy permits a vicarious thrill which is relieved when the villain is defeated. Politically, the defeat of the villain, while it may not confirm the ideology of a society, does assuage social tensions. It supports the delusion that a simple moral order exists in some realm, imaginative if not sociological. Because of its simplified balance of forces, this kind of show is extremely popular, but also severely restricted. It holds a visceral, dreamlike attraction because of the effects it produces but even more because of the distinctive transformations it takes us through.

The possibilities of the dialectic presentation open up when the potentiality of the antagonism in this type of show is exploited more subtly. Aristotle's injunction that a tragic figure should be neither wholly good nor bad, but more good than bad, has a psychological explanation. It also has an esthetic basis. In melodrama, where the moral status of opposing forces is sharply divided and the audience's allegiance is predetermined, the excitement of the show is somewhat quantified. By that I mean that the moral split prevents the audience from seeing the dramatic conflict in qualitative terms—identifying with evil, for instance. As a result, the interest lies in the relative strengths of the two forces and in the human effects the various confrontations produce. The action thus proceeds by showing relative changes in physical power.

In the more subtle forms of opposition which we associate with tragedy, the clear-cut moral status of the opposing forces is not so precisely set. The tension between performer and counterforce is thus a deep tension because it embodies conflicting allegiances. What occurs is that the performer's thrust and the resistance it faces are balanced not only as energy but also in terms of values. The tension produced by this relationship is highly resonant, dividing the emotions of the audience. That division need not, of course, be only between one character and another. It may lie within a character. In fact, we find that in his tragedies Shakespeare often uses both dialectic possibilities. In *Hamlet*, for instance, he sets in motion a melodramatic action involving the "good" Hamlet and the "evil" Claudius. Simultaneously, he sets in motion Hamlet's will to revenge and the internal resistances that get in the way of the revenge. The first aspect of the show supplies much of the theatrical thrill; the second gives the play its unique dimensions. Neither aspect can exist without the other.

An audience is not always ready to respond to the second form of dialectic presentation. That second form challenges established values by yielding to conflicting claims a measure of justice. Where the conflicting claims are explored fully, as in the drama of ancient Greece, Elizabethan England, and in the late modern period, we find a society in flux, established values challenged yet not so shaken that the state panics, and a people able, if only temporarily, to contemplate unanswerable questions.

The view of presentation that I have offered has examined various ways in which the performer can utilize skill, person, and imagination to create a wide range of shows. There is an organic connection, I have argued, between the form of a show and the content being shown. In shows of illusion, no matter how complex the dramatic material may be, if the material is effective and affecting, it is rooted in the art of show. In Chapter 2, I have also discussed in a general way the imaginative basis of dramatic illusion and how mimesis relates to presentation. Now, we need to consider somewhat further the question of naturalism as a form of presentation.

By naturalism, I include the movement of that name but much more: the entire effort to transfer observed behavior to the stage. That effort has two phases, obviously. The first phase is to choose the behavior to be transferred; the second is to adapt that behavior to the demands of presentation. As we saw, in all likelihood the incorporation of observed phenomena into performance exists from the beginnings of drama. Along with other raw material it is the stuff of theatre. What distinguishes naturalism is the concerted determination to put substantial, undiluted experience onstage. Throughout the eighteenth century we see repeated, though qualified, efforts along this line. I say qualified because the examples we have do not quite reveal a naturalist commitment. George Lillo's *The London Merchant* is a candidate for consideration, but though Lillo drew upon his knowledge of apprentice life and introduced serious treatment of a new class to the theatre, his treatment of the material combines sentimentality and melodrama. He vacillates between presenting the dialectic conflict in George Barnwell and offering him as an iconic image of a moral fall. In no way is it Lillo's object to reproduce life.

Slightly later, Diderot argues for a more naturalistic drama but like Lillo, in actual practice, he creates a clear-cut conflict between moral decency based on romantic impulse and social constraint. True, he advocates fresh and serious treatment of class types not yet fully exploited in drama, and he does suggest changes in performing technique that would appear to lead to naturalism. Still, his argument for a fourth wall is calculated above all to emphasize the isolation of dialectic presentation rather than to lead to the reproduction of nature. But though he is hardly a naturalist, Diderot does mark a stage along the way to serious changes in presentation involving the performer.[5]

Hitherto I have spoken of the performer as a relatively independent figure. And so he is in dialectic presentation at least until the eighteenth century. To understand what happened we need to glance back at the relation between the performer and the context of performance.

Contemporary scenography tends to embrace the entire complex of design which affects the performer. Stage decor, costume, lighting, theatre architecture, and even sound effects come under this heading. But this equalization of elements is essentially a post-Renaissance development that radically distorts the organic ties between performer and various production features. There is a different order of relationship between a player and costume and between player and stage setting, and the difference is reflected in theatrical history. Richard Southern called attention to the peculiar intimacy of performer and dress in *The Seven Ages of the Theatre*,[6] and it is to this intimacy that we need to turn.

Unlike contemporary theatrical practice, stage dress in the pre-Renaissance theatre was not an aspect of stage design as a whole. It was linked more to the actor as a showman than to the play. In Greece the tragic costume of *onkos*, *cothurni*, and robe announced a type of drama and the status of the character. If Pollux, the second century A.D. lexicographer, is accurate about earlier tradition, the mask may have suggested character types, though that is doubtful. Instead, the dress was a kind of appropriate show garment, one that monumentalized the actor. In a sense we can speak of the dress as an icon of the tragic figure. It not only signified his performing role but also celebrated it in its distinctive image.

But though the costume celebrated the performer, it did not immobilize him as the pageant garments of the Renaissance tended to do. Rather, the iconic facade was in fierce contrast to the violent passions expressed by the action. Thus, the actor, instead of being pacified by his dress, became the animator of it; he had to dominate it, just as we see today the actors in Kabuki animate and struggle against the rigid facade of dress and behavior that the social code imposes. In both cases the formality of Greek and Japanese iconic costume is in violent opposition to the turbulent passion with which the fictitious character is endowed. This type of relationship gives the costume a double aspect: it is an instrument of showy display; it is also one of the planes of contrast that compose a dialectic act.

The performer's intimate use of his costume as an apparatus in his show is in contrast to his relation to the stage space. In classic Greece the sharp division between stage and audience space did not exist. It is unlikely that there was a raised platform. Movement, therefore, between acting space and choral space was easy. The *skene* or scene house was more a tiring hut than a scenic feature. Though the scene facade often represented a palace, there is no indication that the palace was individualized in any way. Rather, the actors used the undifferentiated playing space and orchestra for their performance, the contextual or decorative features being most fully embodied in their dress and in the musical accompaniment.

This type of generalized playing space characterizes the popular theatre of Renaissance Italy and Elizabethan England. Partly because of practical conditions, that is, the importance of touring, but largely because of the kinds of shows they gave, these popular performers did not rely on a specific scenic environment. Like the Greeks, they depended more upon their dress than their setting. I do not forget, of course, that the Elizabethan public playhouses were gorgeous playing places, impressive in their own right. But in determining the way the performer interacts with the theatrical and imagined environment, we have to make several distinctions. In considering the effect of space upon a show, we should determine the degree to which the effect is functional. In that case we are concerned with the *specificity* of the space and its *proximity* to the performance. Neither in Greece nor in Elizabethan England was the locale highly individualized, and even the neo-classic efforts of the Italian artists, Serlio most notably, produced a type of stage decorum by specifying three types of setting: the tragic, the comic, and the pastoral. These later efforts found their expression in the court theatres, which became primarily celebratory and iconic. In the popular theatre, on the other hand, the performer continued to maintain his independence of the setting well into the eighteenth century.

With the Renaissance, space came to impose more specific attributes upon performance. This was readily apparent in the court shows, such as pageants, tournaments, naumachias, and masques. The performer began to blend into the setting, to become part of the overall design. Inigo Jones designed not only the setting but also the costumes, placing his figures in a visual context that honors them as symbols rather than allowing them to act independently and perhaps even capriciously. From the seventeenth century onward, we find a steady absorption of the performer within a scenic context. Gradually, the performer's relationship to costume changes. Instead of being primarily an expression of the actor as showman, it becomes an aspect of the environment. It is in the burst of antiquarian enthusiasm of the early nineteenth century that the taming of the actor occurs. The symbolic and presentational motives of stage dress become subordinated to historical consideration. More and more the chief actor becomes the unifier of all stage elements, ordered by considerations other than the performing idea. By the time historical example gives way to contemporary illustration in naturalistic theatre, the dominance of stage setting has become complete.

It is no surprise then that the setting should become a kind of performer. As it assumes a more and more specific character and becomes more closely intertwined with the action, it either emerges as an icon of locale (in Romantic drama) or takes on a dialectic role. The setting as a fictitious environment begins to weigh upon the characters or to express them. In several famous instances, it becomes a full character. One of the most spectacular scenes of nineteenth-century drama was the burning of the tenement in Dion Boucicault's 1857 play *The Poor of New York*. A rather conventional melodrama, it had a phoenix-like life: known variously as *The Poor of Liverpool*, *The Poor of Leeds*, *The Streets of Manchester*, *The Streets of Islington*, and later as *The Streets of London*, as well as *The Streets of New York*.[7] The key scene showed the firing of a tenement by the villain in order to burn a secret paper which he

knew was in the building but which he could not find. The hero
rushes to the top floor of the flaming structure and barely escapes
with the crucial evidence. Dynamically, the hero struggles to gain
his end. His opposition is the building itself. The dramatic wonder
lies not only in the character's struggle against the odds, but in our
witnessing what is meant to appear as a thrilling event from the
safety of our seats. The theatrical effect depends upon the greatest
fidelity to "realism." Boucicault worked with immense care to
make the various stages of the burning convincing. Yet the
conviction depends on the most absurd of all conventions: our
assurance that the "real" thing is not real. Like the woman being
sawn in half, we know the act before us, which seeks to give us an
illusion of actuality, is impossible.

Two conclusions emerge from this example. First, the close
imitation of actuality is an element of a stage show, not its
objective. Indeed, the more "natural" an act, the more likely it is to
suggest its essential artificiality. Secondly, with increased inter-
twining of performer and environment, the environment tends to
assume a role in the dialectic exchange, and in some instances the
performer becomes a stage property of the stage space. In an
extreme form, this can be seen in the vast show that P. T. Barnum
brought to the Olympia in London. Supposedly with a cast of
1,200, Barnum depicted the Rome of Nero with all its varied thrills
of chariot races and fighting gladiators, interspersed with circus
thrills and illusionist tricks. Claiming fidelity to history, Barnum
presented this amazing display as a spectacle and as an educational
presentation.[8] In a way it was the ultimate expression of the
antiquarian spirit turned into kitsch.

Theatrical naturalism is closely identified with an emphasis upon
environment. Indeed, without according preeminence to stage
design, naturalism as we know it would be impossible. Furthermore, in order to harmonize the performer's behavior with the
environment, the performer had to partially assume a descriptive
function. That is, the performer began to say and do things that had
as a primary purpose the creation of an atmosphere within the
environment. Low-keyed conversation, genre-like bits of business,
and stage groupings filled in the setting to give an illusion of
actuality. The origins of this naturalistic tendency arose out of
drama that was initially dialectic, yet as the naturalist setting came
to dominate, it tended to blunt the dialectic interchange and
encourage iconic images of bourgeois life. It is significant that the

writer who is probably the most important realistic dramatist of the twentieth century, the Eugene O'Neill of *Long Day's Journey into Night*, *The Iceman Cometh*, and *A Moon for the Misbegotten*, needed the amplitude of lengthy plays in order to move from the creation of environmental reality to the dialectic confrontations that raise these plays to tragic power.

Historically then, the dialectic mode of presentation has passed and is still passing through a number of phases. Over the centuries it is expressed through a variety of potential juxtapositions: performer and audience, performer and performer, performer and environment, performer and self. Later in this work I shall look closely at the dramatic structures that result from these inter-changes.

Chapter 5

Act and audience

A show gives us something and nothing to respond to. The something is in the form of people doing extraordinary things with their voices, with their bodies, with the world around them. Even the ordinary becomes extraordinary when it is lovingly framed for our attention. The glance of an actress, the dash of a magician, the swirl of a costume can become something unforgettable. Edmund Kean's mad rages and Duse's withdrawn solemnity remain as icons of all their performances. They are the something given.

The nothing we respond to is no less important. It is not an amorphous nothing. It is not absence. Rather, the nothing that is so central to theatrical show is a carefully defined nothing, a nothing that captures us, into which we pour our feelings. It is the nothing that lies between Richard III's affability with his princely nephews and our knowledge of his intentions, between the announcement of a high flyer's triple somersault and the moment he attempts it, between a villain's threat and his assault. It is the nothing in the reverberating pauses of Pinter's plays. It is the nothing in the incongruity of humor. It is a nothing compressed by sharply marked boundaries so that the space between is not dead space but resounds with contradictions and ridiculousness. It is a nothing that serves as a screen onto which we project our expectations and emotions.

At this moment in a most preliminary way, we can say that the something to which we respond is the iconic element in a show, the element offered to us for display: sound or color or movement. The texture of these elements is heightened by the fact of their display, and we are granted license to relish them as we will. By contrast, the nothing we respond to we may speak of as the dialectic element. The nothing is the electrified air that crackles from the interchange between one actor and another, between one moment and another. The poles of dialectic action set the space between them in motion, sometimes in a simple dualistic manner, sometimes in a more complex vibration of overtones upon overtones. The difference between simple and complex responses depends upon the content of dramatic action as well as the way it is shaped.

By simple responses I mean responses that are uniform, without ambivalence, single in effect. They can be terribly intense; indeed, one of the great pleasures of simple responses is that they can be overpowering, either in exaltation or in trepidation. One of the attractions of a performing medium is its ability to arouse strong, simple responses.

Complex responses, unlike the simple ones, do have ambivalence. Actually, a complex response might be thought of as the simultaneous experiencing of two contradictory simple responses. Instead of being overpowered by emotion, feeling may be tentative, subject to qualification, contingent and unresolved.

Not every show is designed to arouse both simple and complex responses, nor is it capable of so doing. Those shows that can evoke complex responses can also incorporate simple responses within them. The opposite is not the case, however. Shows primarily designed by their governing form to produce simple responses, exclude the possibility of complex response.

Some shows, as we have seen, use activity that is in its essence presentational. For the most part these are shows of skill. X's attempt to perform the triple somersault demands public display for completion. This dangerous and thrilling feat promises to arouse a double-barreled response: intense anticipation as the acrobat prepares to do the act, and then, depending on his success, either intense admiration or disappointment. In such an act all the spatial and temporal elements are sharply defined: the high trapeze, the absence of a net, the crystallized sequence of announcement, approach, swing, and leap. Our responses are firmly anchored to each phase of action, and indeed blend with the action. Whatever the reverberations of the act, they remain closely connected to the act itself.

In illusionistic feats we can see how content may affect response, although content and action are still closely linked. A magician's search for a new act is invariably a search for material that lends itself to amazement. Whatever the magician chooses—sawing a woman in half, levitating a box, escaping from manacles—he is organizing the act to exhibit its impossibility in the strongest terms. In fact, everything connected with illusionism is intended for show. That is why magic offers so many insights into the nature of presentation. By positing the impossible and then accomplishing it, the magician produces a simple response of wonder. That simple response does continue to reverberate within our imaginations as puzzlement and delight, but as already stated, it too is directly related to the act that aroused it.

We can see the interaction between content and presentational structure most clearly in the magician's use of stage props. The prop crystallizes the impossibility inherent in the act. Some props are solely stage devices: bottomless top hats, trick boxes, etc. But many props retain real life associations and are largely effective for that reason: pitchers and glasses, ordinary playing cards, electric saws, elephants and lions, etc. Such props seem to bear a double sign: their familiarity and the impossibility of control.

Content in a magic show, beyond positing the impossible, also has a secondary function. Depending on the style of the performer, it may suggest the exotic or the mundane, the fashionable or the ridiculous. The better performer will develop a persona and a repertoire of content that will identify him or her. Houdini concentrated upon escape tricks, cultivating the illusion that he did possess unusual powers. Others employ oriental personas, conveying the impression that they bring to the audience exotic mysteries. Whatever the atmosphere created, it serves as a ground against which the performer performs. Through the use of such a ground, the performer attempts to enrich and deepen the response to the illusions.

The interaction between content and structure shapes audience response in dramatic illusion too. By content in drama I mean any of the extra-presentational elements that are included in a work: events from daily existence or images derived from art, objects in common use or allusions to other theatrical shows. It would seem that such content is the necessary substance of every dramatic presentation. Yet certain avant-garde producers like Richard Foreman and Robert Wilson have played with self-enclosed systems of signs. The current fashionableness of this sort of reflexiveness is hard to gauge, for it runs counter to cumulative experience with theatrical art. Suppositions about audience response based on such self-reflexiveness are too amorphous and too recent to warrant generalization. More central to our understanding of how content affects response is the question of how content is transmuted into structure.

First of all, it appears that there is a dynamic give and take between theatrical form and extra-theatrical materials. On the one hand, with the earliest Greek tragedies we see that a general structural pattern has evolved, obliging playwrights to assimilate any new material into that established pattern. Yet in another instance, that of the earliest liturgical play, we see that the church has accepted specific episodes for transmutation from biblical to dramatic form although the form itself is not yet fully developed. These two different relationships between content and structure should warn us that there is a continuous process of accepting and rejecting materials for the stage.

Granting the diversity of content-structure interactions, however, it is still safe to say that most ongoing theatrical systems include a set of accepted presentational forms into which new material is absorbed. The accepted forms are not necessarily rigid; rather they emerge as historical models which a society demands of performers and playwrights. It may do so through the natural response of the audience. Or it may act more coercively, as when the Athenians forbade Phrynichus ever to deal with contemporary subject matter.

Commonly, however, the model serves as an armature for the specific expression of a show. Depending upon the extent to which established forms accommodate a playwright or need to be made to do so, the playwright introduces lesser or greater variations of the core model. Our awareness of the primary structure of the core model and the variations introduced at a secondary level depends on our perspective. For generations, the core model of unified action as manifested in classical and post-classical examples was so widely accepted that any other model was considered deficient, even the Shakespearean model. In the romantic and post-romantic age, the Shakespearean model, even when it could not be clearly described, became accepted as an alternate form. But not until recent years, when we have recognized the validity of oriental and other theatrical models, have we been able to distinguish among the various core models that exist together with the secondary elaborations that individual performers-writers have provided.

To stimulate audience response, it would seem that performers ultimately have to pursue two contradictory courses. On the one hand, they cultivate and refine performing routines that seem to provide immense direct satisfaction. How such routines evolve is not usually clear. But they are recognizable when they crystallize. The mummers' visits at holiday time, the stand-up comedian, a particular dance such as the cakewalk, all are examples of routines that crystallized and endured, sometimes for centuries, sometimes for a few years. The point is that these forms satisfy audiences deeply enough to become a staple for a particular theatrical culture. In the main the individual performers then have to express themselves through a routine acceptable to the audience.

This delight with the familiar routine is balanced by a seemingly intense hunger for novelty. Audiences continually crave variety, the unusual, the unexpected. They want fresh faces, fresh stories, fresh routines. How quickly they tire of performers will, of course, depend on performing conditions. During the heyday of vaudeville, from the end of the nineteenth century to the third decade of the twentieth, it was possible for performers to play the same act or routine for many years. The long-running team of Smith and Dale played their Dr. Kronkite sketch for forty years. During this period the vaudeville circuit took performers through many cities over the course of a year, with an act playing a theatre perhaps once or twice in that time. The audience could get its variety from the succession of acts and therefore welcome the familiarity of their old favorites. Since the advent of television, however, the nation as a whole can see an act at the same time, and novelty therefore becomes the great demand.

At a rudimentary level, performers introduce novelty into primary structures by draping apparently new material on the same form. Characters have new names, the setting of the action changes, minor twists in the story appear, and there is a new work. Most of the great popular forms—melodrama, domestic comedy, farce—work in this way. Writers, while still operating within the accepted conventions of the routine, play with variations that fuse novelty with the comfortably known. The efficacy of this sort of accommodation is evident in the enduring popularity of certain familiar types of shows.

Of the many popular forms, melodrama illustrates vividly not only the interaction of content and form but also the interaction of form and response. Melodrama, as different writers point out, relies on a clear-cut moral choice. It may almost be defined as a dramatic work in which the protagonist(s) and antagonist(s) can be distinguished as good and evil. Thus we have conditions ripe for melodrama when the division between good and evil is strong, and the contest between good and evil is central to the performance. This kind of moral division, discussed in Chapter 4, has both a material and a structural aspect. It embodies social values in fairly absolute terms. By lodging virtue and beauty in the heroine of Victorian melodrama, playwrights merely exaggerated values that had a basis in popular attitudes if not in actual behavior.

Along with exaggerated values, the sharp contrast between good and evil enhances dialectic action. The opposition of vividly contrasted characters arouses excitement almost independently of the actual circumstances. What is necessary, of course, is that the conflict of contrasting figures be imprinted on our psyche. We have to be split psychologically so that opposing loyalties are stirred within us. In melodrama this is done by putting our loyalties into conflict with our expectations. Our loyalty to the heroine, an absolute loyalty in the case of melodrama, is posed against the power of the villain. Especially when we are let in on schemes to harm the heroine, expectation produces empathic anxiety for her safety.

How audiences attach themselves to the various components of melodrama is intriguing. The dramatic patterns suggest that audiences need the framework as a stimulus for their reactions. Since heroines were somewhat conventionalized, it is not always the specific variation that appeals to spectators. Yet the thirst for variation does absorb new material. This can be seen in the readiness with which authors take advantage of new inventions as quickly as they appear. For example, when elevators became popular, playwrights introduced them as instruments that could be used to endanger the lives of heroines. Such devices tend to freshen traditional response.

To reconstruct imaginatively the complexity of response to melodrama, we can say that the components that produce the response consist of (1) defined and clearly identified social values, (2) a range of content from the most familiar to the contemporary, and (3) a pattern of action that repeatedly juxtaposes a vulnerable heroine and a potentially triumphant villain. The values are given, periodically brought to the fore (foregrounded) either in the behavior of the hero or in an explicit speech. In the main the values serve as part of the background of the action, a link connecting the audience's extra-theatrical loyalties and the dramatic characters. The content of the specific action also serves as a background, providing apparently original circumstances to freshen and particularize the fundamentally conventional patterns of action. Perhaps the background content opens the pores so that the modulations in the dramatic structure can effect a response. Occasionally, as when new material is introduced into a conventional form, the content itself comes into focus. This was the case in Dion Boucicault's 1874 play *The Shaughraun*, when the hero and heroine turn out to be fighters for Irish freedom and the villain is in the service of landed wealth.

Response, as we see, is not only tied to the three components described above, but is also a factor in the relative prominence of these components. Whenever new content is introduced into a presentation, it tends to dominate. Audiences notice it, and the formal components recede into the background. But as that material recurs in play after play, it then recedes, and the formal or more minute dynamics move forward. This process of changing perspective, common to all the arts, is intensified in the theatre because of certain distinctive features.

In watching a show, it is physically impossible to absorb the entire presentation. Unlike cinema, where we are subject to the camera's eye, theatre is seldom so contracted that the eye can take in the entire performance at one time. Rather we have to scan a performance, looking first at one player and then another. To whom we pay attention at any one time is partly determined by the performers. Part of their aim is to control and direct our focus. Yet, however astute the performers are, they do not have absolute control. We can always direct our attention elsewhere.

Human perception relies on a relatively limited but fine focus combined with a fairly broad, though blurred, periphery of awareness. Wherever our attention moves, we are not unaware of what goes on about the person or object of our interest. Given the dimensions of theatrical presentation, a show offers ample opportunity for us to focus upon specific points while we enjoy considerable peripheral stimulation. That stimulation is spatial and temporal. When we look at the heroine, we are still aware of the villain. When we focus upon what is going on before us, we also sense that the door may open. In short, the carefully contrived array of signs that the theatre supplies encourages continuous shifts of focus as we follow the action.

The focal–peripheral shift has a figurative as well as a physical basis. As we attend to the theatrical activity that unfolds before us, we perceive it not only focally, that is, in its appearance before us, but peripherally as part of a context of events. We become acutely conscious of such a context when we see plays that deliberately confuse or mask the background of action. Some contemporary dramatists, notably Pinter, provide insufficient or conflicting signals that make it difficult if not impossible to locate the action within a frame of recognition. One of the characteristic responses, in such cases, is to find ourselves continually seeking to normalize the dramatic action by explaining its context. This technique does have the effect of forcing the audience to concentrate on the performer's behavior in uncommon ways. It furthermore undermines the performer's own activity, for in concentrating on the sounds and motions before us, we lose the distinction between a character's and an actor's sounds and motions.

The overwhelming number of dramatic shows, however, do unfold in a specified context, which manifests itself in actual performance as a peripheral ground against which the focal events play. We can distinguish two phases in the establishment of that ground. First, there is the ground of knowledge and experience the audience brings to the performance that will connect with the content of the show. This provides an initial ground for encounter between audience and performance. When that initial ground is conventional, as in the value-system of melodrama, it does not exercise much stimulus. It has a negative role. If the heroine did not meet conventional expectations, the ground of action would be seriously disturbed. Indeed, her meeting these expectations only assures the audience that the conditions for performance are set.

A second type of ground emerges once the performance begins. It is gradually built up by the players. Earlier scenes serve as an imaginative background against which later scenes unfold. Suspense develops through an interaction between the foregrounded action and a sharply defined background of events that contradict or endanger the future of the foregrounded action. In fact, dramatic performance relies heavily upon various kinds of dislocation between past and present, present and future, as well as between an image we are expecting and another that appears before us. That dislocation is built into the performance. We participate in and undergo the dislocation through shifts in focal and peripheral attending. Either we actually find our attention shifting between two facets of the performance or, what appears to be more common, the action is crystallized in such a way that we are acutely aware of the conflicts or strains between our focal concentration and our peripheral awareness. In the case of Pinter's plays, the dislocation is often between the concrete act on which we concentrate focally and our very inability to place that act in an imaginative ground. Like Ruth in *The Homecoming*, Pinter seems to be saying to us: Look at my motions. Don't try to figure out what they mean.

How the audience's initial ground functions *vis-à-vis* a show will vary considerably in different circumstances. Some shows make sense only to an audience that shares a common ground of understanding. Others depend only tangentially on previous tradition. In general, however, we can distinguish between positive and negative use of the audience ground. By positive use, I mean that the performance assumes the ground to support or confirm its action. By negative use, I refer to the deliberate subverting or challenging of the ground by a play or other show.

The iconic show is a prime example of performance that confirms audience values. Pageants and parades illustrate this most clearly. Almost by definition, they affirm common social position through celebrating traditional symbols (as in the case of religious icons) or personalized symbols (as in the case of political or cultural heroes). With parades, the assembled crowd itself provides the physical background for the event. In such an instance, there is no dislocation between focal and peripheral elements, but the focal element, the symbol in most shows, is an extension of given attitudes. It thus serves as a dense embodiment of feelings that do not always have clear avenues of expression. The iconic show provides such an avenue, for there the tension exists in the dislocation between the promise of the hero's appearance and the actual thrill of being in that presence.

Such crystallization of audience belief is the work of other types of iconic show, especially those of a political character. It is widely recognized that political drama does not change people's minds. Rather, it affirms the opinion of believers. It is, in short, a celebration of values. Often these shows take the form of agit–prop sketches in which sharp moral distinctions of a melodramatic nature are applied to class representatives: workers against bosses, one racial group against another, one nation against another. Even when the action seems to be arranged in terms of dialectic struggle, key points are usually celebrations of triumph or reaffirmations of positions despite defeat. During the Vietnam war, one of the acclaimed productions was *The Trial of the Catonsville Nine*. This trial play, celebrating those who opposed the war and defied prison to take action against it, was, as mentioned in Chapter 3, performed for the most part before sympathetic audiences. It offered a vehicle for the expression of deep feelings in the audience, and was an even more effective vehicle because there were so few satisfying avenues of that expression in the world outside the theatre. In this case, the intensity of the response was partly conditioned by opposition to the wider social and political context.

In other instances, an iconic action may provide focus not for a commonly recognized set of values but rather for inchoate potential feelings. It was in this realm that the Open Theatre often worked. In *The Serpent*, especially, it fused traditional biblical images with contemporary events. Its prophetic depiction of the endless round of assassination as a media event came to stand as a symbol of contemporary life. It did not appear as a comment about background events but as the concentrated embodiment of them.

These examples of iconic shows indicate varying relationships to the audience ground. But, however different each relationship may be, they all depend on the audience ground for their effect. Unlike dialectic action, iconic action embodies and concentrates social values and images. In fact, it works by presenting striking signs of those values and images. The means are often quite simple, though the effects can be elaborate.

Part of the utilization of the audience's ground consists in merely providing adequate symbols to release a response. But there is also an inclination toward elaboration. One of the ways to elicit maximum admiration, which is the primary objective of the iconic show, is to place the individual symbols in a rich setting or to replicate the numbers of participants as testimony for the event. Sometimes this elaboration takes the form of enriching costumes, floats, flags, and other accessories. Another method is to introduce quasi–dramatic identification that links the symbols to figures or ideas that carry considerable psychological impact for the audience. Dressing a May Queen as Cleopatra would endow the queen with some of Cleopatra's fancied wit and sexuality. Sporting a Mardi Gras King as Hercules gives him some of that demigod's power. Since the iconic figure is already supreme, his further celebration is achieved not only by showing him overcoming obstacles but by relating him to other accepted tokens of grandeur.

Where iconic action celebrates values, dialectic action subjects them to challenge. More than iconic action, dialectic action relates in indirect ways to matters of value. While the projection of sets of values is seldom the purpose of such action, the triangular relation of audience, values, and dramatic action is critical. Unlike other kinds of show, dramatic illusion unfolds in a value-free context only with considerable difficulty.

This is a factor directly related to its human medium. Because the performer is used as the medium, and moreover, as an embodiment of another persona or agent, the performer establishes an initial concern on a concrete human level. Furthermore, as we saw earlier, dialectic action by definition stands for interaction and contrast with one person straining against another. The human attachment we have for one or another person calls on us, the audience, to make choices, which in turn involve a context of values.

Melodrama operates within a context of broadly shared values that serve as a necessary but not a focal ground for simplified action. In fact, the simplified action, operating as it does within a widely recognized convention, also serves as a background for the particular variation in any specific production. Melodrama, however, is not the only example, although it is the most striking one, of accommodation between the first ground, audience values, and the second ground, created by the dramatic illusion. Comedy, especially domestic comedy, shows similar alignment.

As Northrop Frye has made clear in his discussion of comic characters, opposition emerges between different rebellious figures, usually the young lover or his surrogate, the clever servant, and blocking figures—most frequently a stern father, a figure of authority (teacher or magistrate), or an old husband.[1] Action proceeds along the various paths that the rebels take to thwart their elders or masters until the situation becomes so complicated that an impasse threatens. To this whole question of values, the resolution of the impasse is central. In Molière's plays, a final authority resolves the problem. *Tartuffe*, for example, shows the rebels against Orgon's will—his son, his daughter, and his wife—finally joined by Orgon himself, but only after he has passed his authority to Tartuffe. When Tartuffe seeks to invest himself in the full exercise of his new authority, he is finally thwarted through the action of the supreme authority, the king. In an analogous way, Horace and Agnes in *The School for Wives* seem to be threatening the authority of Arnolphe's claims on Agnes. But just as Arnolphe appears to conquer the "rebels," the arrival of Agnes' true father reveals that Arnolphe's authority is false, and a true authority is established in its stead.

All these denouements reaffirm conventional values. As with melodrama, the audience's stake in one side or another is not in question although the balance of one character's claim against another is not so schematic. The tortured history of *Tartuffe* shows that Tartuffe, villain though he is, bears in him not only the sign of hypocrisy but also the sign of religious devotion. It is that side of him that appeals to Orgon. As a result, he projects a problematic image that engages the audience's loyalties in different ways. In his own day, some members of the audience read Molière's depiction of Tartuffe as an attack not on religious hypocrisy but on religion itself. The version of the script we have is an attempt to minimize this disparity.

What this case illustrates is the genuine danger that dialectic action can pose. In my initial discussion of dialectic action, I observed that it involves genuine risk. At the level of skill, as in acrobatics, that risk is mainly the performer's. Our response then is isomorphic, paralleling in imaginative tension the arc of risk the performer faces. In shows of dramatic illusion, the risk is no longer located primarily in the performers, though in certain circumstances it can be located there too. Rather, the risk is shifted to the audience. It continues to be an emotional and psychological risk. But in addition, it takes on the nature of a moral risk. The poles of action place the given values of an audience in opposition to subversion or challenge. Where the challenged values are deeply cherished and the dialectic opposition has genuine appeal, the imaginative risk we experience is more than game.

In traditional comedy, the rebellion, which at first seems to challenge authority, turns out to be sanctioned by it. Either the rebels submit to enlightened understanding or it turns out that the rebels themselves are the true embodiment of genuine authority. In either case, social values are confirmed. Audiences can delight in threatened disruption, safe in the knowledge that all will be put right. Popular forms, such as melodrama and farce, because they are close to iconic action, abound in this comfortable and comforting exposure. They allow the audience's values to remain undisturbed in the background, so that the audience can merely concentrate on the give and take in the action.

Quite different are the shows that use dialectic action to attack or challenge the audience's value system. Henrik Ibsen is the prime example of a dramatist who did this although the very definition of modernity includes such attack. The clearest instances of Ibsen's dialectic attack can be seen in *A Doll's House* and *Ghosts*. The outcry that the first provoked testifies to the accuracy of Ibsen's aim. In the guise of melodramatic action, Ibsen establishes an initial action between the vulnerable heroine, Nora, and the supposed "villain", Krogstad. Audience sympathy in its own day and even now goes to the "heroine." But then Ibsen shifts the focus, and we follow. It turns out that the real conflict is between Nora's concern with herself and Torvald's claims for the family. Set against a period when wifely self-sacrifice was a common theme both in life and in drama, the new antagonists complicate the audience's lines of sympathy.

For an audience rooted in nineteenth-century beliefs in the supremacy of the family, Nora's challenge to Torvald is a challenge to its own values. So powerful was that challenge that initial performances did not permit its full exercise. That is why instead of having Nora stride out of her home, the first German performance substituted Nora sinking down at the door of the children's room. In effect, through Nora, Ibsen was putting the audience's deep-seated views at genuine risk. When, however, the challenge and subsequent history mitigated the most overt signs of opposition to Nora, the polarity of the action shifted radically. As audiences accepted Nora, they no longer associated with Torvald. Torvald became a silly, old-fashioned, stuffy individual who held the "heroine" in his sway. The play tended increasingly toward an iconic demonstration of endurance and escape since the genuine dialectic of values no longer operated. However, in the 1981 production of the play by the Royal Shakespeare Company, the claims of Nora and Torvald were more nearly adjusted. Torvald was no longer a benighted materialist, but a genuinely cultivated young man who did love Nora and thought he was acting for her good. What he lacked was understanding of her emerging self-discovery. The effect was to restore the dialectic action of the play. One could admire Torvald's desire to protect Nora at the very same time that one deplored his inability to help her realize her self-sufficiency. In this instance, the alignment of values was not neatly divided *between* two characters, a characteristic of melodrama, but divided *within* two characters. The prevalent inclination to champion woman's independence—that one can suppose characterized the audience of The Other Place where the RSC production opened—

had to deal with the evident naïveté of Nora and the heartfelt love of Torvald. In this way, the audience's values were unexpectedly challenged.

Once more we can resort to Aristotle's admonition. A tragic character should be more good than bad though not entirely good. In this observation he is enunciating not only a moral prescription but a dramaturgic one. For dialectic action to fully work, its terms of opposition must make comparable if not equal claims upon our allegiance. There must be a possibility that our empathy can be turned against itself. Perhaps the most disturbing and shocking presentation of that danger occurs in the tragedy of *Macbeth*. Shakespeare creates a figure who at one level of action relentlessly alienates us. He is everything Aristotle says a tragic hero should not be: increasingly more brutal as the play goes on, increasingly more isolated. Against this alienating development, Shakespeare forces upon us the play of mind of a high-strung, finely sensitized man. To the extent that the actor seduces us into sharing his mental action and allowing our empathic nerves to vibrate with his emotions, we are on his side. One set of values, our horror of murder and tyranny, is juxtaposed against another set of values, our sympathy for an anguished human being. In the lore of the theatre, the Scottish play is jinxed. It is one of the most difficult for an actor to play effectively. I suggest that this is so because few actors go far enough in committing themselves to the contradictions of the two terms. Until an actor arouses our full engagement with Macbeth's interior anguish, we shall not ourselves suffer the complete risk to our values that this action demands.

Dialectic action, then, always holds the potential for risk to the audience. That risk does not stem from direct challenge to audience beliefs or fancies. History seems to show that when a performer or a production provokes an audience frontally, the response is equally direct. Initially, when the confrontation is novel, an audience tends to reject challenges. As it becomes familiar with the content or the form of a challenge, it might very well co-opt or absorb it. This pattern is certainly evident in the modern period, for example, in the reception to Ibsen's work, in the reaction to Alfred Jarry's *Ubu Roi* in 1896, and later in response to Dadaist spectacle.

When, however, dialectic action penetrates a spectator, activating one value-potential against another, then the risk is genuine. Then the audience must face itself. The type of conflict I have in mind was sharply presented at the conclusion of Dario Fo's *accidental*

death of an anarchist as it was given in London. The final action deals
with the way a revolutionary group treats a journalist who has
witnessed its destruction of several policemen. At first the
journalist is chained to a window in a room where a bomb is about
to go off. For the audience it is a horrible act, sure to alienate it
from the revolutionists. But before the bomb explodes, the
revolutionary chief stops the action and addresses the audience. He
observes that the drama critics deplored this ending, going as it
does against all one's liberal instincts. Therefore, the revolutionists
have decided upon an alternative ending: permitting the journalist
to go free. We see this alternative ending acted out. The consequences
are as devastating, perhaps even more devastating, than the first
ending. The chief revolutionist looks at us and says, "Which ending
do you choose?" Through this device the production sets different
sides of our liberal sensibility into conflict with one another. We
have to confront our own allegiances. It is in this way, through
dialectic action, that Fo achieves what Brecht advocated: simultaneous
engagement and detachment that force the audience to resolve
emotional disjunction through thinking about the implications of
the play.

Here, as in iconic performance, audience response is a direct
consequence of engagement with performing structures and
content as they alter, challenge, and confirm our attitudes. We are
still far from knowing fully how audiences mesh with presentation,
but we do know that there is no simple pattern. I have argued,
however, that we can isolate and examine the chief factors that
operate in theatrical exchange. This is possible because by its very
nature presentation is an act of giving, and thus the primary
structure is one of the performer projecting activity to receivers. At
the same time, the performer picks up cues from the receivers and
the receivers send overt and covert messages to the performer
about the show. The result is that shows are both independent of
and yet completely connected to their receptivity. As we examine
presentational forms more closely, we can better appreciate the
relative strengths of presentation and reception.

Chapter 6

Act and show

On 1 November 1920, the Provincetown Players presented Eugene O'Neill's *The Emperor Jones*. Without intermission, it ran for under an hour. On 27 June 1970, the New York Shakespeare Festival offered for one night the *Henry VI* plays followed by *Richard III*. This performance began at early evening and concluded at dawn the next morning.

Aristotle tells us that a tragedy should have a beginning, middle, and end, and he further advises that the drama should not be too long, or it will lack proportion. But what he says of a single drama does not seem to apply to an entire show. In his own day, what was the show of the Dionysian festival? Was each of the three tragedies a separate show? And what of the satyr play? Or when Aeschylus presented a trilogy of plays based on the same narrative, was not that *the* show? Indeed, the entire festival was a Chinese box of shows within shows. The full five-day celebration with its procession, its three days of tragic performances, and its dithyrambic contest was a show of shows. And each autonomous element of the celebration was another show, each of which had briefer but clearly differentiated performances within it. In other words, the Greek festival, like turn-of-the-century vaudeville, consisted of "numbers," "acts," and "shows."

The contemporary practice of equating a performance with an evening's entertainment is misleading because it sets a seal of approval on a two or two-and-a-half hour show as though that were the norm. But in fact this practice is a product of nineteenth-century middle-class need. The two-hour show came with commercial development in the Renaissance, and was geared to attract a broad but random clientele. A performance had to be long enough to draw an audience but short enough to be fitted into the daily activities of an urban population. Through the eighteenth century, however, the shows continued to be lengthy by modern standards, but then audiences had a looser sense of attachment to the product. The English practice of half-price admission after the second act testifies to the casual way much of the audience related to a performance. By the nineteenth century, the theatrical and musical performance became part of the elevated interests of a well-to-do, working middle class, and performances were scheduled to fit within the frame of dinner and social exchange. Gradually, a concentrated production of moderate length was evolved.

But this model is not representative of theatrical production throughout history. Moreover, it shows signs of breaking down. The proliferation of festivals, the importance of tourism, the more varied work schedules and increased leisure enable producers to experiment with show length. While the majority of plays and other kinds of shows conform to a conventional length of two hours plus, shows of unusual length are not infrequent.

When we speak of a show then, it is artificial to speak only of the isolated act. A specific work is always embedded in a context of performance, and that context affects the reception of the individual item. Moreover, the extravagance and wonder of a show are enhanced when the show is part of a complex performance. When it is not, when it stands as a totally separate presentation, then it has to struggle more to make its effects. Yet in a true sense, no performance stands alone. An audience sees the performance in the frame of its entire experience with similar presentations, and makes up in memory what may be lacking in actual presence.

What should be kept in mind as we think of the full presentation of performance is that a show may be a brief, independent work or it may embrace a sequence of acts that can extend over a considerable time. In the history of presentation, there have been as many times when performances went on for days as when they lasted an hour. Queen Elizabeth's entertainments at Kenilworth in 1575 extended over a period of more than two weeks.[1] A full performance of a Kabuki drama could last more than twelve hours, and indeed today the presentation of four different acts in a Kabuki program can take four hours. And it is common for the Javanese shadow puppet shows to go on for nine continuous hours. In music we have seen how the Woodstock rock festival lasted for a weekend. Thus, when I speak of a show, I am referring to the full idea of related acts that are connected not necessarily by style or theme but by the idea of common presentation.

Together with length, indeed as a consequence of length, the idea of an extended show involves the matter of variety. So strong is the contemporary conception of unity that we hesitate to see quite disparate elements as constituting a single work. In thinking of a theatrical production, especially of a play, we assume a coherence of style and matter. We expect the language and gestures, as well as setting and costumes, to be uniform. In contrast, the experiments of the last generation have stressed the juxtaposition of contrasting, often violently contrasting, elements. This demonstrates again that uniformity is not characteristic of presentation in general.

When we regard the entire range of performance, whether of the popular circus or the more austere theatre, we encounter a rich mix of acts. The entertainment for Queen Elizabeth that I mentioned consisted of speeches, playlets, water shows, serenades, and pageants. The popular entertainment for Georgian England, as has been noted, combined Shakespearean play, ballet dances, lively farce. The distinctive American art of the musical theatre includes romantic narrative, songs, dances, and spectacular display. Even the much-admired high theatrical art of Greece offered a heady variety for a single day's program. It gave the audience three tragic narratives, a tragic parody in the satyr play, and a comedy. And within each of the plays, there were dramatic scenes, choral songs, and dances. The appropriate meters for the different verses further stressed the rhythmic and tonal variety of the presentation. Thus, when we look at Greek theatre as a show rather than as a piece of literature, we see how it embraced many different performing features.

In general, it is accurate to say that shows which have emerged from the give and take of performing tend to incorporate great variety into their work. We should not forget that Shakespeare's plays were followed by jigs, and that within the plays Shakespeare mixed one story with another, music with dance, comedy with tragedy, soliloquies with processions. The quite alien notion, that theme, character, language, and movement adhere to the neo-classical French school's notion of a single harmony, is an ideal realized by Racine. Rather, Racine took the idea of a single concentrated effect to an extreme. So powerful was his attempt that it dominated the European image of drama and divorced it from its connection with the very nature of presentation, leading to both the achievements and constrictions of modern theatre. The revolt we have experienced since the end of the nineteenth century, a revolt involving both form and content, is largely directed against this alien idea of uniformity of show.

If we are to understand the relationship between performed and non-performed literature, we must recognize that there is a fundamental antagonism between literature and show. Though they did not cast the distinction in these terms, both Plato and Aristotle made a sharp distinction between the poet speaking in his own voice and speaking through the characters. Plato saw it as fundamental. For him, the poet speaking through others was creating a lie, providing a pale imitation of an imitation. In his own voice, at least, the poet kept closer to the truth.

Aristotle did not hold the same moral position regarding the distinction, but he did recognize it as an esthetic matter and sought to describe the peculiar features of the dramatic mode. The effect has been to mute the critical conflict between the literary and the presentational mind.

That conflict has to do with control and point of view, the subject I first raised in discussing the idea of show. If we follow Plato's line of reasoning, the poet speaking in his own voice maintains his own point of view. He shapes his emotion or thought in the lyric, his narrative in the epic to express a consistency of outlook, a consistency over which he can exert control if he wishes. The result is that the literary work, in its very being, tends toward coherence.

But when the poet allows his characters to speak in their own voices, he has to attain an objectivity or effect a disappearance so that the characters seem to be autonomous creatures. Moreover, conceived as show, that independence is magnified by the fact that the roles of the characters are assumed by actual human beings, performers with their own identities. To this one must add the fact that the process of creating sustained attention in performance is very difficult. The same meter or the same subject continued at moderate length seems interminable. The need for variety makes itself felt. Consequently, the autonomy of the performing elements, together with the constant change required to hold an audience's attention, undermine many of the values so dear to the writer. Only a writer who is knowledgeable, cunning, and imaginative can devise a subterranean control over work that is intended for show.

If, then, the show medium has an inherent resistance to a unitary point of view, how is coherence achieved? To deal with that question we have to recognize first of all that it is not always achieved, nor even desired. In expounding the doctrine of unity of action, Aristotle set in motion an ideal for part of the presentational medium that was not native to it. In effect he transferred the literary orientation toward uniformity to another mode of expression. But in doing so he was commenting upon an established dramatic form that already possessed showlike elements: variety of rhythmic meters, alternation of song–dance with narrative episodes, shifts from performing group to performing duets. Nor were his injunctions affected by the scattered recommendations of Horace in the *Ars Poetica*. It was only when the Renaissance humanists adopted an increasingly restricted reading of the *Poetics*, eliminating much of the variety necessary to presentation, that Aristotle came to stand for a forced notion of dramatic unity.

Native to the show form is a loose idea of connected acts, an idea that derives from the nature of the acts themselves. Shows that tend toward celebration, that is, iconic shows, often provide a motif about which related acts may cluster. Again, a parade illustrates one of the most diffused cases of coherence. Whatever the occasion for the parade, traditional or special, there is a theme: celebrating independence, honoring a ruler, crowning a king, worshiping a god. The individual units that compose the parade have some connection to the themes: they support or illustrate. For the most part, each band, float, guild, is a variant of every other. Each may try to outdo the other in colorfulness, cleverness, or discipline. In essence, however, each element does not build upon another but complements it. Whether or not the parade has a climax depends upon its nature. Triumphs of any sort, whether of a Roman general, a prince on progress, or the Rose Bowl Queen, have a natural climax in the appearance of the key figure. In that instance, the peak element, of course, is traveling. As the triumphant figure follows the established route, for each group of spectators he or she passes, the high point is reached. Still, it is not uncommon for parades to have no peak, especially today in countries with mass populations.

In such a show, particularly when great care is taken in the planning, as was the case with the Renaissance pageants and entries, the variable units are chosen to complement each other in a complex fashion. Considerable artistry is expended on finding the most apt or startling motif to amplify the central theme. For this purpose the pageant-makers impressed the Olympian and biblical figures into service in order to provide allusions and compliments in ingenious fashion. This type of artistic variety enriched the show by providing the diversity that it required along with a relatedness, so that each act reinforced the others.

In other forms of entertainment, such as vaudeville or theatrical shows that mixed different kinds of performance, a theme did not supply the knot that held a performance together. Sheer variety for variety's sake often prevailed. First, one might see an acrobat, then a singer, then a monologist, and so forth. The sequence did not have a thematic continuity in those cases. These kaleidoscopic shows had another rationale for the way they unfolded, and that was one of theatrical excitement or appropriateness. In vaudeville, the performing bill was arranged in a rough form of mounting interest. The penultimate spot on the program was reserved for the headliner, whoever the headliner might be and whatever the headliner might do. It could be a singer, an actress, possibly an illusionist, a notorious figure of the day, etc. Building to that key spot involved a skillful assignment of places on the bill in order to vary and intensify the attention of the crowd.

In dramatic terms this arrangement was fairly crude, but it does illustrate a fundamental aspect of a show: the performers must juggle the twin demands of variety and intensification as the work moves forward. In vaudeville, which was a transitory kind of show with a weekly change of bill, the sequence could be set by the availability of particular attractions. The kind of variety found in the London theatre of the eighteenth century was more traditionally set. The main production was interspersed with song and dance for diversion and followed by a shorter, lighter afterpiece. This formula, which included tragedy, farce, and musical entertainment, was very popular and endured for many years.

These last-mentioned patterns of coherence arise from the show medium itself, and though my examples come from popular forms of presentation, we should not forget that the human responses they satisfy need to be aroused even by the highest art. Too pure a conception of theatre can purge it of all the vital juices that flow from the pleasures of a varied and intensifying series of acts.

So far I have described the organic coherence that inheres in all shows, but particularly that type of show that tends to be iconic. Absorbing this form of coherence but going beyond it is the unity that arises from the dialectic act. In acts of skill there is a natural sequence of acts that are increasingly challenging. Considered structurally, the sequence is ordered so that the obstacles or resistance become increasingly greater or the consequences of failure more devastating. Implicitly, such acts juxtapose a performer who persists in choosing the most demanding feat against a condition that seems all but impossible to overcome. In such a dialectic opposition there is a natural climax or rather a series of climaxes that mount to a pitch. Each number has its own challenge and climactic release which contributes to the excitement of the next number until the performer does the feat that lies at the forefront. In this sequence we have the schematic structure of the Aristotelian concept of action.

But whether we are considering the classic form of the performing athlete or the more complex forms of dramatic illusion, the dialectic structure supplies the foundation for the coherence of a performance. Whatever the elements that constitute the conflicting forces, the development of their possibilities suggests the growth of the performance but also its resolution. The nub of danger that the performer–character faces must ultimately be overcome or he or she must finally succumb to it, and in that teleological imperative lies the potential for a coherent show. How to achieve that unity and to provide at the same time the variety that the show form demands is one of the most challenging aspects of theatre art.

The answer lies in continuity. But how to achieve it? In pursuing the answer, a caveat is necessary. Although I have treated the problem of coherence of the iconic show separately from that of the dialectic, it should be apparent that the two types of acts do not exist exclusively within a show. As I pointed out about Greek tragedy, the iconic nature of the ode is set against the dialectic episode to create a complex effect. This sort of mixture of structure is common throughout the history of the theatre. While the iconic or the dialectic mode tends to dominate the drama in certain periods, there are few instances of periods in which a show is exclusively of one sort or another. Perhaps the French drama from the seventeenth through the nineteenth centuries most completely realized the dialectic mode, but even there the dialectic form was often so carefully refined that it assumed an iconic effect. The important point is that until the twentieth century the dialectic mode was preferred, and even though Shakespeare was greatly admired, it was often despite the fact that his dramatic form was regarded as faulty. Still, the principal characteristic of his art was the subtle blending of the two show modes in a host of variants. In later chapters I shall discuss this mixed form in some detail. A more obvious example of using a mixture of modes lies in Ben Jonson's work for the Stuart court. It was he who took the Elizabethan masque, which was a dance form only partly theatricalized and made it more complex. In its pure dance pattern, the masque celebrated love and valor. Its form was iconic. Jonson added a prologue in the form of a dramatic anti-masque that supplied a dialectic feature. In that way he attempted to have the celebration of the Stuarts (Queen Anne, Prince Henry, and more indirectly, King James) arise from a triumph over an opposing principle. Among twentieth-century writers, Brecht and Genet have most successfully blended the iconic and dialectic modes.

One further feature of the *mixed mode* is the matter of tightness in the relationship of the subordinate acts. It might be apparent that the show that is most purely dialectic will also be the one that is most intensely unified. The more closely every aspect of the performing act is tied to the root opposition of the action, the less likely is it that there will be extraneous numbers. But where there is a rich mixture of iconic and dialectic elements, the connections among them are looser. The pull of variation and juxtaposition is greater, and so the introduction of self-contained show elements is more likely. The unity of effect, so lauded by nineteenth-century critics, is therefore remote and even incidental.

Up to now I have treated in an inductive fashion the matter of how a full show is formed out of separate acts. That is, I have started with the act itself, and considered what inheres in its structure and its potentiality that will give rise to an extended work where the parts will be more or less related. Let us now consider the full show by reversing the point of view. What resources do the performers draw upon to frame their separate acts? For shows of illusion the answer is narrative materials. Telling a story by means of a show is not only widespread, but it often seems the only important feature of theatrical art. The staging of narrative is so native to illusionary shows that I have deliberately delayed discussing the matter lest we fail to see how the show form is really independent of narrative, no matter how closely it is associated with it. Now I wish to make some general observations on how presentation and narrative relate to each other, reserving for later chapters a more detailed discussion of dramatic narrative structure.

Presumably, narrative originated in oral storytelling. The language was rhythmic and poetic rather than prosaic in form. In a sense literature and presentation were united. Only with time did the telling of stories become distributed among more than one medium. In all likelihood the first branching may have involved dance or dance-drama, but, of course, we cannot be sure of this. Whatever the sequence, however, over the centuries narrative became an abstraction, an idea of storytelling which found its individual expression in many different forms: epic, folk tale, romance, drama, painting, novel, opera, cinema, and most recently, television. Despite the fact that contemporary criticism has appropriated the term narrative for the medium of fiction, in actuality there are many arts that make use of some type of narration.

Among these arts is the art of presentation or, it might be more useful to say, the various arts of presentation. And among those that utilize narration regularly or intermittently is the art of dramatic illusion as it is manifested in one or another form. Spoken drama, opera, dance, pageant, and mime are the principal cases. Related in form though not of the same order of presentation are cinema and television. Each of these arts relies on narration to some degree though how each tells its story will differ to some extent. Nevertheless, there are some common practices.

A single story dealing with a limited group of people and tracing a finite set of situations provides a basic continuity. Any presentation that sticks to such a narration is bound to have a minimal kind of coherence. But, as Aristotle warned, not all the events that happen to a particular character may relate to a single action. That is why he insisted on one and only one action. But despite his authority and great good sense, medieval and Renaissance drama, especially of England and Spain, proved that a powerful art of dramatic presentation could be based on extended narrative. Certainly, the religious cycle play, with its numerous plays (acts), drew upon a sustained biblical narrative in order to create a dramatic continuity based on figurative juxtaposition. The Japanese theatre also has shown that a valid show can be made out of a string of episodes associated with one narrative line. Thus, the way in which presentation can employ narrative is not predetermined by any organic need.

The cycle plays also illustrate the fact that a dramatic show does not necessarily have to deal with a limited body of characters. Each of the plays in the cycle introduces new people, and only a few figures appear in more than one play. This very impulse to introduce characters when they are needed (without being confined to them) is reflected even in Shakespeare's work when he does not hesitate to drop a character from a play without explanation (the Fool in *King Lear*) or add one late in a show (Osric in *Hamlet*). These examples supply even more evidence that there is no fixed way in which narrative can be used for theatrical purposes.

Nor is there a precise correspondence between the length of a narrative scene (what some critics now call a narreme) and a presentational number. In actual practice, most presentations seem to require a certain duration in order to develop an action. What a fictional narrative may put in a few words, a dramatic narrative may require time to expound and build. But again that is not a necessary condition of performance. Episodic drama has many scenes of great brevity that may make a narrative point and quickly come to an end. In *Troilus and Cressida*, for example, Achilles' murder of Hector takes only a dozen lines. So length too does not determine the relation between show and narrative.

Just what the relation may be is perhaps best seen by looking at several different theatrical forms. Dance is particularly instructive. More than opera or drama, it can dispense with narrative, and often does. Yet it frequently employs a narrative to supply either a superficial or a deep continuity. Non-narrative dance is often a non-presentational dance. Ballroom or disco dancing has no narrative, but neither is it always presentational. When it is, as in the art of the Castles or in that of theatrical tap dancers like Bill Robinson or Ray Bolger, it usually omits narrative. This is also true of the work of Fred Astaire, almost all of which is quasi-presentational. Though dancing for film, Astaire sought to retain some tie to presentation by insisting that a dance be filmed as a continuous rather than an edited work. Non-narrative dance could be given a story, as Astaire occasionally did, though rarely did the story enhance the quality of the show.

Other dance forms, in particular modern dance and ballet, build their work on some kind of narration. The great classical ballets were indeed dramas in physical movement. But in those cases the ballets had to develop a storytelling technique through mime which framed the true heart of the work: the pas de deux, the corps de ballet, etc. In some instances, as in the marvelous achievements of John Cranko, a pas de deux may be a fully worked-out drama of the passion of one person for another, as in *Eugene Onegin*, but more frequently the story merely provides the basis for the dance. Here we have a partial clue. In ballet, the presentational elements that are available for telling a story consist of solos, duets, trios, quartets, male and female groups. While there is no set sequence in which these must appear, some form of alternation is imperative. Therefore, whatever the story, it is arranged in a sequence to allow for variety of dance. In many cases, narrative occasions are invented to justify the introduction of dance numbers, as in *Swan Lake*, where in some productions the different princesses bring with them national dance groups.

A similar though not quite so loose arrangement between narrative and show exists in opera. The recent vogue is to bring opera closer to drama, and thus integrate the narrative into the music. But the major operatic works strike a balance between the musical show and the dramatic show. As in dance, different combinations of performers alternate to provide variety and contrast. In both forms we can distinguish clearly between two different relations, between narrative and presentation. In one form, the narrative provides the context for the act, as in the *Swan Lake* dances or in the children's march in the second act of *La Bohème*. The dance and music do not advance the story, but fit within it conveniently, sometimes arbitrarily. In the other form, the narrative unfolds through the dance or song. That is the case with the Cranko pas de deux from *Eugene Onegin* and the ball scene from *Don Giovanni*. Yet again the forms are not so sharply separated. In Mozart's operas, for instance, where recitative separates aria from aria, each aria, however much it may advance the narrative, has an autonomous quality as a number in a show that interrupts the narrative flow.

In drama the same range of looseness also exists. The more tightly organized dialectic plays incorporate the narrative more fully into their action. They do this by dramatizing only a portion of the available story and alluding to the portion excluded. In effect, they follow Aristotle's advice. But this is by no means the only way to handle narrative. Plays more episodic in structure maintain a loose tie to the narrative flow, including not only the sequence of events that we closely associate with stories but also commentary and other types of show. But what is actually part of the narrative and what is not?

Let us take a simple narrative event: a girl and boy making love to each other. As an event, this narreme is quite abstract. It has no substance until the lovemaking assumes some form. Suppose it assumes the form we find in *Romeo and Juliet*. Shakespeare divides the initial lovemaking into two "numbers": the meeting at the ball, the expression of love in the orchard. In the first scene the young people do not know each other. They are at a formal gathering. They flirt through the thrust and parry of a sonnet. In the Prokofiev ballet of the same event, the emphasis is less on the lovers and more strikingly on the famous Pillow Dance. In other words the situation provided a justification for the production number.

In the orchard scene Shakespeare stresses Romeo's impetuosity while Juliet is mindful of his danger. She is on a balcony, he below. They are physically separated, and that spatial separation is a tangible demonstration of the familial separation they have to overcome. It also accents Juliet's fears. Thus, the moment of the lovers expressing love for each other is structured not merely to supply a lyrical expression but to define a gap between them that their feelings close.

The same event in the ballet does not admit the same solution. Juliet cannot remain on the balcony while Romeo remains below. That is why in most versions of the ballet the lovers dance a pas de deux which in some general manner signifies their passion for each other. It is clearly not a working out of their relationship but a kinesthetic lyricism in choreographed form.

The same scene in the opera *Roméo et Juliette* by Gounod illustrates a handling of the incident in quite another way. Gounod arranges the action in three segments: an introductory love duet, a comic intrusion involving the Tybalt-like figure of Gregorio searching for Montagues and for the nurse Gertrude, and then an exchange of vows leading to the farewell between Roméo and Juliette. In the love exchanges the sentiments are taken directly from Shakespeare, but the dialectic conflict between Juliette's love and her fear for Roméo's safety is virtually eliminated. Instead, everything is simplified. The love duets produce a union of feeling that is altogether distinct from the sense of incompleteness in the drama. As in the ballet, this union is confirmed by the physical proximity of the lovers. Preliminary to the farewell, the stage directions specify a sequence of moves that brings Juliette into Roméo's arms as they sing their second duet. In the opera as in the ballet, the medium and the audience's expectations associated with it lead the performers to emphasize that feature of the story which joins the lovers while dramatic presentation, which permits more complicated nuances, can deal with the contradictory attitudes that Juliette undergoes.

In each of these arts, the story provides the point of departure for developing the material in an individual manner. Each art uses story elements in its own strategic fashion. The presentational demands of dance and opera are perhaps more intractable and, therefore, we find more instances in which the story is merely the frame for the type of presentation natural to these arts. But this is not fundamentally dissimilar from the drama. This again may be seen most readily in Shakespeare's work. No matter what the story or the genre, Shakespeare, with only two or three exceptions, always moves his plays toward some form of ceremonial finale. He shares this practice with virtually all of his contemporaries.

The finale may be the occasion for a duel at court (*Hamlet*), or a formal visit (*Twelfth Night*), or a trial (*Measure for Measure*), but whatever the event, an audience could be sure that the play would move toward such a conclusion. It is as though the presentational form has built into it a movement toward such finality. This is exceptionally evident in such plays as *Measure for Measure* and *A Winter's Tale*, whose finales include revelations. To a certain extent the finales of the last two plays appear forced. Criticism of the bed trick in the one case and of Paulina's secrecy in the other reflect dissatisfaction with the narrative connection between the story and the scene. In the theatre, however, these two finales are enormously effective because, despite the apparent narrative problem, they strike in an unusual way the tone of wonder that is so appealing in a show.

In sum, then, a narrative is a bundle of situations or functions upon which various kinds of shows can draw. The continuity inherent in the narrative helps to supply coherence to a show. But the performer may freely use the narrative materials to create effective presentational acts. In doing so, the performer may integrate the narrative materials in a closely packed sequence or may merely use them as a point of departure. In fact, given the requirements of performance, the performer tends to use the narrative as a resource. It thus serves as a background against which the figure of the action unfolds. Sometimes the background is a complex history against which the concentrated time of the play is acted. At other times the background runs parallel to the unfolding episodes as concurrent but unseen events.

Chapter 7

The act-scheme and the act-image

Every show of illusion is a double-faceted presentation. The actor is himself and simultaneously "another." As we have seen, Cosimo de' Medici is Cosimo the Prince and Jason the Argonaut. It is not necessary that he surrender his own identity in order to assume the fictive one, for the theatrical significance of his appearance lies in the audience's simultaneous awareness of his twofold identity. In similar ways all dramatic acts possess this double nature. Since, by definition, what is presented to an audience brings it into contact with beings or events that do not actually inhere in the performers or their activities, we are repeatedly reminded of the separation between the acts before us and the "living" they embody. To clarify this relationship between the two, we need to re-examine the distinction I made in Chapter 2 between the act-scheme and the act-image. Let us designate the acts in the form that they play before us as *act-schemes* since they all conform to set patterns. Act-schemes exist on at least two levels: that of the theatrical conventions of a given period, and that of the immediate act of presentation that we witness.

What the act-scheme "represents" or "signifies" is the *act-image*. That image may have an historical basis (*Richard II*), a legendary origin (*Phèdre*), or a wholly fanciful source (*Finian's Rainbow*). Whatever the root or source, the act-image which is generated by the act-scheme has or may have an independence of its own. Indeed, in talking about a play, we usually discuss its act-image (plot and story) rather than its act-scheme (presentational forms) unless we are unusually absorbed by esthetic matters. In fact, that the act-scheme and act-image merge into each other in popular consciousness only makes discussion of drama that much more elusive.

In saying that an act-scheme "represents" or "signifies" an act-image, I am posing alternatives that raise the issue of the exact relationship between two types of acts, one that is purely presentational (the act-scheme), the other that may be purely imaginary (the act-image). This relationship is partly determined by the nature of the presentational medium, partly determined by cultural conventions. Perhaps it might be more accurate to say that what we accept as representation actually consists of signs that are related in a fundamentally schematic manner. When the actor playing Lear "dies" onstage, he exemplifies the elements of the act-scheme; he organizes a sequence of "failing signs" to convey cessation of breathing and relaxation of muscles in order to "indicate" rather than to "mirror" or "represent" the process of dying.

The example of the death scene further highlights two other factors in the act-scheme/act-image relationship. While the act-scheme can approach the appearance of the act-image, it does so only in relative terms. There is always an absolute separation between the two. For example, in order to create the illusion of weakening, the actor must expend considerable energy to sustain a high level of concentration. Secondly, the signs that compose the act-scheme always work contextually, as I have suggested. No single sign conveys the illusion of dying; instead, this illusion is created through a sequence of motions that stand for "natural" signs of dying but that are not true significations in themselves. It is through their patterning that these signs or motions project an internalized effect. In essence, then, the meaning emerges at the level of the act-scheme, not at the point of the separate motions or signs.

How cultural conventions influence the act-scheme is not easy to determine. If we compare death scenes in Kabuki with death scenes in Shakespeare, no sharp distinctions emerge. Both types of performance utilize contextual patterns although Kabuki actors appear to be able to abstract the pattern more completely than our contemporary actors of Shakespeare. Kabuki actors can, for example, create an impression of life seeping out of a body by slowing down their stage activity. In fact, differences in enacting the death scene may be greater between genres than between cultures. Comic death scenes often isolate a character's spasm (as in Pyramus' comic death scene) and through the isolation render them ludicrous rather than pathetic.

While it may be most graphic in death scenes, the discrepancy between act–scheme and act–image is evident throughout theatre. Consider the soliloquy, for example. In the most general sense of the term, the soliloquy is a presentational act. It designates a solo speech within a play involving more than one character. (We don't usually speak of a monologue or a monodrama as a soliloquy.) A more restrictive notion of soliloquy associates the speech with the expression of inner thought, and in a further extension of this idea there is an assumption that the inner thought so expressed is the revelation of the true nature of the character. Thus, the soliloquy promises to give direct access to a character's mind.

Even more than the death scene, the soliloquy poses an absolute contradiction between this scheme as presentation and the act–image it reflects. The act–image is that of an uninhibited flow of mind. The means for conveying that image in the theatre which is noted for soliloquies, the Elizabethan theatre, are rhetorical. Hamlet's soliloquies are the ideal examples of the revelation of private thought. Yet these soliloquies are astonishingly regular in their versification, with little attempt on Shakespeare's part to indicate any irregularities in the rhythm or progress of idea. By contrast, the speeches where such irregularity is tried—Brutus' speech on Caesar and Richard III's awakening from a nightmare—are less effective as either soliloquies or dramatic revelations. In the soliloquy, it then appears, the act–scheme has an integrity of its own that can be used to "signify" the working of thought without actually "mirroring" it.

Nor is more realistic business any more amenable to mirror-like representation. Take the business of eating onstage. No matter how naturalistic the performance, the actors do not duplicate the exact process of eating a meal. The pace of eating as well as the amount of food consumed are arranged in a carefully rehearsed sequence in order to coordinate with the action. Though the inclination of naturalism is to have the act–scheme of eating be an exact copy of the act–image, in actual practice that is not possible. Instead, the act–scheme presents a pattern of motions or signs that creates an image of eating. Often that pattern serves as a background for the focal action of a scene (as in the first act of *The Three Sisters*), and occasionally it assumes central importance (Azdak teaching the grand duke to eat cheese in *The Caucasion Chalk Circle*), but, as we have seen, once the act is designed for presentation and consequently rehearsed, it becomes an act-scheme.

If, then, exact correspondence between scheme and image is not possible even in the most naturalistic of activities, how much less possible is it in the entire range of performance types throughout theatrical history. In fact, it is far more likely for the act-scheme *not* to be a copy of the act-image but rather a conventionalized set of activities with a conceptual but not a mimetic relation to the act-image. For example, the various metric forms of oral expression that underlie stage speech, such as the closing couplet in some Shakespearean scenes, are not so much means of imitation as they are instruments of expression and action.

An unclouded look at the earliest dramatic presentations demonstrates, in fact, a startling relation of act-scheme to act-image. Whatever fanciful notions of the origin of drama we may have, by the time the verifiable examples of Greek drama emerge, we encounter highly sophisticated act-schemes. Their characteristics are widely known: alternating sequences of individuals and groups (odes and episodes), costumes that distort and monumentalize the performers, groups moving and speaking in formal patterns, individuals speaking in set meters and following strictly defined paths (e.g., stichomythia).

Thus, in our earliest knowledge of the drama, we find a schematic structure that does not relate to the act of mirror-like imitation, however much that subject may occur in ancient Greek criticism. Indeed, as Gerald Else seems to argue,[1] the notion of mimesis may refer to the mode of expression, that is, to the act-scheme, rather than to the object of the expression, the act-image itself. Later periods have displaced this reference by directing attention to the act-image, and so removed analysis from the treatment of the act-scheme. In ancient Greece that act-scheme arises from the social balance between individual and community, with the individual endowed with an appearance that heightens his superhuman qualities. Whatever passions or circumstances these schemes signify, the schemes themselves embody forces other than the fictive or mimetic.

What we find among the Greeks is similar to what we find at the initial stages of any dramatic tradition and what we are finding in the developments of the twentieth century. Noh drama, which emerged from religious dance, coalesced into a theatrical scheme that serves admirably as an instrument for evoking certain metaphysical states, but it is hardly a reflection of the appearance of life. Whether the form that did arise came about purely because of socio-religious influence or was partly the result of esthetic play, may be impossible ever to discover. But whatever its genesis, an act-scheme embodies in its structure a resolution of impulses stemming from deep social causes. As presentation, these act-schemes not only provide a form for displaying these varied impulses but also serve as a means of transcending the limits that contain them.

The act-scheme in any theatrical period is, as we see, a complex of many elements. To observe more clearly how this complex produces the act-image, we might first explore the code or system of conventions within which an act-scheme operates. I have mentioned this in a preliminary way. In a broad sense the act-scheme has a dynamic, though not necessarily causative, connection to the encompassing code.

In ancient Greece the code includes performance for large numbers, the use of performance to resolve opposition (through the contest), and a formal program that unites disparate features. Although we may not be able to show a direct correspondence between dramatic form and the inclusion of the dithyrambic contest in the Dionysian festival, still we can see the act-scheme as a formulation of an echoing agon that reverberates throughout the festival. Not only do we have a complex of contests (dithyrambic, tragic, comic), we also have tragedy set against satyr play, one tragedy against another, chorus against individual, and ultimately individual against individual. Thus, the structure of the festival, with its oppositions and modes of reconciliation, provides a sympathetic context for more specific act-schemes within the separate plays. The same reverberation between presentational contexts and act-schemes occurs in other societies. The privacy of the Noh performance, the ubiquity of the medieval mystery, and the commercial variety of the Elizabethan theatre all offer distinctive settings for quite different yet appropriate act-schemes.

In other words, the governing conditions of performance go a long way toward determining the kinds of act-schemes a society will generate. The mystery cycles, developed in association with the Corpus Christi festival and presented by religious or secular guilds, had much to do with the growth of the short play in England in contrast to the longer passion plays in the more centralized cities of the Continent. The number of the guilds interacting with the extended narrative of the Bible produced the model for the discontinuous but related performances involving from twenty-five to forty-eight plays. It is within such a presentational framework that the act-schemes of individual plays emerge.

Again, the medieval example illustrates a general condition of theatrical history. Conditions of performance set the terms within which creative artists work. By influencing scale, length, and variety of performance, these conditions incline the theatre to one or another kind of act-scheme. It would be desirable to study such conditions in each historical period, but that is beyond the scope of this book. Here it has to be sufficient to provide a few examples in order to establish the influence of performing conditions on presentational structures.

Perhaps the feature most readily observed as a manifestation of these conditions is that of length. Despite the prevalent assumption that a play should encompass the "two hours' traffic of our stage," the length of dramatic performance has varied greatly throughout history. At dinner in a Tudor hall, an interlude lasted but an hour or so. Each Greek tragedy took less than two hours to perform, though the three offered each day of the festival plus a satyr play went on for eight to ten hours. Shakespeare's plays—as they have come down to us—run from under 2,000 lines to nearly 4,000; that is, they could run from less than two hours to over four. The Javanese shadow plays unfold over a nine-hour period throughout the night, and the medieval cycle drama went on for several days. Currently, we are in a volatile state in which shows of eighty minutes or less play cheek by jowl with shows of four, five, and, in the case of *Nicholas Nickleby*, eight-and-a-half hours. The breakdown in conventional length reflects changes in patterns of leisure and experiments in form, and focuses on the need to reestablish a commanding impact on theatre going. In all of these instances, the act-scheme emerges within the initial limits set by the overall length of a performance together with the system for designating formal subdivisions (plays, acts, scenes, numbers).

Within these initial limits the individual schemes follow equally systematic patterns. In shows of extended duration, we seem to have two basic sequences. While both types of sequence include self-contained, highly defined "plays," one type endeavors to link one "play" to another (the medieval and the Kabuki cycle plays); the other type merely frames the autonomous "plays" (Dionysian festival, contemporary arts festivals). It is within the given conventions of these presentational frames that we can discuss the individual act-scheme.

To what extent is the act-scheme shaped by performing needs and to what extent by its subject matter? Again, a glance back may help us provide a framework for examining present practice. Although it is hazardous to generalize about any historical development, several common characteristics appear in the early stages of performance. First, as Richard Southern has noted in *The Seven Ages of the Theatre*,[2] the performer initially appears in some fantastic guise: Greek tragedians in raised boot, high headdress, mask; the comedians with mask and phallus; numerous tribes in grotesque costume and mask; Chinese actors with painted faces, etc. Second, invariably the early stages of theatre freely utilize dance, music, and song. Thus, from the very beginning the act-scheme has a highly defined theatrical appearance. That appearance, it is often claimed, has the purpose both of striking awe into the audience and arousing belief. Though that may be true at times, it also has an esthetic purpose of delighting and astonishing the onlookers. Motives are complex, and pleasure mingles with observance and tradition.

Of equal importance in shaping the act-scheme is its relationship to the material enacted. Here contemporary practice differs considerably from the practice that has hitherto prevailed in theatrical history. In its most extreme form, the performer (someone like monologist Spalding Gray) draws from a life experience elements that he wishes to transform into an act-image through an act-scheme that will be congruent with it. Repeatedly through the 1960s in the United States, theatrical groups sought to present events as they actually occurred (*Dionysus in '69*, *The Concept*, etc.). This type of congruity is antithetical, however, to other, more abstract practices in the same period. While drawing from experience in similar ways, groups such as the Living Theatre and the Open Theatre created structures that were metaphors of their interpretation of events or, in some cases, metaphoric vehicles for creating the experience in front of and with the audience. In effect, they used an act-scheme to create an experience that was actual, not virtual. Yet even in doing so, they often drew from history or legend to provide the metaphoric vehicle.

Myth and history are the first sources of dramatic performance. The distinction between the two, however, is not entirely clear. In utilizing the resurrection of Christ as the initial situation for their trope, the *Quem quaeritis*, the Winchester monks thought of the event as both symbolic and historical; indeed, it was symbolic

because it was historical. Their performance of the visit of the
Marys was a surrogate for the congregational witness. They made
the moment vivid by bringing its essential features into play.
Similarly, the Greek plays employed shared myths to provide the
stuff of performance. It is, of course, true that in dealing with the
Quem quaeritis trope, we are examining a form of presentation
which was at a far earlier stage of its development than we are when
examining the Greek tragedies. The tragedies are fully realized
artistic works while the trope is a rudimentary effort, the fullest
expression of which can be seen in the complex system of
figuration within the cycles, as explored by V. A. Kolve.[3] What we
find among the Greek tragedies are circumstances replicated
throughout theatrical history. For much of drama, performance
combines a system of presentation with derived narrative materials
leavened by the sensibility of the artists concerned. On the level of
an individual play, the system of presentation involves an alternating
sequence of odes and episodes. Why this precise performing
structure evolved seemed at one time apparent but at present is not
satisfactorily explained. Are we dealing with a vestige? Are we
dealing with the practical difficulty of two or three actors playing
before 15,000–20,000 people? Whatever the genesis, the poets had
this system, limited in duration, through which to communicate
extended narrative material. Now it all seems inevitable.

But when the Greek poets were faced with the mass of legend—
much of it in oral form—what a challenge it must have been to
find suitable means for transforming it into presentation. To excise
the narrative connectives and merely put conversation onstage was
not their way. We have only the results, and do not know the
phases of growth that led to the act-schemes we now find. But it is
clear that they were led by given conditions to concentrate on a
specific event and then to shape that event into a series of
confrontations. Since we learned that *The Suppliants* was not
Aeschylus' first play, we no longer see its narrative mode as an
argument for dramatic form arising from storytelling. Even if we
accept the theory that the first actor arose from the chorus, he may
have done so in order to challenge and so confront the group rather
than to confide in it. By the time the act-scheme emerges in the
early plays of Aeschylus, it is already a fixed system of debates,
verbal wrestling, and lamentations.

In short, a repertory of primary-level structures existed for the
poet's use, and though he might modify them, as Euripides
certainly did, he did not abandon them entirely. These structures

survived both because they answered the needs of the poets and because they proved efficacious in performance. The act-images that these schemes induced, we must assume, reflected what the poets wished to express. At the same time, these act-images embodied principles and attitudes that have come to stand for Greek thought as a whole.

Variations of this interaction between act-schemes, narrative sources, and act-images occur throughout history. We cannot consider them all. But our discussion of Greek tragedy permits me to put forth some tentative observations about the illusionary act that arises from the successful fusion of act-scheme and act-image. For diverse reasons a specific theatrical culture formulates distinctive act-schemes. These schemes are the presentational forms through which theatrical workers create act-images. In attempting to create personalized act-images, the worker reshapes existent act-schemes to accommodate a variety of pre-existing and conceptual materials. Much of the vitality of a performance comes from the struggle of reshaping. The model of the act-image need not be—in fact, usually is not—an image of an actual world or an action in an actual world. It is far more likely to be a construction of possibilities—or, in Aristotle's words, of probable or necessary events. But since it is based on a communal act-scheme, it also captures a firmly grounded structure of behavior.

Seen from another perspective, a dramatic presentation is a structured act that combines several levels of impact. At the act-scheme level it offers a theatrically effective pattern that has inherent interest for the audience. It also contains in the dynamic of its structure a social enactment that serves as a particularly meaningful level of exchange among members of that society. Its heightened form—the fact that it is sufficiently intense to sustain audience interest—further embodies a trace of the extraordinary; that is, no matter how much it utilizes *actual* features of the audience's life, it transforms these features into a pure state. It is this resultant and complex act-scheme that holds immediate theatrical interest.

While compelling on a purely phenomenal level, the act-scheme continuously intimates the act-image. In certain theatres, the interaction between act-image and act-scheme is so rudimentary that interest centers on the perceptible features of the performance, as in ballet. Whatever the balance between them, though, an act-image arises from an act-scheme which is rooted in the presentational potentialities of a particular theatrical culture.

Chapter 8

Actor to audience

"Showing off," when it is a matter of skill or glorification, can be direct and open. The very nature of a display of skill invites audience admiration in an acknowledged exchange between performer and spectator. It is true that the center of a gymnastic act requires the athlete to shut out the audience and concentrate on the feat; still, the feat is framed within an address to those attending. In displays of glory, such as a float, the "hero" openly waves and smiles to the crowd. In virtually all instances of non–illusionary show this openness prevails.

Even in some shows of illusion the performer regularly "plays" to the audience. This is true of magicians. When they assume a role, they do it within a continuous persona so that the audience is never aware that there may be a distinction between the performing persona and another type of behavior. When the magician temporarily assumes a persona such as an oriental wizard for a single act, the identity is more a superficial sign than a full role. It is a lightly held "as if," which the audience is not expected to treat seriously.

It is when we are presented with fully developed acts of illusion —those we associate with drama—that direct presentation becomes complicated and provocative.

Traditionally, a distinction is made between presentational style and representational style. This distinction suggests that one form of theatre involves direct communication with the audience while the other does not. It is here, in discussing representational style, that critics tend to isolate drama from the performing process, denying the fact that in a true sense, all drama is presentational. Even the most introverted, self-contained scene is intended for performance, and to the degree that it is prepared and an audience brought to witness it, it is a work of presentation.

Still, the distinction presentation/representation is valid on other terms. What is normally called dramatic presentation is actually a form of *direct* presentation. The performer acknowledges the presence of the audience and presents the show making that acknowledgement explicit. This type of playing differs from the *indirect* form of presentation where the performer supposedly does not "admit" the presence of the audience and acts as though the activity performed has an autonomous existence. Such indirect presentation prevails in most of what we recognize as drama, but the implications of this autonomy have not been explored.

In actual performance practice there is no razor-sharp separation between direct and indirect presentation. All sorts of modifications of both types appear, and we shall consider these later. Meanwhile, let us look more closely at direct presentation of dramatic materials.

Direct presentation, as I've said, is an open exchange between performer and spectator. But drama, by its very definition, has a double nature. In performing drama, the actor assumes an identity, plays a fictional action, or does both. There is thus the actor and the act which are fundamentally at odds with each other. The result, for direct presentation, is that the openness of a dramatic actor is a sham. It is another illusion, but an illusion that proclaims it is what it appears to be. The modulations of this illusion are most evident in dramatic prologues.

The fashion for prologues and epilogues in the direct vein is long past, at least in the form that was traditional. Such framing devices ranged from two-line appeals for applause (in Plautus) to witty verses in the eighteenth century. Here I shall discuss speeches rather than scenes that serve as prologues (in the line of Shakespeare and Brecht). These supposed extra-dramatic devices might represent the performers speaking in their own person. In England this was quite common. For instance, a friend of the author may defend the work, or an actor may ask for praise or support. Such direct appeal often sought to put the audience in the proper frame of mind or strengthen a favorable response. Its very existence may be rooted in class distinction; that is, such direct appeal characterizes those social situations in which the players are regarded as servants and their playing as amusement for a superior class. This certainly is the case with Elizabethan actors and is in strong contrast with the citizen-like status of the Greek actor.

The essentially non-dramatic prologue and epilogue shade into instances where the direct exchange assumes a quasi-dramatic character. The Chorus in *Henry V* is not merely an actor guiding the audience into the action. He assumes a more lofty status, an impersonality that makes his voice not that of the performer-as-working-player but performer-as-voice-of-historical-drama. The longing for a muse of fire is a longing resident in an imagined mind, not the actual mind of the speaker. Yet here the passage of the performer beyond his own identity is limited, and designed to mediate between the audience as it is and the action as it will be.

The epilogue of *As You Like It* is quite another matter. There the actor plays with the audience both in his character and in his person. Currently, when Rosalind is played by a woman, the delicious teasing in the passage is somewhat lost. But in its original form, as spoken by a boy actor, the playfulness is cunning and changeable. The actor, retaining his role of Rosalind, first admits that "It is not the fashion to see the lady the epilogue," but nevertheless goes on to conjure the men and women separately to like the play. Toward the end, the boy actor confesses that "If I (he) were a woman, I (he) would kiss as many of you . . . that pleased me."[1] This playful transsexual seduction is nicely managed, and shows the performer crossing the line from character to player, making use of both aspects of dramatic presentation.

Many more are the instances in which the prologue is enclosed within a character who never drops that role. Coulmier, the director of the clinic of Charenton in *Marat/Sade*, is such an example. In his address to the audience, whether as prologue or intermittently throughout the play, the actor always retains his fictional identity. Such a form of direct presentation is quite different from the other cited, and introduces new esthetic considerations. By maintaining a fictional identity and yet communicating with the audience directly, the performer poses questions of overlapping worlds: the world of the audience and the world of the play. How the character can remain in his world while the audience remains in theirs, and yet have an open exchange, offers opportunity and introduces problems to be explored shortly.

So far I have considered direct presentation only in terms of a single performer's relationship to an audience. But direct contact can involve groups as well as individuals. How does that contact differ in the case of groups, if it does so at all? And, in fact, what are

the characteristics of direct presentation when one goes beyond the
individual exchange?

As we have seen in examining mass performers in non-dramatic
shows, distinctions between individuals are minimized and common
behavior is stressed. Large groups may be subdivided into smaller
units that bear a hierarchical link to the whole. This is especially
true of shows of glorification. Purely dramatic shows, with few
exceptions, involve more modest masses of performers though there
are even exceptions to this (Reinhardt's *The Miracle* and *The Eternal
Road*). The most common form of mass performer today is the
chorus, whether in opera, musical theatre, or play. The mass may
or may not utilize direct presentation. For example, the crowd that
gathers to hear Stockmann's speech in *An Enemy of the People* is
rarely presented as in direct contact with the audience. This is in
stark contrast to the final moments of *Marat/Sade* when the inmates
of Charenton march upon the audience as though about to attack.
In this latter instance, mimetic assault is heightened by utilizing a
large group, and thus adding physical intimidation to the psychological.

More usual is the mass group as entertainer. In the American
musical theatre, singing or dancing choruses often play directly to
the audience even when they maintain a fictional framework. One
of the most effective and startling acts in which a group of
characters reached a dramatic climax by playing directly to the
audience occurs in *A Chorus Line*. After revealing their struggles
individually, the characters drew together as a chorus to show their
unity and to dazzle the audience. Even the shape of the production
number conveys the very nature of direct presentation by massed
performers. Arranged in a triangle with its apex pointed at the
audience, costumed identically, their bodies replicated by the
mirrors behind them, they display themselves proudly both as
actual dancers and as chorus characters who triumphed over
adversity to achieve this glorified image.

In this example we have emphasized some basic principles of
direct presentation. For a group to function, especially directly, it
needs unity. In the case of *A Chorus Line*, the unity is absolute.
With rhythmic and kinetic precision, every member is subservient
to the overriding image. But even where slight differences may be
introduced, as in *Marat/Sade*, the total unifying effect is stressed,
not the differences. Often a single, powerful idea is compressed in
that direct contact, and the presence of a large number of bodies

makes that simplification necessary in order to produce an effect upon the audience. The individual actors themselves are expected to fit a scheme and carry through a common process. In essentials, they replicate each other, sometimes in a system of subordination, sometimes in a harmonic pattern.

The narration is handled differently in *Nicholas Nickleby*. The entire company is involved in the narration and it is delivered by them directly to the audience. Instead of utilizing a mass chant, the company employs the storytelling style of a single narrator, but with the story distributed among all the cast in short passages. Thus, a mass narrator emerges. Interestingly, these narrators who are specific characters in the scenes merge when they engage in the narration. It is another example of that type of unifying effect that the stage imposes upon performers if they are to be effective.

While the massed performers do not quite constitute a single character, they do assume something of its dynamic nature. In order to enforce contact with the audience, which is itself a group, some form of concentration is essential. Therefore, all the constitutive elements of the performing group have to be subordinated to a single impression. In effect, the group produces a single point of contact.

It is true that certain theatrical experiments, notably by the Living Theatre, have attempted to disperse contact, but the problems of that sort of structure can be better considered in the discussion of indirect presentation. For the most part, throughout theatrical history, where groups of performers engage in direct contact with the audience, they do so by unifying the group and concentrating its energies.

To what extent, then, do these principles hold for all instances of direct presentation? How effective are smaller groups of three, four, or five in such a performing situation? Instructive in this respect may be the way groups are organized, particularly popular-music groups that tend to create performing personae. Usually, such a group has a lead singer with others playing or singing back-up. The unity is perhaps not as great as we find in purely dramatic presentation, and that may be due to the fact that music allows greater use of harmonic structures in which separate voices can be maintained in delicate balance with one another. Nevertheless, there is a tendency for these groups to function in a hierarchical way with a point-man or -woman and reinforcing secondaries.

At the non-musical dramatic level, it is rare to have duets and trios play directly to the audience. In the few instances that occur, as with the rumor-mongers of *Amadeus*, two characters in redundant relationship to each other confide in the audience, that is, they work as a single unit. Consequently, in exploring direct presentation further, while taking account of the variations in performing size, I will treat only the individual and the group in its direct relationship to the audience.

A generation ago, direct presentation was an incidental rather than a central concern in theatre. But with the breakdown of the self-enclosed system of naturalism and the rising interest in popular and alternative theatrical forms, the open involvement of the audience in performance has come into the circle of interest. The virtual disappearance of the stage curtain, the spread of variants of the open stage, and the loosening of dramatic causality have further enhanced the directness of the actor. As a result, many plays now utilize narrators, commentators, or confidants to promote an exchange with the audience. So widespread is the practice currently, that direct address is often introduced for fashion's sake rather than as an element intrinsic to the action. However, where that directness is central to the action, complex and daring exchanges can occur.

Direct contact, whether by a single actor or by a unified group, can take many different forms. As we saw, the "actor" may be a relatively neutral figure, as is the Chorus in *Henry V*. Or he may be one who radiates a highly charged association, as does the figure of Machiavelli in *The Jew of Malta* or Iago in the middle of *Othello*. The crucial distinctions do not concern the character but rather the nature of the exchange between the character and the audience. At one end of the scale, the exchange may be low-keyed and diffuse. The performer may play a narrator who tells the audience a story. Often the story is personal, and there may be a compelling reason for confiding in the audience. But the storytelling function tends to defuse the potential intensity of the exchange. The Stage Manager in *Our Town* performs the role of storyteller. He commences in a gentle manner, and only by indirection and irony gradually makes his personality felt by the listeners.

Along with a generally impersonal storytelling, we find more active performing that is essentially a form of display. A musical production number is often such a show even when the singers and dancers sustain characters. The series of national dances in the *Swan Lake* ballet are ostensibly performed for the prince, but are so staged that they are displayed to us. They have a tenuous connection to the action, existing almost solely for the esthetic display that they make. In spoken drama display of this sort is less frequent, though it does occur from time to time. In the Kabuki drama, key moments such as the *mie* are moments of intense emotionality in which the performer objectifies his state in a traditional pose. But display in western drama, rather than working on an audience, appears as an occasional act. A performer making an entrance, an actor taking a bow, or a singer doing a patter number—each verges on mere display.

Quite different from these relatively restrained exchanges are those far more frequent instances in which the performer works upon the audience. In Peter Shaffer's play *Amadeus*, Salieri, the leading figure, addresses the audience as the "Ghosts of the Future" who will judge his actions. It is a neat conceit by which Salieri makes us the mind of history, and throughout the play he can turn to us for justification. In this regard he asks for our mental acquiescence, though obviously the action he takes with Mozart sets off conflicting emotions within us. In this play, as in many others, the speaker invites the audience to sympathize with him or with the events that unfold. Such an attitude is in the tradition of the winning performer, appealing to the spectator for applause or hearty response. Variations on this type of exchange are legion. Dolly Levi in *The Matchmaker*, Launce in *Two Gentlemen of Verona*, and the parabasis from Aristophanes' *The Birds* give us some idea of the range.

Related to this type of emphatic exchange but much more circumscribed is that act which we so often associate with audience exchange, namely, the aside. Now considered an artificial device more suited for comic parody than serious expression, the aside is usually thought to be an awkward means for letting the audience know what a character is thinking. But initially, and as it often appears throughout dramatic history, it is a means of highlighting an action by allowing a character to pull out of the boundaries of stage events and create a link with the audience. As it develops in England, it is not always a means of direct exchange with the audience but is often a spoken thought of the character. I shall reserve a discussion of this type of aside for the moment.

Perhaps the single most important type of act that involves direct communication to the audience is the soliloquy. Its rich and widespread use enables us to see the varied ways in which a character can deal with an audience. Furthermore, in the soliloquy we find the clearest instance of the crossing of dramatic concept with presentational form. In no possible way can we consider the soliloquy as a reproduction of actual behavior. It is a wholly contrived means of exposing a character through the medium of presentation. The progress of a particular soliloquy may reflect psychological or intellectual impulses as well as performing requirements, but the performing nature of the act is always evident.

Because of the contemporary predilection for audience participation in theatre, actors who perform soliloquies—mainly the Shakespearean ones, of course—tend to play them all as forms of address to the audience. As a general policy, this practice has invigorated many productions and added dimension to the plays. But not all soliloquies are written for direct address. Most of Hamlet's soliloquies suffer if the actor insists on using them to confide in the audience. They so much embody internal dissension or dismay at what Hamlet sees about him that efforts to externalize them often dilute their impact. In considering soliloquies, then, we should distinguish between those that are distinctly outward directed, to the audience, and those that have a somewhat different focus.

In pre-Shakespearean England the soliloquy is dominated by the surrogate devil, the Vice. With rare exceptions his soliloquies are aimed at the audience which he teases, titillates, and seduces. By no means passive, he works upon the people in order to disrupt and mislead them. Much of the exchange is marked by mock intimidation, and it is apparent that audiences were thrilled and delighted by his sallies. In contrast, the Virtues, when they addressed the audience, were more sober. They enjoined the populace to obey the tenets of the wise and saintly. Together, Vice and Virtue provoked a tug of war within the audience though, of course, Virtue always won, at least onstage.

As employed by Shakespeare and his contemporaries, the soliloquy not only appears less frequently but is less determinedly focused on the audience. More gradations of contact creep in. Many soliloquies, Petruchio's in *The Taming of the Shrew* and Hal's in *I Henry IV*, appear to be exchanges with the audience. In the first, Petruchio muses over his treatment of Kate and then challenges the audience to improve on his method. In the latter, Hal confesses to the audience that his apparent behavior does not reflect his true intent. Other soliloquies are easily played as exchanges or as private thoughts. Benedick's response to the news that Beatrice loves him is such a case. And still others, as I mentioned earlier, are only satisfactorily realized when they are treated as expressions of an internal process.   .

But whatever the degree of contact the Renaissance soliloquy suggests, its direct address usually takes the form of admonishment, as when Anne Frankford in *A Woman Killed with Kindness* warns women to learn by her example or by her challenge. It is in the earlier plays that we see the two approaches in their clearest form. By showing off, telling stories, or deliberately teasing individuals among the spectators, the Vice plays upon the sentiments of the crowd. That is why his soliloquies are so much richer than anyone else's. In his act we have an alternative to the more sympathetic, more confiding type of relationship that obtains in the speeches of a Dolly Levi or a Viola.

Yet however much the Vice may tease the audience, he makes no effort to transform the audience itself into anything but what it is. In this respect the direct contact of the Renaissance differs from some of the innovations in the twentieth century. Within recent years we have seen many efforts to use direct contact with the audience in order to foist a role upon that audience. I mentioned the clever conceit Peter Shaffer uses in order to allow us to be ourselves by calling us the Ghosts of Salieri's future, which in a sense we are. But we find many more radical efforts.

These efforts are rooted in experiments with audience participation such as in *Waiting for Lefty*, where the audience is fictionalized as union members attending a crucial strike meeting. As originally played, the premise stirred tremendous excitement as the audience was carried away by the final words, "STRIKE, STRIKE, STRIKE!!!" But though audience members were treated as members of the union, they were not asked to assume a role at odds with their own status, unless of course they were well-to-do, anti-union people. In more recent productions, however, direct address may involve more radical adjustments. In *Miss Margarida's Way*, the school teacher addresses us as recalcitrant children who need strict discipline. When played before adolescents, the play becomes a lark of taunting between actress and audience. In such a show, the performer no longer seeks sympathy or confirmation from the audience but challenges and attacks it. The difference, however, is that whereas the Vice had something of the privileged jester about him, the newer "Vice" or challenger often attacks and subverts the audience.

The challenge to the audience may achieve its apogee in Peter Handke's *Offending the Audience*. In this work, which is a descendant in spirit if not in fact from the Dada tradition of Tristan Tzara, the performer seeks to provoke the spectator to an overt, irrational response, hoping to break through the audience's veneer of civilized behavior. That assault upon the audience, also characteristic of many avant-garde productions in the 1960s and 1970s, struggles against the absorption capacity of an audience. Through some form of psychological immunity, as we shall see, audiences soften or absorb direct attacks and neutralize them more readily than they do indirect attacks.

Allied with direct attacks upon their own persons, are those attacks which rely upon the audience playing a role. *Marat/Sade* is again a classic example. It is cast in the form of a play-within-a-play. We in the audience are supposedly guests at a performance of a play by the Marquis de Sade given at the mental asylum at Charenton in 1808. Coulmier, the director of the institution, treats us as allies, enlightened Frenchmen who favor play therapy and reject revolutionary violence. What makes the director's address to us something more than forced role-playing is the way he appeals to us in terms widely familiar to liberal humanists. The fiction of our role is thereby subordinated to the actuality of our sentiments. And this subtle blending of past and present works effectively until the rampaging inmates of the asylum march on us at the end of the play. Then the actors try to actualize what has been a delicately balanced ambivalence.

In marching on us as a unified group, in order to stimulate true fear, they also seek to go through a transformation from characters to actors by applauding the audience in mocking fashion. In effect, they try to make the transition from character to performer as Rosalind does, but at a provocative rather than seductive level. That is where direct contact fails. It is at this point that *Marat/Sade* illustrates the problem of imposition upon an audience of a role it may not welcome. When the actors carry forward the attack of the inmates, they are forcing us to carry on the sentiments attributed to the French we played. It cannot be. Despite their efforts to make us guilty, we refuse the guilt by continuing to applaud, thereby insisting that in dropping the role of inmates they show us the role of antagonistic actors. In short, they are still performing.

Direct address captures in its baldest form the triad of doer, act done, and receiver; or sender, message sent, and receptor. The role the performer assumes, and the action aimed at the audience, are under the performer's control. The audience is not. Only by working astutely on the audience can the performer gain its agreement to play the game of the show.

We may indeed be seeing the end of direct assault upon the audience. Its limited utility and the audience's immense reserve of self-protection may make sustained attack futile. This is quite distinct, however, from the occasional sally that strikes home. The aside or even the topical comment that is embedded in an otherwise indirect action, as are Shaw's comments on Englishmen in *Caesar and Cleopatra*, can be immensely effective. But for direct address to justify itself, it must enable the performer to penetrate the audience most deftly. Usually it does so when the performer achieves effective byplay or confirms or challenges common values.

Byplay between performer and audience is most easily confirmed in comedy. The stand-up comedian, though he may not be operating in a strictly dramatic medium, engages in direct byplay, and through the immediate response of the audience knows he is doing so. Occasionally, plays incorporate the format of the stand-up routine, as I indicated earlier. However, an instance of the comedian in reverse is Harpagon, in *The Miser*, who calls upon the audience to tell him who stole his money and then accuses it of complicity.

As an example of byplay with audience values that shows an extraordinarily keen challenge, we have the end of Dario Fo's *accidental death of an anarchist*. Let us again recall the scene. The play appears to end with a journalist, caught in the dilemma of freeing four policemen or not, and refusing to free the murderers.

Then the leading character, a revolutionist Maniac, stops the action. He confesses that critics and others have protested this harsh ending and, therefore, the company is restaging it. This time the journalist, Ms. Feletti, saves the men. When she does so, they are grateful at first. But then, realizing that she knows of their crimes, they chain her in the room where a bomb is about to explode. The revolutionist turns to us, asking which ending we prefer. This challenge, touching our deepest values in a satiric manner, more effectively assaults us than any of the direct attacks, and in doing so, highlights a central aspect of theatre. No matter how much performers try to involve the audience directly in the action, the greatest involvement will be mental and emotional, with no physical contact. Even direct involvement cannot substitute for the reverbatory engagement that is stimulated obliquely.

In seeking to grasp the dynamics of the actor-audience interchange, we have the benefit of the wide variety of experiments in the 1960s and 1970s that tested the limits of dramatic effectiveness. The assault upon the audience's values and even its very being took several forms, two in particular. As we have seen, there was the deliberate act of provoking the audience, a provocation that may be purely existential, as when the Living Theatre probed the extent to which the audience would tolerate boredom. The second main type of provocation involved performers' efforts to project upon the audience an unpleasant or indeed even offensive persona. In a regional production of *The Merchant of Venice*, George Tabori and his then wife, Viveca Lindfors, presented the play as occurring in a Nazi concentration camp. The actors were Jews who were forced to act out the play before the camp's officers. Shylock was a stereotypical image of a Jew. Throughout the performance armed guards paced the sides of the stage. Shylock played quasi–directly to the audience and thereby continually reminded its members that they were the hated Nazis. This example of offensive projection indicates the extremes to which one may go with revisionism of the classics and the desire to shake the spectators.

However momentarily effective it may be for the actor to confront the audience, the impact rapidly diminishes. That is why so few of the techniques of confrontation find their way into the common vocabulary of the theatre. As occasional spice, such direct challenge can be incisive and suggestive. As unrelieved attack, it degenerates into grandstanding. Moreover, its limitations reveal a deeper reason for the modest use of confrontation. Audiences come to a show voluntarily, and that expression of free will is embodied not only in their physical presence but also in their minds. We shut out things we find painful or that are forced upon us. Just as psychological assault proved transitory, so did physical challenge prove titillating for a brief period. But in short order virtually all theatres that attempted to coerce audiences had to give up the effort. If drama is to employ direct presentation, it must do so in a way to win the audience's participation (as in *Nicholas Nickleby*), and as a means of building a structure that can startle and penetrate its imagination. The conclusion of the Dario Fo play combines intellectual challenge with a magician's manipulation of events in a wonder-working way.

The ultimate impact of direct presentation depends, of course, upon its function within a complete work. Central though it is to the essence of theatrical show, in drama it is seldom employed unremittingly. And for a very good reason. In the exchange between performers and the audience that is the basis of direct presentation, the initiative comes from the performers. Whether displaying themselves or working upon the audience, they set the direction the show will take and strive to bring the audience along with them. But there are limits to how much they can manipulate the spectators who will respond to suggestion—that is, play off the actors—but cannot in turn initiate any action. Nor can the actors count upon specific reactions from the audience. At some point an actor may safely project upon the audience attitudes that it might reasonably hold but not exhibit. But such guessing does not permit a sustained dramatic structure to emerge, and that is why most examples of direct address are relatively brief. They make up a "number," an "act" within a longer performance.

Direct presentation normally takes one of several forms. It may appear as sallies: for example, the actor's passing acknowledgement of an audience's presence. As I have said, such passing acknowledgement may lend spice to a scene. An actor may wink at the audience, seem to throw a line at it, or actually deliver a short aside to the hearers. Certain productions feature these occasional sallies (melodrama, for example). Often the gestural nod has comic potentiality. By breaking the frame of what is an indirect style, these passing moments of contact can be both pleasurable and powerful.

Also occasionally used, but more substantial in effect, are the passages of direct presentation that we associate with the soliloquy. They have more than a passing effect because they are usually of sufficient length to promote a sustained impression. To what extent they produce the same effect of a sharp stylistic break that we found in the aside, depends on the explicitness of the contact. Sometimes the speech is so integrated into the style of a play or production that we do not have a case of direct presentation. This seems to be the case in the fourth act of *The Sea Gull* when Kostya comments to himself on Trigorin's writing. On the other hand, many soliloquies deliberately use direct contact to enable a character to escape the frame of the action (*The Matchmaker*). How powerful that intermittent but concentrated contact can be is evident in the way Shakespeare plays with it in *Richard III* and *Othello*. The early soliloquies, aimed as they probably are at the audience, are marvelously seductive, fascinating us with their mocking villainy.

Fairly widespread also is the use of direct presentation as a frame for a production. Often this is effected by utilizing a narrator. Tevye in *Fiddler on the Roof* is an example of this technique. In *Our Town* the narrator is the Stage Manager who stands, for the most part, outside the action and has a global understanding of what is happening. By contrast, Tom in *The Glass Menagerie* is a narrator who plays a vital role in the action. He cannot escape the consequences of events, and therefore his narration is an exorcism for abandoning his mother and sister. In these plays the narrator appears repeatedly, frames the events, and serves as a mediator between the play and the audience. In a sense he is a ringmaster or master of ceremonies.

The narrator as frame appears in novel form in *Nicholas Nickleby*, as I mentioned. In that production a gradual sympathy is built between performers and spectators. Before the play proper begins, the actors, in costume but in their own persons, come into the auditorium and speak in a relaxed, non-theatrical manner to many members of the audience. Even the stage design extends out to embrace the audience. When the time comes to start the show, the actors unhurriedly gather together onstage, and begin their joint narration until, at a given point, they dissolve as narrators and emerge as characters. The narrative frame thus is paradoxical. While it is delivered by the entire company, the fact that the company has had a "personal" relationship to the spectators keeps the narration direct and unpretentious.

Lastly, there is a type of performance in which direct presentation is a more central part of the action. Not only is a larger proportion of a play cast in direct form, but the very structure of the action stems from the balance of direct and indirect presentation. Of a formal nature are those dramatic shows that use a continuous chorus, the Greek plays and musical theatre, for example. While the Greek chorus is occasionally introspective or engaged in indirect action, as in *Agamemnon*, more generally it comments on the action for the benefit of the spectators. In the texts there are seldom specific forms of direct audience address, but in the formality of the dancing and singing, the chorus is in effect giving a performance for the audience. Their expression is usually iconic in that they crystallize a set of values or concretize an observation in an autonomous, detached manner. Their closeness to the audience is further heightened by contrast with the characters. Within the episodes the characters never address the audience directly. As a result, the chorus mediates between the events and the audience. Again this effect is heightened in the Greek theatre where the chorus would be physically close to the audience. At Epidaurus that closeness between chorus and audience is intensified by an unusual acoustical phenomenon. As the chorus approaches the dancing circle nearest the audience, the sound of their voices appears to originate from the midst of the audience. The contact is complete. We are addressed by the chorus and address ourselves simultaneously.

In the modern theatre, the use of direct presentation as a central element in production may take several different forms. Besides its appearance in musical theatre, it may have thematic significance. An extraordinary example is that of John Osborne's *The Entertainer*, commented upon earlier. The play presents scenes in the life of an aging entertainer: some involving his family, and some as "turns" to us, cast as his music hall audience. His failures in the one resonate in the failures of the other. In his performances he pathetically tries to arouse the kind of response that will salve his ego, but to no avail. As he moves toward his last stage performance, he moves toward the end of his life. In this play the quality of exchange between the character and the audience is unusually complex. On the performing level, especially as realized by Sir Laurence Olivier, the entertainer is fascinating. He entertains us truly. But fictively he is a worn-out old trouper. His act is dreadful. He mocks us for not responding to his gags. And here we have the primal paradox that makes drama so explosive. There are two performers and two audiences. There is Sir Laurence Olivier and Archie Rice, and there is Olivier's audience and Rice's audience. In one fell swoop Olivier dazzles us by the brilliant way he has Archie appall us. In that intricate way direct presentation is essential and brings us close to the wonder-working performing world of the magician.

Repeatedly in this chapter I have touched on those examples in which the primary structure of an act is not so explicit as to make it certain whether direct address is involved. There are many such examples, especially of soliloquies, that are of this type. In addition, performers have styles of playing that utilize an appearance of direct contact, or point to such contact. These styles may not be manifested in the text but are evident when a performance is given. This latter practice is widespread in operatic productions. More often than not, a singer will deliver an aria straight to the audience with only a nominal nod to a partner. In some houses the pervasiveness of this style may be due to acoustical necessity. However that may be, we can describe this practice as direct delivery or display to the audience within a frame of inter-actor exchange. This is the case not only when the singer is alone on stage but even when he or she may be intensely engaged in an intimate action with another person.

A similar sort of frontal orientation is characteristic of comic sketches, such as those played in burlesque shows or musical revues. In these cases the performer does not make specific contact with the audience but generally throws his lines or projects his body at the audience. This type of indirect directness is perhaps more widespread than direct contact. In many ways it has the features of "distancing" or "estrangement" that we associate with Brecht's notion of alienation. It is fundamentally a comic technique, though, as we see, it can be used within the formal structure of musical tragedy.

One step removed from this style of direct delivery that is independent of the text are those scenes or speeches in a play that allow latitude of delivery. In poetic drama the matter is further complicated by the habit that playwrights have of introducing into the speeches such devices as apostrophes (O, Heaven, etc.) and offstage figures whom the characters address. Often the question of whether or not those sections involve direct contact can be answered only in performance when a specific actor makes a decision on the matter.

There is yet another aspect of these sections that involves an alternative type of act. As examples of what I mean, I will turn to two dramatic speeches, one written by Ben Jonson, the other by Sam Shepard. That by Ben Jonson is Sir Epicure Mammon's speech as he anticipates the triumph of the alchemical process (*The Alchemist*). That by Sam Shepard is when Miss Scroons conflates the movie stars she sees on the screen, with her self (*Angel City*).

Sir Epicure projects himself into an imaginative state of luxurious wealth. The future is no longer the future but the present, as he tastes all manner of sensual delights, sexual and otherwise. His flight of fancy is a display to the audience of his inflamed state. What we witness is a heightened state of being. In an analogous way Miss Scroons encapsulates the blending of herself and her image. Time disappears. Pure idea exists. Like the speech of Sir Epicure, hers is not so much talk as it is revelation and elaboration: "I look at the screen and I am the screen."[2] Compare this to a soliloquy by Hamlet ("To be or not to be . . .") or Macbeth ("If 'twere done . . ."). Those soliloquies reveal internal struggle. The dialectic is inward. But the speeches of Epicure and Miss Scroons do not progress historically toward a decision; rather, they establish a theme and play its variations. In such cases the audience perceives a performance that is for them whether or not they are addressed directly. The performance is by way of display rather than by interchange.

Historically, these iconic forms of audience contact are significant. They are frequently found in medieval and Renaissance drama and appear less frequently in the eighteenth and nineteenth centuries. But it is within the last generation that the iconic acts of display have reappeared in the drama as significant elements. The creation of the Tree of Life by the Open Theatre in *The Serpent* is one example. But more important is the increasing introduction of storytelling into plays. The semi-autonomous story, distanced by being made a self-conscious recital, assumes an iconic character. Even when the story is told to another character, it is simultaneously being delivered to the audience. The fact that it is not a working through of an action but a summary of an event gives it a completeness and autonomy that we find in iconic structures. Admittedly, these acts do not make full use of actor-audience contact. They are bound within an indirect framework. Nevertheless, they peep through and operate both as an aspect of action between characters and as a performance for us.

As we have seen, the convention of the actor-as-character making direct contact with the audience is widespread historically and stylistically. It assumes many forms and degrees of emphasis, and the importance of such contact is readily apparent. Yet despite its obvious significance for the performing medium, it has critical limits. I have indicated one of these: the problem of the performer sustaining a complex action by having only the audience to play against. There are other, equally serious limitations in advancing a fictional situation through a single concentrated exchange. To sustain an impact on the audience, the performer adopts a distinct stance. The performer may charm, may seduce, may confide, but ambivalence cannot be taken very far. For that a partner is needed, and since the audience cannot be an effective partner, someone else must be found: the second actor, the subject of the next chapter.

We saw yet another problem in those efforts to project a fictional persona upon the audience. While the audience may accept any fancy thrust upon it, unless that fancy catches the audience at a subliminal level, it will not take it to heart. Indeed, the most effective communication with the audience occurs when it is accepted for itself and not asked to assume a persona. The RSC *Marat/Sade* was effective as long as the actors did not try to enforce the idea that the audience was from the early nineteenth century, and *Amadeus* adroitly introduces fancy in such a way as to leave the audience to be itself. Neither *Our Town*, *The Entertainer*, nor *The Glass Menagerie* asks us to be anything but an audience. In these plays the writers utilize, in an especially rich manner, the audience in its own act of witnessing. But this is not easy to do, and we have many examples of productions that use narration merely as a device rather than as interaction. If the audience is used in its own person, the range of exchanges that an actor can create with it is minimal. Outside of the general conventions of "playing to the house," the actor or writer must search diligently for ways to utilize direct contact in an exciting fashion. The difficulties involved in this process explain why dramatic presentation must rely so completely on action between actor and actor rather than between actor and audience.

Chapter 9

Actor to actor

Once the actor shifts his attention from the audience to a fellow actor, he produces a crucial change. We don't know, and cannot truly know, which comes first: the actor-audience relationship or that of actor–actor. Legend has it that the *hypokrites*, the answerer, stepped forth from the chorus in Greek drama to address the chorus and through it the audience. But even if this were so, it does not go back to the origins of theatrical presentation. The shaman in a trance or the ritual dancer in the sun tells us little about the genealogy of the actor-audience exchange. Indeed, there is something futile in trying to discover origins of so ephemeral and transitory an endeavor as performance. What is important is that in the forms we have come to know as presentation, we find examples of both kinds of exchange: actor–actor as well as actor-audience.

Moreover, in the drama as distinct from shows of skill and glorification, it is the performer-performer relationship that is most widespread. In virtually every cultural context the bulk of fictional presentation depends on actor playing with actor. The centrality of this relationship to drama is so great that it is not even perceived as a structural choice but assumed to be axiomatic to drama. It may well be. But it is also an alternative to direct presentation, and since its dynamic both replicates and differs from overt audience contact, we might well consider it in its most fundamental nature.

When engaged directly with the audience, the actor may display himself or work upon the audience, as we saw. But what happens when an actor deals with another actor? These actors no longer display themselves to each other, at least in any primary way. While they may appear in situations that imitate the performing structure (Antony addressing the Roman crowd), even here the first emphasis is not on display, because the second actor must do more than play the receptor. He must provide a more active partner if the utility of indirect presentation is to be realized. It is instructive to remember that the root term for the Greek role-type was *agon*— as in protagonist and deuteragonist, the primary and secondary strugglers in the action. The model actor working on the audience is what is replicated between actors: one working upon the other and then responding.

The shift in concentration is critical. To impress an audience, the actor exerts considerable force of personality which is redirected when he deals with another actor. It is focused on the partner, sometimes so forcibly that it is palpable. The levels at which these energies are projected may not change radically. Where an actor may maintain a fictional understanding with the audience, a different but nonetheless fictional understanding is developed with other actors. As with so many areas in the drama, we have a double process. The actor-as-performer does project a vital force at other actors. It may not be measurable, but when it is absent, fellow actors note its loss. That projective energy, actually emanating from the actor, carries the fictional "energy" of the character. The system of signs employed by the actor frames the exchange so that the audience reads the actor's energy as belonging to the character.

When the actor is projecting that energy directly at the audience, the audience does not need to be shown that the energy exists. Its effects are felt, not abstractly, but through the gestures and words the actor uses, that not only register as information but impinge as sensations. The vibrancy of the actor kinesthetically reverberates in the audience. When the actor no longer aims those impulses at the audience, however, but directs them at fellow actors, then a new manner of perception emerges. Were the actor to direct his energies at an unresponsive, neutral partner, then we could not perceive its intensity. Beckett has experimented with a version of the neutral other in *Not I*, in which a woman, called Mouth, represented by a pair of lips, pours out a story to a mute Auditor. From time to time the Auditor gestures, but always in a non-committal manner. In this work, the Auditor stands in for the audience, and we have a slightly fictionalized state of direct presentation. But where presentation is completely indirect, the partner, the deuteragonist, responds by providing a resistant force to the first actor. It is through the encounter of one actor's projective energy with that of another that the audience becomes aware of the vital force that sustains the dramatic situation.

The primacy of acting concentration has a transforming effect upon the actor's shift of focus from audience to fellow actor. It is not only a matter of where the attention goes, but of the kind of event that can be created. With the actor-to-actor exchange as the basis for the character-to-character portrayal, a self-enclosed world is created. It makes the exchange between the two autonomous from the world of the audience. The actors are no longer completely bound by the spectators' presence. As we saw in the last chapter, some dramas attempt to break the stranglehold of the audience's presence by projecting upon it a fictive character. By and large, these attempts succeed only if they do not violate that presence. When an actor plays a scene with another actor, however, both can transcend that presence and invent an alternative space and time.

The redirection of performing energy has another effect. In direct presentation, the actor can fully control only one side of the exchange, and though experienced actors or actresses can generally predict how an audience will play its part, they are never absolutely certain. Moreover, dramatist and performer are limited in the situations they can show. On the other hand, the actor-actor exchange frees writer and player to control both poles of the action in a rich variety of ways. As we shall see, the terms of the exchange, that is, the ways in which one actor can engage another, are finite. Yet the ways in which the actor can manipulate these finite relationships are unlimited.

Control arises not only from the nature of the exchange itself, but also from the fact that the actor-to-actor exchange, like all theatrical presentations, is not open-ended. The end is foreseen and pursued from the beginning. This is true of direct presentation too. But because the audience can be shut out of immediate engagement with the dramatic situation, it gains a perspective that enables it to observe the evolution of the exchange. The audience traces the pacing of the action as the actors wrestle with yet another doubling contradiction. Just as the actors' own energies are theirs and yet also the characters', so too an action proceeds on two different planes: as known action for the actor, as unknown action for the character. The delicacy of this progression emerges as a balance between spontaneity and determinism. The actor plays each moment as if he doesn't know what will follow—although of course he does—in order to convey the impression that the character pursues an open-ended action. By distancing this process in a self-enclosed world, the actor–actor exchange also has the effect of unifying the audience's perspective. The audience focuses on the autonomous world of the actor, often to the momentary exclusion of its own.

The power over an audience that the actor–actor exchange can generate is so great that with very few accoutrements, it can grasp and hold the audience's attention. I have raised the question of the role of scenery in drama and will discuss this matter further in Chapter 12, but any discussion of scenic elements—props, costumes, setting, etc.—cannot deal accurately with the presentational process without accounting for the compelling force of acting that is independent of these elements. The rich scenes of the English Renaissance theatre constantly remind us of the primal attraction of actor with actor. Even one actor alone can compel that degree of attention, but actor-with-actor is, I repeat, the foundation of the drama.

So far I have spoken almost exclusively about the actor. It is, of course, the peculiar partnership of actor and dramatist that provides the situations for a pair of actors. In using the term dramatist I include not only the independent poet who may himself never act, but also the actor who may create his own scripts. We may equally speak of the deviser of the act that the actors perform. Whether that deviser plans a scenario, writes its dialogue, or directs every phase of its production, that person assumes a dramaturgic function. But whoever performs the dramaturgic function, the act itself is transmitted by the actors in such a way that it appears to arise spontaneously from them. The deviser then has to allow for the natural forms of the medium, in this case, the dramatic medium that emerges when one actor plays a fictional situation with another. Therefore, I shall continue to speak of the exchanges as taking place among actors, it being understood that I also include in these exchanges the entire range of scenes devised by dramatists.

The creation of an autonomous event through the redirection of an actor's attention seems to contradict the primacy of presentation. If the actors concentrate on each other, how can they be said still to perform for an audience? Are they merely being observed? Or are they performing "to" us? Common sense and practical experience tell us that they perform for us. They act out the situation for us. Although there was a period in the 1960s and 1970s when actors and directors fell in love with the rehearsal process itself, to the exclusion and detriment of public performance, this unhealthy

introversion was a passing phenomenon. Actors playing together
do so for us, not themselves.

We return to the question: how can one actor concentrate upon
another and still present his act to an audience? Here we can return
to our distinction between performing energy and character
energy. The actor controls his performing energy in such a way as
to make the character's impulses, thoughts, and emotions evident
to us in a variety of ways. He paces the exchange to maintain the
spontaneity of the situation and yet to reveal the steps of the action.
This involves crystallizing intentions and responses. Pacing may
incidentally correspond to actual time, but it more usually responds
to action-time. The actor decelerates events, accelerates them,
builds them into a coherent sequence. What he does with time he
also does with space. He fills it with his presence so that
movements and gestures assume significance beyond the customary.
The business he performs and the words he utters already are
highly selected and related to one another in a deliberate sequence.
The more the actor can give a concentrated clarity to each element
of pace, space, gesture, and language, the more presentable it
becomes.

To these techniques of crystallizing action, the actor may add
explicitly presentational conventions. Take the matter of bodily
orientation. There may be some instances—and these tend to be
rituals more than presentations—where the actor may perform
regardless of how he relates physically to the audience. But they are
not the norm. The fact that presentation relies on the living
performer gives primacy to frontal orientation. This is especially
true when we have one actor playing with another. Even allowing
for theatre-in-the-round and for the thrust stage, the actor tends to
play toward the most important part of the audience. That part
may be personified in a single figure, a monarch, or it may be
diffused among a crowd. But seldom is every member of an
audience accorded equal emphasis, and the actor tends to orient
himself toward one part. Theatre-in-the-round demands special
handling, and in the contemporary theatre actors have developed
techniques (or conventions if you will) to enable a pair of actors to
face a substantial part of the audience at all times.

The intermingling of frontal orientation with indirect presentation
occurs, however, in theatre that is principally "in front of" an
audience. That theatre is represented by the Greek, the Roman, the
Renaissance, the modern, the Chinese and Japanese, as well as

many other types from other cultures and periods. In all these theatres the tension between actor-to-actor exchange and frontal orientation is most acute. On the one hand, the structure of the dramatic action impels the performers to relate to each other. On the other, the need and desire to present that action encourages them to play to the audience. Naturalism sought to resolve the dilemma by providing situational motivations for frontal orientation so that the logic of the environment and events would account for the actor directing his performance sufficiently forward for the audience to gain an effect. That is why we hear actors in realistic productions talking so much of "cheating," that is, playing a scene with another actor, partially facing the actor, and as much as possible "opening up" toward the audience. These surreptitious means of attaining frontal orientation are clearly conventional. Attempts to defy that orientation, by having actors turn their backs upon the audience, are merely occasional. They operate as signals of exclusion, but are so intermittent that they do not really change the frontal orientation.

Far more conventional are those styles of performance in which the actor maintains one type of orientation and suggests a character who operates in another. Perhaps the most vivid example of this duality occurs in comic playing, and most particularly in the performance of comic sketches. In such sketches it is common to have a comic and a straight man. The straight man propels the action, often by questioning or admonishing the comic. They invariably play full front to the audience, throwing their lines to each other so that as characters they are playing with each other but as actors they are playing the house. Maintaining this double kind of exchange requires many small adjustments in the way the head and body are controlled and in the way lines are delivered. Such performances are frankly "presentational," yet still indirect. They illustrate one balance in the tension of orientation and indirection. And in the range of comic sketches there are degrees to which this frontal orientation is explicit or tacit. Some skits have actions that are virtually "realistic."

What I have been describing is a performing style. The text on which this style is based may or may not contain any explicit indication of the degree of frontal orientation. After all, a script arises organically out of the theatre to which it belongs, and unless it deliberately seeks to change the playing style, it silently utilizes what is available. Only when a script is revised does the problem of appropriate style arise. The conventions that one theatre devises for resolving the tension between frontal orientation and indirection may not be the same. Adjustments must be made. But whatever the adjustments, each theatre solves the problem of that tension in a distinctive way. The innovative vanguard of the twentieth century loudly rejected the naturalist conventions and sought to introduce its own more authentic conventions, at times defying the imperative of frontal orientation. But the problem is unsolved for the present, and most contemporary theatres operate in a kind of *ad hoc* style.

So far we have considered the way the actors adapt the enclosed form of dramatic fiction to the open demands of the stage. Now we shall shift our attention to the fiction itself, or more precisely to the scene patterns through which the fiction is presented. We shall start with the simplest form: the scene between two people.

While any two people can be placed in a scene, it is traditional, and traditional because efficacious, for the two to be in some contrast to one another. The contrast may inhere in the persons. Comic burlesque relies on the strong contrast between the straight man and the comic. The straight man is apparently knowledgeable, nattily dressed, articulate in his use of high-class language. The comic has a baggy appearance, seems at a loss, needs to be instructed, and fumbles with language. Their interchanges are usually propelled by the straight man though it is the comic who, by a twist of logic, gets the better of the situation.

Less conventionalized though equally set off against one another are many of the juxtapositions of characters of different sex, temperament, nature. Indeed, one of the evidences of dramatic art lies in the skillful structuring of a duet of characters who set off sparks in one another. When we think of great scenes in drama, we have the royal Oedipus interrogating the humble shepherd, the idealistic Antigone defying the practical and political Creon, cunning Iago misleading trusting Othello, the daring Lovborg seeking explanation from the cowardly Hedda. We could go on indefinitely listing scenes where crucially contrasting figures are brought into critical play with one another.

To this contrast in agency can be added the contrast in circumstances. One character may want something that another has: information, actual objects, a particular response, or dominance. One character's situation may be vulnerable and may be deeply affected by the other person. It is impossible to summarize all the permutations that exist between two figures, yet for stage purposes there is a marked inclination to devise events in which meaningful disparities exist between characters caught in specific circumstances. From these initial contrasts the action is constructed.

As we have seen, events that concentrate on the passage of time, that suggest the uncertainty of the successful completion of an action in the future, tend to emphasize the dialectic mode. Conversely, those that tend to reveal themselves without stressing the passage of time but instead stress their presence in space, operate in the iconic mode. Dramatic scenes likewise tend toward one or another of these modes though it is obvious that in some way all scenes have both temporal and spatial features.

These contrasting dualities unfold through time and space, the duet being particularly receptive to temporal development. Because the duet originates with an initial contrast of person or situation, it contains an imbalance, an unresolved impulse that cannot remain suspended indefinitely. Furthermore, since the medium does not offer any external force for resolving that imbalance, it must arise from one or another of the characters in the duet. As illustration, we can take one of the most common scene types in theatrical history: the persuasion scene. Persuasion is one of the basic aspects of Greek rhetoric, and certainly prominent in Greek drama. But it is equally prominent in Renaissance tragedy, modern comedy, and indeed in a wide repertory of plays. Its elements are simple.

In one of the great persuasion scenes of drama, Volumnia tries to convince her son Coriolanus not to destroy his city of Rome. Others accompany her but the persuasion is hers. The contrast between persuader and one to be persuaded is provocative in several ways. Mother strives against son. Roman citizen pleads with Roman outcast. The person who used to rule is now forced to beg. And the circumstances add to the resonance of the scene. The success of either, pleader or listener, destroys the other so that the consequences always impend.

In this context, mother pleads; Coriolanus listens. The mode of persuasion moves from rational argument to evocation of personal attachments. That is, Volumnia tries to convince Coriolanus to save Rome on grounds of advantage to both Rome and his allies. She then attacks by mocking his manhood and, finally, mutely pleading for his family. Each stage of the persuasion becomes more intimate. This is reflected in the verse which commences in measured rhetoric and then breaks up in fragments. In response to this powerful persuasion, Coriolanus is largely silent. At one point he attempts to run away from his mother's importunities. Only at a critical turning point, just as his mother is about to leave defeated, does he confess that she has won. This mode of silent resistance does not convey what is going on in Coriolanus' mind and heart. At the beginning he tells his mother he will not save Rome and, therefore, her pleas seem directed at a granite surface. Through it all, because of his silence, we the audience can project into it our reading of the conflict going on within him. When he finally breaks, he releases a pent-up anguish.

To abstract from this scene, we see that we have four components. First, there is a persuader. The persuader moves the action forward, driving with determination toward a resolution of the initial imbalance, the imbalance that composes the precipitating context of the action. Next, there is the person to be persuaded. Since the nature of a persuasion scene is that the person being persuaded may or may not yield to the persuasion, the object of persuasion can respond in a variety of ways, from answering directly to listening silently. The third component is a type of persuasion. The persuader, the mover of the action, has to find a way or ways to convince the other person to act voluntarily. Aristotle tells us of some ways recommended to persuade a person: pointing out past allegiances, painting future good or bad, evoking attitudes deeply based in the person listening or watching. In other words, the persuasive act has specific avenues of development though it may contain unlimited illustrations of that development. Lastly, there is a type of resistance on the part of the listener. Direct argument is possible, but usually the least interesting of possibilities. To strengthen resistance, a character may reveal deep-seated reasons. This occurs when Pastor Manders' efforts to persuade Mrs. Alving to act finally lead to her revelation of her husband's behavior. Often the resistance is internalized, either by leaving a suggestive silence (as in *Coriolanus*) or by expressing internal conflict in asides (as in *The London Merchant*). Whatever the means, the compelling instance of the mover, the persuader, working upon the resistance of the listener ultimately comes to a point where the mover succeeds or fails. Shakespeare adroitly indicates that Volumnia has failed before he turns the action about by revealing her devastating success. This point of crisis (crux) resolves the initial imbalance and sets the ground for the next phase of action.

In this model that I describe, there are many variables. The degree of contrast between persuader and receiver may be extreme or delicately shaded; the intensity of the persuasion may be sharp or relatively relaxed; the crux may occasion a sharp break or a gentle understanding. All of these components are amenable to control both by the one who conceives the scene as well as by the one who performs it. The primary level of engagement that the dramatist has devised in this text is invariably modified in some respect by the performers. They in fact play with the relationships that the writer has introduced on the primary level.

The model I have described embraces a vast number of situations in drama. Again, one person working to gain something from another without full power to secure it is fundamental to drama. Outright use of force has great but limited attraction onstage. It makes for an excellent finale but cannot sustain a narrative. Where emphasis is placed on the exhibition of conflict, we have a sporting contest: wrestling, boxing, gladiatorial combat—what Alberti termed Shows of War. When such shows are transferred to the drama, they spin out quickly or they are transformed into symbolic actions where esthetic or acrobatic play replaces physical encounter. Such is the case in the Chinese theatre. But in drama, for an encounter to be sustained, it not only requires relative degrees of strength between the pair in an exchange, but those degrees of strength must convey the full effect of the fiction. The actors are not what they seem. In the same way the action is not what it seems. Another realm of living is suggested, and one way—the main way—that realm is conveyed is by the performers highlighting the dislocations between characters throughout the work. The persuasion model allows the actors to play with a wide variety of dislocations which have a potential for considerable nuance.

This core, the persuasion situation, is a dynamic model of a larger category of exchanges that are inherently *active* in structure. By an active structure I mean a dramatic situation in which there is a mover who has a concrete purpose and who exerts the force to achieve that purpose. The initial moment of the sequence introduces a problem about the future. Will the mover achieve the goal?

The event itself operates on a double level, as is the case so often in the theatre. There are the tangible features of words spoken, movements made, space occupied. There are also the suggested features—usually (though not always accurately) called the subtext —which are perceived as dislocations between one state and another, or between one will and another. As we saw, the most vivid and significant aspects of Coriolanus' resistance are not manifested in the script. Should they be made evident by the actor? How could this be done? It is a seething conflict that Shakespeare leaves us to imagine. He illustrates for us the power of structuring a scene so that the lack of convergence between two people, or their disparities of intent or need, leave room for us to project into them our sense of what goes on beneath the surface. In crude scenes of suspense, those disparities produce physical effects of excitement. In more subtly organized scenes, the disparities resonate unexpectedly.

The persuasion model goes beyond argument, of course. In fact, persuasion is a category of action that embraces many subdivisions such as seduction, exhortation, groveling, urging, etc. Every transaction in which one person moves in on an issue and another person may or may not concede to it is a persuasion scene. Hence, we have scenes in which the persuader is dominant but needs acquiescence from the listener. In reverse, the mover may be subservient and require consent from the person who has been approached. Further variations have one or the other appear to be in a dominant position when in truth they are dependent on each other.

Will the mover fail? The audience is alerted to an unsettled present. Information given to the audience and knowledge available to it serve as pointers toward a relatively defined future. We are continually directed toward that future, and it is in this respect that Langer correctly speaks of drama as the art of the virtual future.[1]

A large part of drama employs an active structure, a structure that is not only shaped in terms of persuasion but also in modulations of that mode. On the one hand, we find scenes in which a dominant figure moves beyond persuasion to coercion: threat, sarcasm, shaming, and so forth. On the other hand, where persuasion is less insistent, it becomes asking or offering. The entire range of active structures may in fact be represented by the following diagram.

$$\begin{array}{ccc}
 & & \text{involuntary} \\
 & \text{coerces} & \\
A & \text{influences} & B \\
 & \text{offers} & \\
 & & \text{voluntary}
\end{array}$$

A represents any figure in a duet who acts as a mover, precipitating the action by pursuing a goal along one of the three paths: coercion, influence, or offering. *B* is the figure upon whom *A* acts. Where the mode of action is coercive, *B*'s responses tend to be more involuntary. *B* has less choice in meeting the onslaught, and the limits within which *B* makes a choice are much more constricted. As the mode of action shifts toward exerting influence or ultimately toward extending an offer, *B* enjoys greater latitude. *B*'s response becomes more voluntary and *A*'s pursuit more problematic.

In this basic format, where *A* is the initiator (the mover) and exerts force upon *B* (which we may represent as $A \rightarrow B$), the shifts of emphasis and the variations in the degree of emphasis may be considerable. This format, though closed in upon itself, with character *A* concentrating on character *B*, still is a presentational unit. It is therefore structured so that the parts interrelate and progress toward a point of crux. When the pressure of *A* meets an appropriate counterpressure from *B*, then we sense a compelling intensity which shapes the action of the scene. As presentation, the intensity is that of the actors, but by transference, the audience reads it as belonging to the characters. Depending upon the scheme of the scene and the stress given by the performers, the active structure may be arranged for presentation in several different ways.

While in any duet the interest is shared to some extent between *A* and *B*, it may be directed more at one than at the other. Our attention may be directed toward the mover or the receiver. As we have seen, the mover (Volumnia) can dominate the action as the receiver (Coriolanus) listens but makes little overt response until the end. This type of dynamic is one that Pinter is fond of using (*The Homecoming*, *No Man's Land*). On the other hand, *A* and *B* can share the attention from the very beginning although the major interest may be focused on the reaction rather than on the mover (*Hedda Gabler*).

Along with variations in focus of interest, there are variations in length and wholeness. Active units can be extremely brief, especially if the context is readily apparent (those in Chekhov especially), while in many instances the sweep of a single active movement may extend for some time. In short, the active structure is a flexible means of building an exchange between two figures. As we shall see, this flexible exchange between a moving force and a resistant force is often limited to two people, but it is not mandatory that it be so limited. The same structure may also be organized with more than two. We shall explore this in the next chapter.

In the dynamic of the active structure which we have just examined, the balance of pressures that gives a scene its tautness depends primarily upon the quality of resistance that *B* offers *A*. Not only must it be sufficient to meet the efforts of *A* by containing a strong enough counter effort, but it also should engage the pressure in such a way that the potentiality of the conflict is exploded. Through the meaning of the resistance, the exchange either stands or falls.

In illustrating one's arguments, it is usual to select the most excellent of examples. But here, in order to illustrate the crucial role of resistance in an active structure, it is more useful to compare works of different qualities. Let us look at a once popular but now discarded Boucicault play, *The Corsican Brothers*, which was first performed in 1852 and held the stage for many years as a thriller with spiritual overtones. In the second scene of Act II, a young married woman, Emilie de L'Esparre, who has become entangled with an unscrupulous adventurer, Renaud, seeks the return of her love letters. At Renaud's insistence, she explains why she sent him the letters and then pleads for their return. He puts her off, the reasons being multiple. He claims to cherish them as the "only relics of our unhappy attachment."[2] He does not have them with him. He is jealous of the man who urged Emilie to secure the letters. He asserts that while she seeks the letters, he has been trying to help her find her sister. Behind these evasions or refusals is Renaud's wish to take Emilie with him to a party and so win a bet. His scattered resistance thus puts her off. But the varied elements of it do not individualize or deepen the nature of the exchange between this upright though vulnerable young woman and the callous man. We know no more of her helplessness nor have any greater insight into their conflict. All evolves at the level of plot suspense.

Yet the play was immensely applauded, perhaps not necessarily for this particular scene but still the scene is part of the whole. In respect to this scene, though, the mere outline of a virtuous but vulnerable young wife and a man about town is a cliché of the stage and perhaps of life. The audience could fill in the anxiety that would surround Emilie, and so Renaud's evasions could induce a pleasurable concern for the heroine. To probe the man's vanity, sexual desires, or coldness, all or some of which could lie behind his rejection of Emilie's pleas, was beyond the attempt or concept of this work. One only has to look at the "melodramatic" scenes of Krogstad and Nora in *A Doll's House*, in contrast, to see how effectively Ibsen utilizes an active form of coercion in order to explore Nora's capacity to fight for herself and her family.

The shift from the text to the performance of active scenes depends, of course, on the performers' understanding of the material. The performer activates and fills the lines of force that the text holds *in potentia*. Where the text may be deficient in some respect, the performer may very well compensate through suggestion. An actor playing Renaud can easily indicate a depth of cunning so that his scattered responses can read as astute confusion. He can increase the effect of Emilie's helplessness, developing his amorality by exploiting the lines of solicitousness. In effect, he can extend and complicate the skeletal structure. Indeed, the actor in a thinly realized play is more likely to compensate since so many of the dynamic features of a scene are merely sketched and not probed.

The active structure, although the most prevalent form and the one most fully understood by critics, is not the only arrangement of action. In contrast to a pattern where A works upon B, we find what appears to be a reversal, with B responding to A. It is, however, unlike the type of active scene where B reacts to A's pressure. Instead, it is a form in which the initial pressure that works upon B is concentrated but not sustained. A may tell B that someone is dead. Throughout the scene that follows, A does nothing more. B, however, goes through an extended period of facing the news. Or A may tell B that the latter must perform a task. B searches for a means of fulfilling the assignment. These are models for the non-active, or reactive, structure.

That drama contains a structure quite different from and even opposite to the active has been recognized by others. Bert O. States makes the distinction between the dramatic mode and the lyric.[3] He tends to see the lyric as antithetical to the dramatic. But the reactive is as much at the heart of theatrical presentation as is the active. It has merely not been so widely perceived. In his book on musical theatre writing, Lehman Engel distinguishes between two types of songs: the active and the reflective.[4] He recognizes the quite distinct lines of movement in these two kinds of material, and by stressing the song emphasizes what we have to do with a presentational form. Instead of a movement aimed at changing or shaping the future, the reactive or reflective unfolds what some might call a state of being. That state of being is elaborated in a world of retarded time. The passage of time in fact is minimized, and in its stead the impact of the initiating impulse is explored in terms of its effect on the character.

The precipitating impulse that sets off the extended reaction need not be personified, even when it is carried by a messenger. In the format where B reacts to A ($A \leftarrow B$), A need not be onstage at all. Often in Shakespeare a character will enter, already responding to an accumulation of events that have occurred in previous scenes or offstage (*Othello*). The main difference from the active structure is that the character, instead of moving forward to resolve the question in the future, is adjusting to a core of pressure from the past and attempting to deal with it. It is a form widely used by the Elizabethans, and interestingly enough returned to popular usage in the contemporary theatre. In *Strange Interlude* Eugene O'Neill attempted to arrange an alternating active-reactive structure by placing the active structure in conscious dialogue and the reactive or reflective structure in the internal monologues. More organic incorporation of the reactive structure, however, appears in the work of the Expressionists and recently in such dramatists as Genet and Shepard. The range of reactive structures can best be summarized in the following diagram.

$$\begin{array}{ccc} & \text{laments} & \\ A & \text{reflects upon} & B \\ & \text{rejoices at} & \end{array}$$

Between the *active* and *reactive* structures there is a third possibility, a theoretical interaction that we might term a *balanced* structure. That is, if $A \rightarrow B$ treats scenes where A is mover and B is resistant, and $A \leftarrow B$ treats scenes where A's impulse is finite and B has an expanding reaction, it is still theoretically possible to describe a structure in which the pressures of A upon B and the resistance of B to A are so nearly the same that one cannot say either figure is the mover or the moved. We do find scenes in which A and B are virtually matched ($A \leftrightarrow B$). The range of situations is limited, but in certain cases significant. We may diagram the possibilities as follows:

$$\begin{array}{ccc} & \text{fights} & \\ A & \text{debates} & B \\ & \text{meets} & \end{array}$$

While scenes of meeting occur in drama, more useful to dramatic presentation are the activities of fighting and debating. In essence, the latter is only a verbal analogue of the former. Fighting onstage appears from time to time, but it requires peculiar conditions to be effective. It is no accident that the most fully realized form of stage fighting is the sword duel. By nature, the duel allows the kind of control that makes fighting feasible. For example, we don't find many instances of rock throwing onstage, and though we have occasional examples of the pistol duel (in *The Corsican Brothers* most importantly), it too does not afford many useful opportunities. Fencing, however, allows sufficient distance between the antagonists and yet enough closeness to allow the fighting to be sustained and turned into an exciting stage performance. In theatrical history, the two main approaches to dueling have been the realistic and the symbolic. In the West we have had actual contact of sword with sword and simulated the actual thrust into a body. In the East symbolic forms of combat have appeared in which the acrobatic rather than the mimetic elements receive fullest elaboration.

The verbal analogue of fighting, the debate, has also had a significant growth, though largely confined to the Greek theatre. In both tragedy and comedy formal debate occupied a substantial part of a dramatic work. Through a mixture of matched speeches interwoven with stichomythic wrestling, a neatly balanced exchange emerged. Later theatres, while occasionally utilizing the debate, never quite gave it the central importance that the Greeks did. More recent debate plays, such as *Inherit the Wind* (dealing with the Scopes trial) or *Abe Lincoln in Illinois* (which includes the Lincoln–Douglas debates), depend upon active structures and not the balanced structure in which *A* meets *B* head-on. In *Inherit the Wind* the opponents do not engage face to face but work through persuading third parties.

The three structures—active, reactive, and balanced—then, are the foundation for dramatic scenes. They provide the dynamic basis for transforming narrative material into dramatic presentation. Of the three, the balanced structure is the most limited, though it can be significant. The reactive structure varies in importance from age to age. It appears more and more frequently in the contemporary theatre and we respond to its special appeal. However, the active structure is and has been the most frequently used. Although as the diagram shows, the elements of the active structure are limited, they do allow a wide range of expression.

There is another way in which we can distinguish how these structures of action work in terms of presentation. The effectiveness of the active structure depends on a balancing of forces between A and B. The balance is not complete. Quite the opposite. B has sufficient strength to hold off A, though not necessarily sufficient strength to produce an impasse. Furthermore, the tension between A and B makes the future uncertain. Events can go one way or another. Moreover, in the scenes that produce the most complex and evocative effects, the values that underlie conflicting impulses may be mixed. We can often empathize with both sides. These are the very elements of the dialectic mode. In effect, then, the active structure is the presentational expression of the dialectic sensibility.

On the other hand, the reactive structure may or may not tend toward the iconic mode. In some cases a reactive scene may lead to working through a temporal sequence, the adjustment moving from one moment in time to another. A frequently recurrent reactive structure has the character recalling the past, focusing on the present, and imagining a future. (This subject has been introduced in *Dynamics of Drama*.)[5] But even so, the reactive does incline toward displaying the consequences of an act, and so becomes an exposure for the audience. This has an iconicizing effect on the scene. But the true iconic mode arises from a balanced relationship in which performer reveals self to audience.

If these duets are indeed the basis for dramatic presentation, then we must ask how they relate to the initial idea of a transcendent act. How does the human being exceed the self through such forms? Setting aside the matter of subject, which in itself may be extraordinary, we have to consider the very nature of the structured exchange. The root idea that a performer can both merge with and yet remain distinct from an act is itself transcendent. Only by being structured can the event be controlled. But control belies the illusion, which is to suggest spontaneous life. If it were possible (and attempts have been made) to present unstructured existence where no one knows what would happen, or where matters would end, or where or how one would even recognize an end—then we would lose that dynamic tension in which finite humans are juxtaposed against their own capacity to exceed their finiteness. But given the knowledge of the conclusion and the condition of repetition at least in performance, that double nature appears. In order to utilize that double nature most richly and to crystallize the finite-infinite possibilities most fully, the performers need structures in which they can submerge themselves and yet play. At the primary level they have the three structures that I have described.

Chapter 10

Actor and actors

My favorite actors A and B seem to be doing all the work. They run the gamut of action from intense aggressiveness to deep recoil, from persuasion to reconciliation. But what about C and D and all the others? Where do they fit into the model of activity that I have laid out? That Cs and Ds abound in dramatic performance is obvious. Despite the handful of two–character plays that do exist, drama is not confined to the twosome. Nevertheless, the model I have suggested is not entirely hypothetical, but reflects the actual way in which successive scenes are organized.

To envisage how the two-person model exists in practice, we need to appreciate two conditions. First, in dealing with scenes we are concerned with the number of people onstage at any one time. The characters who occupy the positions of A and B will change from action to action, but the juxtaposition of A exerting influence over B or B reacting to A will remain constant. Therefore, the story of a play may unfold as $A \rightarrow B/\ B \rightarrow C/\ A \leftarrow C/\ D \rightarrow A$, B, C, that is, A urging B, B threatening C, C reacting to A, and D bringing a message to A, B, and C. In this scheme, a succession of duets becomes the means for telling the story and revealing the essential action. At any one time only two people may be involved, though of course more than two are involved in the entire action.

The second condition that exists has to do with the relation of persons to dramatic impulses. In the active segment, for example, one character may be working on one or more people. Antony delivers his oration to a crowd out of which representatives answer him. Yet whether they warn him against speaking ill of Brutus or urge him to read Caesar's will, they act in unison. We can thus notate this relationship as Antony $\rightarrow$ Crowd or, more accurately, as Antony $\rightarrow$ Citizen 1 + Citizen 2 + Crowd. Thus, although the number of persons increases, the dramatic impulse emitted by one actor and directed at another does not multiply. In exploring a scene's dynamics, then, the interchange of impulses rather than the mere number of bodies should be noted.

With these two principles in mind, we can now consider the degree to which the dialectic model I have proposed actually represents dramaturgic practice. After all, it is hard to believe that a substantial part of dramatic presentation can be reduced to this binary type of action or even to a succession of binary actions. Short of anatomizing every production, can we even examine the hypothesis?

V. Propp developed his theory of narrative functions after scrutinizing a vast number of folk tales.[1] However, in dealing with the entire range of theatrical performance such a procedure is unfeasible. Instead, a judicious selection may adequately demonstrate the extent to which this binary mode may serve as a working hypothesis. Let me start at the beginning—with the Greeks. In the forty-four works from the classical period we should see some evidence of this model if indeed it has any validity.

Obvious in the comedies as well as in the tragedies is the prevalence of simple duets. The duet may occur between two characters or between one character and the chorus, which often is an explicit surrogate for the actual audience. The chorus is always present, of course, but its role keeps shifting. Sometimes the chorus is an audience; sometimes it assumes a distinct character and thus substitutes as a character. Putting the chorus aside for the moment, the character proper frequently engages in a duet with only one other person.

The limitation of the number of characters is often attributed to some rule or convention that bound poets to use no more than two or three speaking characters onstage at one time. Aristotle, after all, tells us in the fourth chapter of the *Poetics* that it was Aeschylus who added the second actor, and Sophocles the third. But the rule —if it did exist—was not mechanical, and as we shall see, there may be other reasons for restraining the number of actors onstage at any one time.

Simple duets, as I've said, prevail by far. But there are many episodes where more than two characters are onstage. Such scenes come readily to mind: Jocasta separating Creon and Oedipus (*Oedipus the King*), Iphigenia interviewing Orestes and Pylades (*Iphigenia in Tauris*), etc. Due to the Greek practice of using no more than three actors, we seldom find scenes with more than three characters onstage simultaneously. But the effect of a great number could be achieved by using the chorus or even individual chorus members as secondary characters. The crucial issue, however, concerns the ways in which three or more characters function on stage.

One of the most common ways in which a Greek dramatist deals with more than two characters is to render them mute. Seldom do children speak when they are brought onstage. Instead, they act as objects of pity. In contrast, mutes often are curiously eloquent in their muteness. There are several scenes in which a prominent character is brought onstage, only to remain silent while two other characters argue or speak. During Clytemnestra's welcome to Agamemnon, Cassandra says nothing (*Agamemnon*), speaking only when both of them leave. In a similar way the captive maiden Iole says nothing to Deianeira, standing only as a mute symbol of Heracles' passion (*Trachiniae*). When Peace is rescued from the pit by Trygaeus, she refuses to speak aloud although she does whisper into Hermes' ear (*Peace*). In these scenes, the muteness of certain characters is used for dramatic effect. But it also preserves the concentration of the duet. While Force and Hephaestus argue at the opening of *Prometheus*, Prometheus' silence prepares us for his tortured cries when left alone. Of all characters, Pylades is probably the archetype of the mute. He appears in five tragedies. More often than not he is mute. As Orestes' companion, he reinforces the tormented hero. Aeschylus uses his muteness to striking effect by having him deliver only one speech in the entire *Choephori*: the injunction to Orestes to kill his mother.

But lest we attribute the use of mutes solely to the limitation on the number of actors, we should note several illuminating scenes. Turning back to the often muted Pylades, we find an example in *Iphigenia in Tauris* in which Orestes and Pylades are brought before the priestess of Diana, Iphigenia. Throughout the segment, Iphigenia speaks only to Orestes. But once Iphigenia leaves, Orestes and Pylades speak to each other. Thus, the actor playing Pylades is not a permanent stage mute but his silence is dramaturgic in purpose. Similar cases occur in *Oedipus at Colonus* and *Antigone*. Thus, it is not true that the person who remains mute onstage is a non-speaking actor. The dramatist's failure to make the *Iphigenia* scene a three-way conversation is not due to performing limitations, but again to some dramaturgic purpose. And that purpose appears often in the Greek plays. Aristophanes' *The Wasps* opens with two servants, Xanthias and Sosias, speaking to each other. When their master, Bdelycleon, awakens, Sosias becomes mute and the duet continues between Bdelycleon and Xanthias. This practice is so widespread that it constitutes a conventional element in dramatic construction among the Greeks. While not invariable, in most instances where more than two characters appear, only two carry on the substance of the segment. The result is to sustain a duet despite the additional characters.

Allied with the use of mutes, though not confined to their use, is the division of an episode into a sequence of duets. When three people are onstage, the arrangement may follow this sequence: $A \rightarrow B$ with C mute/ $B \rightarrow C$ with A mute/ $C \rightarrow A$ with B mute, or some such variation. Indeed, writing a story by means of a sequence of duets may not even include mutes. Aristophanes introduces a leading character who remains onstage while a succession of people come to him. This arrangement is analogous to that of Prometheus who has Oceanus, Io, and Hermes visit him. Together, the use of mutes and the duet sequence raise the number of binary episodes to a vast majority.

Less significant but still important is yet another way in which an apparent trio is actually structured as a duet. This occurs in those scenes where two or more people act in tandem. In the *Choephori*, at the end of the *kommos* Electra, Orestes, and Pylades are all active, joining together in praying to the spirit of Agamemnon. Their impulses thus are welded into one powerful call to the late king. The same sort of alliance is apparent at the opening of *Peace*. As in the opening of *The Wasps*, two servants are speaking, but when the master enters, instead of one speaking and the other remaining silent, both speak in support of each other. They in effect compose one impulse. Still, this introduction of echoing or seconding is an advance in dramatic structure. It keeps more than two people active on the stage and at the same time retains the concentrated structure of the duet.

The Greek dramatists thus have three principal ways of maintaining the binary form. They allow characters to keep silent onstage, they arrange their narratives into sequences of duets, and, on some occasions, they link two or more characters along a single line of impulse. Of these three methods, the one involving the mute requires some further consideration.

On the surface I seem to relegate the mute figures to a subsidiary if not a virtually nonexistent status. This does not seem to allow for the character's physical presence, reactions, relationships, and so forth. Though characters may disappear from a text, they do not disappear from view as long as they are onstage. But with what emphasis do they remain onstage? I have already cited scenes in which the mute is particularly eloquent, and the focus is on this figure. We must, however, distinguish these emphatic figures from those who recede into the background. The issue concerns the degree to which the action arises from the mute figure or is directed at it. Where either of these is the case, then it is obvious that the figure has a speaking silence. But in the majority of cases, the mute figure recedes into the background. This figure's reactions may enhance the performance, but the reactions are supportive, ancillary, rather than focal and the vital movement of the action arises from the speaking figures.

Of the focal figures I mentioned, only Peace and Iole are truly central. Even Cassandra is subsidiary, though the way a particular production stages her entrance will give her greater or lesser prominence. Otherwise, the greater number of mutes in Greek drama tends to be subordinate. They undoubtedly contribute to the total effect of the scene, but by providing a supporting ground rather than as a focal figure.

In summary, then, Greek drama, while formally utilizing an alternating structure of ode and episode, dynamically organizes the episode as a duet or a sequence of duets. Often the chorus acts as an audience to these duets, though the chorus leader (*coryphaeus*) sometimes is a partner in a duet with one of the characters, usually the Messenger. At other times the *coryphaeus* will provide transitional comments between the duets in a sequence. Besides these variations in the ways that the chorus relates to the characters, there are departures from the duet structure. In a limited number of scenes, three characters appear onstage and engage in a three-pointed exchange. These scenes are trios in a true sense; I shall reserve discussion of them for the next chapter. Here it is essential to stress that, despite the handful of trios that do appear, the fundamental unit of the Greek dramatic scene is the duet.

The dominance of the duet, especially the simple duet, found in Greek drama, passes down through Roman to Italian and French drama. Induced partly by example, partly by native preference, the Italian and French playwrights adopted a concentrated dramatic form and utilized limited numbers of characters. These practices, by narrowing the range of both subject and means, found the duet a congenial form. But even this propensity for duet scenes does not fully explain the extremes of some dramatists in this regard. A comedy such as Machiavelli's *La Mandragola* is virtually a sequence of duets with occasional transitional trios and one or two sustained scenes that involve more than two people. With the disappearance of the chorus, the alternation of duets and group scenes no longer existed. Instead, duet succeeds duet, sometimes with transitional sequences, sometimes not.

In Racine, moreover, this reliance on the duet is virtually absolute. There are thirty French scenes in *Phèdre*. Not one is a true trio or group scene. There are a number of scenes in which more than two people are onstage, but in most instances only two are engaged in the scene, the other or others are mute subordinates. In four scenes (I.iv; II.iii; II.v; V.vii) three people actually speak during the scene. But though three speak, there is never a triple exchange. Instead, Théramène delivers a message to Hippolyte, and then Aricie persuades Hippolyte to act (II.iii). In this scene we have a simple duet sequence. The same is true of Act II, scene v. The last scene of the play (V.vii) is Phèdre's confession to Thésée. As she dies, Panope observes this in half a line of verse. In essence, the scene is another duet.

Most of the play, however, relies on the quite simple form of bringing two people together without the presence of others. The play has about 1,650 lines of verse. Over two-thirds of the lines come from simple duets. Only some fifty-three lines or 3 percent are spoken in soliloquy. All the rest come from scenes of complex duets, though the complexity is minimal.

We do not frequently encounter so concentrated a form, for few dramatists have the style and command to sustain so compact an action. Yet the connection between simplicity of means and dynamism of effect was not lost on others. While no other playwright restricts himself as much as Racine, others do utilize the duet with similar intensity.

In certain of his plays, Ibsen is the dramaturgic heir of Racine, particularly in the plays of his middle and greatest period in which he employs a limited palette. He too uses the duet, but without the strict exclusivity that Racine observed. In these plays, such as *A Doll's House*, *Ghosts*, *Hedda Gabler*, and *The Master Builder*, Ibsen deftly balances duets with occasional trios or one or two group scenes to suggest the flow of life in a natural way. Yet we have but to examine the sequences in these plays to see how heavily he relies on the simple duet. The comings and goings in *A Doll's House* cannot obscure the importance of the duet culminating in that historic confrontation between Nora and Helmer at the end. The first act is built around four major duets and one trio: Nora and Helmer, Nora and Mrs. Linde, Nora and Krogstad, and Nora and Helmer again. The trio occurs among Nora, Mrs. Linde, and Dr. Rank. Between these scenes occur more or less brief transitions that give an impression of daily life. Between the first Nora–Helmer scenes and the Nora–Mrs. Linde scene there is a five-line transition involving Helmer's departure and the maid announcing Mrs. Linde. But this type of "natural" transition is not the only one. Between the second Nora–Helmer duet in Act 1 and a final but significant duet between Nora and the nanny, Anne-Marie, occurs a brief soliloquy by Nora. This use of a character alone onstage, speaking, is a vestige of earlier dramatic convention, which in this play Ibsen has not entirely discarded. However, he has minimized it—Nora's soliloquy is only a line and a half long, but it is a connecting link between duets.

It is interesting to note that the first act of *A Doll's House* serves as an example not of Ibsen's maximum use of the duet in this play but rather its minimal use. The second and third acts are more severely restricted to the duet, again mainly the simple type, although there are several examples of complex duets. The only fully realized trios are those involving Dr. Rank. There is one in each act. It is significant, moreover, that the Dr. Rank motif concerns a man who is an outsider, an outsider always doomed to look in upon others, who is never to join in family life. In the second act the use of Nora's solo speeches increases as transitional passages between duets. Despite the so-called realism of the play, then, the structural arrangement follows more conventional forms.

The use of the solo speech as a transition between duets harks back to Roman and Renaissance practice. It appears regularly in Italian plays, such as Machiavelli's *La Mandragola*. In these plays it is true that the solo speeches tend to be longer than those of Nora, but they serve similar purposes: to reveal reactions to events, to allow planning, and also to separate the duets. Where the solo speech is not used, the two characters onstage can simply leave and another pair comes on. The earlier tradition accepted the convention of distinct units which could or could not be bridged by motivated business. Even where an entrance or exit is motivated, there is something arbitrary in it. In *La Mandragola* at the end of one duet Nicia tells Ligurio, "I'll be with the missus meanwhile, and we'll see each other later" (I.ii). Ligurio then has a host speech in which he comments on Nicia's fatuousness, concluding that "Callimaco has grounds for hope. Ah, there he is now."[2] In comes Callimaco and the two have a duet. The formality of scene divisions is cemented with the institution of the French scene. While some of the same techniques for providing transitions between scenes still are employed, they are not so numerous, and the distinctness of each scene is sharper.

With the rise of naturalistic conventions, dramatists made concerted efforts to decompartmentalize the action. They sought to blur the divisions between scenes, and therefore began to introduce overlapping action and transitional passages dealing with the details of life in order to create the impression of the continuous stream of existence. *A Doll's House* is at the conjunction of two styles. It contains transitional units of comings and goings that overlap. Rather than have one person leave and then another arrive, Ibsen has the new arrival, such as Mrs. Linde, appear before Helmer actually leaves. At the same time the use of Nora's reactions between duets adheres to an older practice.

This tradition of intensive drama does not disappear with Ibsen. It is alive and healthy in the twentieth century. The plays of Beckett, Pinter, Orton, Miller, Williams, Albee, and many other contemporary playwrights continue to depend on the simple duet as the key structure. They may put it to more varied use than their predecessors, but nevertheless, it is central to the way they build action. Their type of play, with few characters and changes of place, has the classical features that link these writers to that tradition in which the duet occupies so central a role.

When we turn to the tradition of looser narrative drama, the tradition of Shakespeare and his contemporaries, to what extent does the duet still dominate?

In a previous study of Shakespeare's *Two Gentlemen of Verona*,[3] I demonstrated that 85 percent of the play consists of duets or solos. Of this figure less than 15 percent of the text involves solos, some of which have a character speaking directly to the audience. That leaves more than 70 percent of the text arranged as duets. Again we need to distinguish between simple duets, with only two actors onstage, and complex duets, with more than two onstage though the action dynamically resolves itself into two impulses. In *Two*

Gentlemen simple duets take up 46 percent of the material, complex duets 24 percent. As in the complex duets of the Greek drama, the principal means by which multi-personed scenes are resolved into duets are these: by keeping certain characters mute; by arranging a long scene into a sequence of more or less brief duets; and by utilizing parallel impulses in a redundant manner, redundant here meaning that the same message is conveyed by more than one carrier.

In this play as well as in others, Shakespeare shows how heavily dependent he is upon the duet. Critics have often been puzzled by Shakespeare's failure in *Measure for Measure* to give Isabella any lines to her brother Claudio after she discovers he's alive. And they might be equally puzzled by Sylvia's silence in the last scene of *Two Gentlemen*. In these cases Shakespeare is only obeying his instinct to de-emphasize certain characters when his attention is elsewhere. Not only does he employ mutes widely and wisely, but he arranges scene sequences artfully, often in a triptych order.[4] In his handling of redundant figures, that is, those who essentially serve to echo or mirror one another, he goes well beyond the Greeks. Indeed, just as Pylades may be considered the archetype of the mute character, Rosencrantz and Guildenstern may be regarded as archetypes of the redundant characters, two persons who compose one sycophancy. In tracing their appearances throughout *Hamlet*, we see an adroit shift from redundancy to muteness.

The two friends of Hamlet appear in eight scenes (II.ii; III.i–iii; IV.i–iv). The eight scenes fall into eleven segments. Their opening remarks immediately link them as a single voice. Rosencrantz responds to the appeal of Claudius and Gertrude that they help Hamlet by saying:

> Both your majesties
> Might, by the sovereign power you have of us,
> Put your dread pleasure more into command
> Than to entreaty.

Guildenstern picks up the thread with the continuation of the half line:

> But we both obey,
> And here give up ourselves in the full bent
> To lay our service freely at your feet,
> To be commanded.

(II.ii.26–32)

Here Shakespeare uses redundancy not only to assure dramatic concentration but also to characterize these figures. But lest we think redundancy in *Hamlet* is only confined to Rosencrantz and Guildenstern, we should note that in the same scene Claudius and Gertrude also act redundantly to entreat Rosencrantz and Guildenstern to visit the Queen's "too much changed son" (36).

Later in the same scene, Rosencrantz and Guildenstern do visit Hamlet. Their remarks continue to be echoes of each other. Shakespeare stresses this by the way he orders their dialogue with Hamlet. At first, Rosencrantz and Guildenstern alternate speeches to Hamlet so that the dialogue runs as follows: Guildenstern, Rosencrantz, Hamlet/Rosencrantz, Guildenstern, Hamlet/Rosencrantz, Hamlet/Guildenstern, Hamlet. This last sequence is repeated. Then for three pairs of speeches it is Rosencrantz, Hamlet, followed by Guildenstern, Hamlet. Then both answer Hamlet, after which there are sixteen pairs of speeches, eleven involving Rosencrantz. The fact that it is rare for Rosencrantz and Guildenstern to speak sequentially in the meeting with Hamlet only emphasizes the singleness of their dramatic presence.

In their next scene (III.i), Rosencrantz and Guildenstern report to the King and Queen. They give a continuous report of their encounter with Hamlet. Unless we know the text by heart, we would be hard put to divide the lines between them:

> He does confess he feels himself distracted,
> But from what cause 'a will by no means speak.
> Nor do we find him forward to be sounded,
> But with a crafty madness keeps aloof
> When we would bring him on to some confession
> Of his true state.
>
> (III.i.5–10)

The Queen then asks, "Did he receive you well?" They answer:

> Most like a gentleman.
> But with much forcing of his disposition.
> Niggard of question, but of our demands
> Most free in his reply.
>
> (III.i.11–14)

Having thus established this kind of redundancy, Shakespeare begins to vary his handling of Rosencrantz and Guildenstern. Later in the action, after the debacle of the play-within-the-play, he introduces Rosencrantz and Guildenstern to convey the King's distemper. But instead of using the two characters redundantly this time, Shakespeare adopts the mute technique. First Guildenstern has a duet with Hamlet (III.ii.284–306), then Rosencrantz has his duet (307–30), and lastly a second duet with Guildenstern follows when Hamlet challenges him to play upon the recorder (331–87).

Thereafter, Rosencrantz increasingly comes to speak for both. In the remaining five scenes in which they appear, Rosencrantz speaks twenty-seven lines, Guildenstern only five. Moreover, Guildenstern speaks only one line in the last four scenes while Rosencrantz speaks thirteen. Thus, through the course of the play Shakespeare has shifted from reliance on redundancy to the use of Guildenstern as a mute in order to maintain the dramatic line through duets.

The care that Shakespeare takes in fitting Rosencrantz and Guildenstern's roles to the action is equaled by the care he takes in every other respect. With a few deft strokes, he creates an impression of an entire court, the center of an empire that can dispatch warnings to Norway and exact tribute from England. Yet it is a court of pleasure, even drunkenness, readily responsive to an apparently indulgent monarch. Moreover, it appears to be an exceptionally vulnerable court, easy prey to its people once they are aroused. The vividness of this contradictory picture, moreover, is only an outline, barely filled in. This sketchy yet vibrant image of the Danish court is only the background to a narrative that traces the fortunes of two families, one royal, the other gentle but inferior. Shakespeare unfolds that narrative through a sequence of scenes, the great majority of which fall into a binary form.

In *Hamlet*, as in *Two Gentlemen*, Shakespeare transforms his narrative source into a sequence of simple and complex duets. Nearly 70 percent of *Hamlet* is so arranged. Somewhat less than 7 percent is in soliloquy, but here as in so much of Shakespeare, the impact is greater than the means used to achieve it. Psychologically and imaginatively the soliloquies seem to occupy a far greater portion of the text than they actually do. Of the remaining 23 or 24 percent of the text, about half is composed of trios and the rest of group scenes. In general, these proportions are not so different from those in *Two Gentlemen*.

But if the quantities are similar, the actual scenes are not. By the time Shakespeare came to write *Hamlet*, he had learned to use the binary structure of drama with considerable finesse and efficiency.

He relies heavily upon complex duets, over 40 percent of the play being cast in this form. By utilizing techniques for maintaining dialectic concentration while creating variety and verisimilitude, he expanded his ability to produce both concentration of action and complexity of effect. Throughout the play he relieves the starkness of the simple duet with two–line or three–line transitions from one scene unit to another or by allowing a seconding, that is, a redundant, character a line here and there. Yet in the main, he sustains the thrust of action by juggling mutes, duet sequences, and seconding voices.

In the first court scene we can see how he accommodates a group yet refines the dramatic movement. Though this scene is sometimes staged as a council scene, it requires a general assembly. The Second Quarto calls for a flourish of trumpets to open the scene. But flourish or not, the two authoritative versions specify the entrance of the King, Queen, Hamlet, Laertes, Polonius, the two Ambassadors, and others, Lords and Attendants. They make a goodly show. Presumably they gather in some ceremonial fashion, suggesting a serious meeting of a potent court.

In production, the director can treat this entry in a variety of ways. He can emphasize the busy routine of an inner circle. Or he can elaborate the ostentation of a powerful and magnificent court. He can build the entrance by the order of the procession or by revealing the court already onstage. In short, the actual assemblage allows considerable choice. Nevertheless, whatever the choice, the court itself rapidly becomes part of the background as the action proceeds.

Claudius first addresses his courtiers as a body. He thanks them for their support, and presumably they acknowledge his appreciation in some fashion. Amidst this general goodwill, Hamlet in black strikes a discordant note. How strident the note depends upon the staging, for he can draw attention to himself from the beginning or remain a peripheral disturbance until Claudius addresses him. The more prominent he is at the beginning, the more the action assumes a triadic quality.

The scene continues with Claudius sending off his ambassadors to old Norway. They share a single line of response between them, an obvious mark of redundancy. All others are mute. Next Claudius turns to Laertes and his request for permission to leave Denmark. Polonius seconds him. In this action Claudius invites a petition, checks that Polonius is in accord, and then grants Laertes' request. Again the brief segment has a single line of action in which Laertes and Polonius share the same objective. The next duet engages Hamlet. Claudius and Gertrude join together to persuade Hamlet to "cast (his) nighted color off" and to remain at court. The thrust of their persuasion is identical: they both assert that death is common and mourning should end; they both beseech Hamlet to refrain from going back to Wittenberg. In this exchange, Gertrude is obviously differentiated from Claudius by her sex, her appearance, and her affinity for Hamlet. Her action, on the other hand, is co-active with Claudius'. Indeed, one of the reasons that Gertrude seems to lack inner fibre is a result of the fact that, at least until the last scene, she repeatedly is seconding Claudius.

After the court departs, Hamlet undergoes a deep-seated revulsion at his mother's marriage. While the segment is not a duet, it does have a dialectic character because Hamlet reacts to the accumulated pressure, not only from his father's death but even more from his mother's behavior. On the heels of Hamlet's reluctant acceptance that he must keep silent, Horatio and the two members of the watch arrive. Again in this segment there is a single line of action. Horatio and the soldiers come to report what they have seen; Hamlet questions them about it. Structurally, the scene consists of a brief unit of greeting (I.ii.160–7) in which Hamlet recognizes Horatio, guesses at or knows Marcellus' name, and may acknowledge Bernardo's presence. In these few lines Shakespeare conveys three different degrees of familiarity with the visitors. But then the scene becomes a duet between Hamlet and Horatio with some reinforcement from Marcellus and Bernardo. Marcellus has one line alone; several times they answer in tandem. They second Horatio and in a single line comment on Horatio's estimate of the Ghost's time by together insisting "longer, longer."

Taken as a whole then, the linear movement of this scene proceeds through a sequence of three complex duets, all relying on Claudius' active direction, a soliloquy of pained reaction, and then a final complex duet of report and reaction. At the spatial level there is the potentiality for modulating the contrast between a grieving Hamlet and a busily functioning council. These two planes of action, because their structures are uncluttered, are capable of being presented effectively and yet developed complexly.

This structuring pattern recurs throughout the play. Although the narrative techniques of *Hamlet* and indeed most Elizabethan plays are quite different from those of Greek drama, there is the same reliance on the duet. In the case of the English drama, however, the reductive process is more widespread. Because Elizabethan and Jacobean plays employ large casts and introduce new characters without reserve, the manner in which many characters onstage at one time are organized along binary principles is more varied. In general, there is widespread use of mutes. Sometimes the hierarchical organization of society, as shown in a court scene, allows a verisimilar appearance to this suppression of certain characters. But even when that hierarchical justification is not present, playwrights regularly render characters mute when the story so demands. When a playwright has a large group onstage and each member has something to say, the scene tends to be diffuse. One of the writers who constructs scenes in this manner is Robert Greene, and that may be why when compared to Marlowe, Shakespeare, and Kyd he was so much less a success. Despite the popularity of his *Friar Bacon and Friar Bungay*, its story development is marred by a number of exceptionally diffuse scenes such as the first one.

It is not my contention that every scene is either a simple or complex duet. Almost a quarter of *Hamlet* consists of scenes or segments that have more than two centers of action. Trios and other group scenes will be discussed in the next chapter. My argument at this point is that there is a powerful tendency in drama to cast any chosen narrative into a sequence of duets. Whatever the number of characters that may be involved in a particular segment, the writer tends to align them into two camps or more properly to align them so that they share a common active or reactive thrust. In my view that tendency does not primarily have a mimetic but rather a presentational purpose.

For an action to be sufficiently vivid and possess the minimal force for projection to an audience, it must be differentiated from other actions. Since presentation relies so much upon temporal and spatial contrasts, it is essential that the elements of a dramatic scene have those contrasts. Once the presentation turns inward, that is, stops being a direct offering to the audience and becomes indirect, the generation of projective energy has to increase. In this indirect performance the initial contrast between performers, and then the give and take of effort, create the vital by-play to which the audience attaches itself. The duet provides the structure for such indirect action. That is why Sir Laurence Olivier can say so feelingly that "the greatest heights in drama are always between two players."[5]

The concentrated power of the duet, however, when it is embodied in two people, can be tedious when confined to the same two people throughout the play. That is why there are relatively few plays with only two characters. Just as there is a powerful tendency in presentation to shape action into duets, there is an equally powerful inclination to stretch resources beyond that narrow limitation. One way playwrights have done this is by utilizing a larger group of characters but managing the action into sequences of simple duets. As already pointed out, the neo-classical drama of Italy and France follows this course for the most part. Another way is to increase the number of roles but to maintain the dual structure not in terms of bodies but in terms of dramatic force. As we have seen, by breaking action into shorter or longer sequences of duets, by keeping some characters mute, and by giving two or more characters a common line of action, dramatists can provide the base strength of the duet while taking advantage of minor variations in tone.

So far I have made my argument on the basis of play texts. It could very well be argued that I am ignoring what actually happens onstage. A character may have no lines, and yet be a significant figure in the action. That is undoubtedly true. Not only may characters in scripted plays exert considerable force by their actions, but often key features of performance, especially in comedy, are never adequately embodied in scripts. Furthermore, the audience, having the freedom to look where it will, may pay attention to a silent actor more than to one speaking. Yet with all the truth of these objections, the fundamental argument I have advanced remains valid.

Earlier, I stressed that a presentation does not occur in a vacuum. It is appreciated within a context. This also is true of shows of skill and glorification, and far more true of shows of illusion. Not only does the narrative have a cultural and often historical context, but every feature of the presentation has a potential resonance. To handle the horde of potential overtones that emanate from the numerous signs in a play, the producers—dramatist and director and actors and so forth—arrange their materials in depth, that is, as background and foreground features. The artistic arrangement may not always accord with audience interest. What may have been intended as a subordinate element may assume focal interest. But despite these occasional dislocations of emphasis, it is usual for the intended levels of interest to be projected to the audience. In short, the producers establish figure and ground patterns to which the audience responds.

One of the avant-garde arguments of the 1960s was that the presentation of such structures of dominance and subordination was inherently restrictive, and that audiences should be free to respond to whatever they wish at any particular moment. It was claimed that the non-matrixed performance allowed the audience to participate more intimately in the theatrical event. In practice, however, these so-called non-matrixed efforts exerted their own tyranny. When they followed their logic to a conclusion, they sometimes presented works that were in fact all background. There were productions in the 1960s in which the performers projected undifferentiated impulses which encouraged each member of the audience to select what he or she preferred. It was something like shopping out of a great bin in a store-wide sale.

In fact, the practice of providing all background and no foreground merely continued a practice that had begun in naturalism. In Belasco's work and even before Belasco, the fascination of creating a naturalistic background onstage often outran the action that occurred within the frame. In an odd turnabout, the faithful rendering of observed environments became fascinating to spectators. Much has been made of the social appeal of real life, but in truth the placement onstage of an actual locale from life is the ultimate in the fantastic. Is it not the height of impossibility to see before one the exact duplicate of a restaurant that is located only a few streets away? This naturalism, like the non-matrixed performances of the 1960s, tended to dehumanize the theatrical event and reduce the audience's astonishment at the display of human beings exceeding themselves.

In the face of the tendencies to obscure the distinction between ground and figure, the dominant tradition of drama remains contextual, and in that light we can understand how the complex duet works. In discussing the mutes in Greek drama, I noted that occasionally a mute actor was a focal figure. In such instances the very presence of the character exerts an impulse that engages an impulse of a speaking character. Such mutes are no less active than speaking characters. Invariably, the skillful dramatist calls attention to that figure in the script either by a stage direction or a speaking character's action. The majority of mutes, however, are not focal figures, though they may be vitally involved in an action. The actors who play the roles offer appropriate responses, but for the most part these responses are supportive of one or another of the active figures. At such moments they second another character. Or they may recede into the background, behaving appropriately but not focally. The orchestration of varying degrees of emphasis is one of the major achievements of the director's theatre. Yet something is lost. Where actors attempt to be equally alert at all times, they find it difficult to become subordinate at appropriate moments.

It is one of the triumphs of the production of *Nicholas Nickleby* that it created a vivid, bustling, constantly active ground of mid-nineteenth-century London life in theatricalized form and yet permitted characters to step forward in a personal, highly visible manner as the narrative demanded. As one watched members of the company standing about the stage, silently watching a scene before them, one could see how a mute figure temporarily became part of the living ground of action without detracting from the focal duality that was being presented.

The complex duet poses theoretical issues of considerable significance to dramatic structure. On the one hand, we have a scene or a segment with three or more people onstage at one time. On the other, the action that involves this group orders them into two camps, each of which shares a common intention or reaction. Between the binary lines of action and the larger number of characters, there is bound to be augmented tension. Here we must make a distinction between dramatic structure and theatrical effect. The binary structure provides the concentrated basis for the enactment. The larger numbers of characters provide the presentational contrast that augments the structured conflict. Most obviously, those scenes in which a single pleader faces a hostile crowd or a powerful tribunal (Antony and the mob, Katherine and the court) illustrate the way the multiplication of persons can create striking duets. In effect, the complex duet embodies the paradox of confined action and multiple expressive agents. When the expressive agents act redundantly—that is, when they follow the same essential line of action though they may reveal minor variations in temperamental or attitudinal detail—then the use of the complex duet can be richly developed.

As we have seen, the classical line of drama preferred to build on the simple duet, a technique that does permit immense concentration of effect as well as an elegance of dramatic development. In contrast, the tradition of narrative or extensive drama makes far greater use of the complex duet. How much it gains by this method we can see by glancing once again at *Hamlet*. In the play there is virtually nothing that Rosencrantz and Guildenstern do that could not be conveyed by a single character. Such a single character would make an effective foil to Horatio, for instance. Except for a lone aside between them when Hamlet asks them to speak the truth, all other actions are carried out in a parallel manner: insofar as dramaturgic purpose is concerned, one person would do as well as two. Unlike Stoppard's Rosencrantz and Guildenstern, who show temperamental differences, Shakespeare's Rosencrantz and Guildenstern seem copies of one another, even though Rosencrantz emerges marginally as more of a leader. Yet in presentation it is their very duplication of each other that suggests the commonality rather than unusualness of time-serving. By being two, their behavior becomes generalized, and Hamlet's individuality is accented. In this instance as in so many others, the complex duet affords the play-makers the means for achieving a kind of harmonic density while sustaining the necessary concentration upon which effective presentation depends.

One question remains: how important is the duet in the modern theatre? Although it dominated traditional theatre and still dominates certain kinds of theatre at the present time, to what extent does it operate in either the naturalistic-styled plays such as those of Chekhov or the epic works of Brecht? An illuminating comparison is that between the first act of Chekhov's *The Wood Demon* and the later revision of the play, *Uncle Vanya*. Both versions involve people sitting about, eating and chatting. Many of the circumstances are identical: Voynitsky's love for Helen, the Wood Demon's obsession with protecting the forest (though in the later version this is attributed to Doctor Astrov), Dyadin who is the hanger-on (called Telegin later). Equally, there are differences. For example, Sonya is markedly revised as a character.

But the greatest differences are structural. The way the characters are introduced and handled in *Uncle Vanya* provides a sequence of concentrated actions. While *The Wood Demon* is even more diffuse than is customary with Chekhov, and has more characters, *Uncle Vanya* allows concentration on a series of particular characters. Symptomatic of the changes is a segment initiated and sustained by Vanya's mother. The dialogue in both versions is virtually identical. But there is a considerable difference in its concentration. In *The Wood Demon*, Mrs. Voynitsky addresses the professor she admires and tells him of a pamphlet she received, commenting disparagingly that the author has changed his opinions in the last seven years. Vanya disagrees and the two argue until the professor interrupts. The men verge on a heated argument and Mrs. Voynitsky interrupts. In *Uncle Vanya* the same ideas are expressed, but this time the professor is not onstage. The argument is entirely between Vanya and his mother, and though there are interjections by others, the exchange is far more compressed as a duet.

This type of revision pervades the entire act so that, interwoven with remarks by various people, we do have a succession of interchanges between Astrov and the Nurse, Astrov and Vanya, Vanya's mother and Vanya, Astrov and others, and finally Vanya and Helen. The linkages are adroit, the transitions from genuine trios to simple and complex duets are subtle, and the movement of the act is richer and clearer. It is true that in Chekhov the binary pattern is never so simple nor the confrontation so direct as are those in Greek drama, in Ibsen's plays, or even in the more concentrated examples of Beckett and Pinter. Chekhov usually leavens an argument between two people by interweaving comments by one or another bystander. Yet even he, probably the dramatist who most successfully balanced the binary structure with oblique and diffuse emphasis, relies at crucial moments on the duet.

The dance in the third act of *The Cherry Orchard* appears to be a swirl of comings and goings by a variety of family and guests. Nevertheless, it is arranged primarily in a sequence of duets, with one or two exceptions. It opens with a duet between Pishchik and Trofimov, followed by a brief duet between Vanya and Trofimov. The action continues with a return to Trofimov and Pishchik, and then a duet between Mme. Ranevsky and Trofimov. For a while Charlotta carries the action forward by performing tricks to a group of onlookers whose remarks of pleasure parallel one another. Variation from the duet occurs in the brief trio that follows among Varya, Mme. Ranevsky, and Trofimov. Then there occurs one of the major scenes in the act and indeed in the play. It is the argument between Mme. Ranevsky and Trofimov in which he responds priggishly to her plea for his understanding of her love affair, and she scathingly berates him for being incapable of love. A series of brief duets then serves as a transition to Lopahin's arrival with the news that he has bought the orchard. Inserted in Lopahin's report is a brief exchange between Gaev and Mme. Ranevsky. Lopahin then tells the story of the auction to the guests and their shocked reaction serves as a mirrored background for Mme. Ranevsky's consternation. The last segment of the act is a final duet between Mme. Ranevsky and her daughter, Anya, with Trofimov looking on mutely.

Undoubtedly, Chekhov uses the duet in his own distinctive manner. He often relies on mere fragments. He also enfolds one duet within the framework of another. He overlaps duets so that they seem to flow into one another. But when he wishes, as he does in the confrontation between Trofimov and Mme. Ranevsky, he composes a classical segment of attack and defense. Often it is the tension between the structural duet and the diffusion of characters and background that gives the Chekhovian play its peculiar vibrancy.

Bertolt Brecht, like Chekhov, modifies the basic duet to fit his own needs. Yet, though he plays with the duet in curious ways, he does often rely upon it or a variation of it. Also like Chekhov, he often employs indirection, yet his most effective scenes involve indirection within a binary framework. This is evident in *The Caucasian Chalk Circle*. The play contains three exchanges between Simon and Grusha. All contain a combination of bluntness and indirection. However, their use of third person when they speak to each other, as well as their reliance upon earthy proverbs, allows for a delicacy in their wooing. Brecht's recognition of the strength of the binary form may be further reflected in his organization of the third section of the play. Entitled "The Flight to the Northern Mountains," it consists, as printed in volume seven of the *Collected Plays*, of five segments of action, each preceded by the introduction of the narrator and musicians. In the first segment Grusha buys milk for the infant Michael from an extortionating Old Man; in the second she tries to share an inn room with two high-class ladies; in the third she tries to leave Michael with a peasant woman but then has to rescue him from the soldiers; in the fourth she ritually adopts Michael; and in the fifth she crosses an unsafe bridge over a deep gorge to save Michael from the soldiers.

In all of these segments except the second, the action follows a simple or slightly complex binary form: Grusha pleading with the Old Man, the Corporal challenging Grusha, Grusha pleading with the Peasant Woman, Grusha adopting Michael, Grusha pushing past the Peddlers at the gorge. It is only in the second segment that the action is more diffuse: the Older and Younger Ladies have varying concerns, a latent disagreement between them takes place, the bargaining between the Landlord and them as well as with Grusha has three sides to it. In short, the scene does not have the distinct exchanges we find in the other segments of this part of the play. That is perhaps why it was cut after it appeared in Brecht's first script, and though it was restored for the collected edition, this segment was not included in Brecht's own production of the play.[6] Two factors may have motivated its exclusion: it diverts from the forward movement of Grusha's escape or it makes no concentrated contribution to that movement. In either case, its removal leaves the third part with a vigorously alternating duality as the narrator's recital to the audience alternates with Grusha's struggle against a series of obstacles to her preservation of Michael.

Throughout this chapter, my contention has been that the duet, whether consisting of two actors alone or of groups of actors divided into two dynamic forces, is the key unit of dramatic presentation. The motive behind framing action in this binary fashion is not literary but theatrical. Projecting action in performance demands sufficient clarity of agents and concentration of their energies in order to produce an impact on an audience. That impact also can be produced by a mass of performers addressing an audience directly, as in choral presentation. But once one creates an autonomous action, as though life itself were unfolding independent of narrator or creator, then one has to find effective means for channeling the performers' energies so that the onlooker, the audience, can not only follow the events but feel the effect of the events. That is where the duet comes in.

But, of course, the duet is not the only kind of scene to be used, though it is the main one. Plays are full of trios, quartets, and other multi-personed scenes. How such scenes are given presentational form is the subject of the next chapter.

Chapter 11

Beyond binary action

The courtroom scene, once a popular form of theatrical entertainment, has been disappearing from the stage. Here and there plays may dramatize a trial, but no longer do we find them in major plays. And when a trial is presented, it usually takes the shape of a contest between an attorney and a witness, with the judge serving as little more than a mediating cipher. How unlike such scenes are the adjudications in earlier drama in which the contest between opponents is refereed by an authoritative and commanding judge.

Of the few trios to appear in Greek drama, the first and the most clear-cut is the trial of Orestes. This trio is a true trio composed of the Furies as plaintiffs, Orestes supported by Apollo as defendant, and Athena as president of the court. Significantly, the Athenian judges remain mute throughout the trial—in effect, they act as jurors—and it is Athena who speaks for them and casts the deciding vote when the Athenians render a split decision. In this legal paradigm we have one example of how a dramatist arranges a triple-sided action.

Even this type of scene has a binary basis, of course: the antagonism of plaintiff and defendant. The third force, the judge, mediates between them, and in a sense, then, functions as an audience, but an audience with a participating voice. To the extent that the judge plays the role of adjudicator and not advocate, the scene encloses performance within performance. Athena both witnesses the charges against the defense of Orestes, and so acts as audience, and also issues her verdict, and so subsumes, in a binary way, the opponents within her authority. During this unfolding action, the audience witnesses both the attack and defense as well as Athena's response to this exchange. In that way the triangular model of the stage is replicated as performance within performance.

Not all adjudications have the same structure. The various *deus ex machina* scenes are usually binary in that the god hands down a judgment in a unidirectional fiat (*Electra*, *Philoctetes*, etc.). But wherever genuine opponents engage in dispute before an acknowledged judge—whether or not the scene is in a formal courtroom—the action is triadic. Oedipus' charges against Creon and Creon's defense of his integrity are appealed to Jocasta in *Oedipus the King* so that the scene assumes the shape of a trial, though it is an unofficial trial in which no decision is rendered but an arbitration is effected.

Trials are especially widespread in Renaissance drama. The ruler, be he king or duke, is invariably chief magistrate too. He thus serves as a "natural" focus for a dispute. Shakespeare introduces trials in many of his plays—*King John*, *The Winter's Tale*, *The Comedy of Errors*, *Othello*, *Julius Caesar*, and others. In *Measure for Measure* and *All's Well That Ends Well* the final scene consists of a trial to ferret out the truth about a man's sexual history. In the former play, the duke as judge is also witness and actor; in the latter the king is a somewhat more detached magistrate. In both plays a rather large and complicated action is sustained by means of the judge who asks questions, mediates between opponents, and renders decision. It is by means of this sort of structure that the binary form of thrust and response is most easily amplified into a three-pronged action in which each voice is independent. Where such actions can be meaningfully nurtured, then theatrical presentation can go beyond the restraints of binary action. But, with the decline of the absolute ruler, the judge, when he appears, becomes increasingly neutral as he is in such thrillers as *Witness for the Prosecution*, and drama reverts to its usual binary form.

The trial is not the only type of activity that permits the trio to develop. Again, the Greek drama supplies an incipient example that the Renaissance and later drama develop fully. Throughout the Greek plays, there are instances in which two characters are engaged in dispute either of charge and countercharge or more formal debate. Often when one figure completes a statement and before the next one commences, the leader of the chorus will make a conciliatory or judgmental comment. As Medea ends her accusation against Jason and before Jason defends himself against her, the leader observes, "There is something terrible and past all cure, when quarrels arise 'twixt those who are near and dear."[1] This statement is detached and yet renders a kind of judgment on the quarrel. It serves the practical purpose of setting off one speech from another, and thus letting each stand out more clearly. But it also adds a third point of view to the action. It is quite clearly a subsidiary view and, as the basis for a third voice, rudimentary rather than fully realized. Yet it does indicate one of the forms that a third independent actor might take: that of the commentator.

This type of third voice is developed fully only in the English Renaissance. The plays of the Italian and French Renaissance seem to preserve the binary arrangement much more than do the plays of England or Spain. The multiplicity of characters in the latter plays impelled the authors to find ways of grouping that were not binary. This, of course, was a practical requirement. But the multiplication of characters had more fundamental causes, arising from the interest in multiple perspectives that was kept alive in England and Spain until the early part of the seventeenth century. Whether due to the survival of medieval frames of mind or the delayed influence of the classical revival, the major drama developed in each of these countries before the clamp of neo-classical example closed in on the theatres. As a result, to the primary form of a binary action the dramatists often added a third voice.

In turn, that third voice frequently came from a detached or semi-detached observer of the action or from a bystander emotionally involved in what was happening. Both types of observation can be illustrated by one scene in *Troilus and Cressida*. In this, the most elaborate scene of observation that he ever wrote, Shakespeare shows a love scene between Cressida and Diomedes, the issue of which is whether Cressida will betray Troilus by yielding to Diomedes (V.ii). Troilus with Ulysses watches the game, and Thersites, the scabrous, foul-mouthed hanger-on, watches both the game and Troilus' response to it. Shakespeare thus creates a trio within a trio. The first trio, Troilus noting Cressida and Diomedes, involves someone deeply engaged in events. As he watches what is happening, he can barely control his anguish, and does so only with Ulysses' urging. Thersites' detached scorn is directed not only at Cressida and Diomedes but at Troilus' response to what he sees. Again, as in the trial scene, we have performance within performance, for the root binary event of Cressida and Diomedes is a performance for Troilus and Ulysses on one plane. In turn, Troilus' reaction is a performance for Thersites on a secondary plane, while these two planes together compose a performance for the audience on a third plane.

This structure of receding planes of performance is widespread in

Elizabethan and Jacobean drama. Not only Shakespeare but many other dramatists utilize observation, asides, and commentaries to create action in depth. When the observation is accompanied by commentary, we usually find triadic action remarkably elaborated as in *Troilus and Cressida*. Later dramatic presentation, even when it makes use of the aside, never relies quite so fully on satiric or moral comment to create a third voice onstage.

Where the third voice emerges as commentator in modern drama, it tends to be more serious. A notable instance of a trio based on observation is the scene in *Hedda Gabler* when Lovborg tells Thea how he has destroyed his manuscript. Hedda listens, occasionally making brief interjections, vitally involved, indeed responsible, but exercising her role by failing to act to allay the approaching disaster. In a similar way the Marquis de Sade in *Marat/Sade* remains onstage as a detached yet vitally involved observer during much of the play, projecting a silent third force that manifests itself through the behavior of the inmates. The Director of Charenton rightly calls upon him to act when the inmates get out of hand.

Variations on the observer, but with a significant difference, appear in the twentieth century with a return to Elizabethan-style relativism. The same formal features of the aside and the observer do not recur. Instead, there is a kind of mixed detachment and redundancy, examples of which appear in both Genet and Brecht. In the first scene of *The Balcony*, Mme. Irma is attempting to bring the Bishop's session to a close. Also present is the Woman, as the sinner, who participated in his session. At first Irma is arguing with the Bishop while the Woman stands by mutely, but then the Bishop and the Woman replay a few erotic moments with Irma watching. The Woman as the sinner represents a third level in her role-playing. Yet that third level is the play-acting engineered by the silent Irma. The Woman and Irma thus share an action, for the Woman is an instrument of Irma's. Still, she expresses in her role an action detached from Irma's. On the surface then we have an apparent trio, but it actually reflects only a binary action.

This blending of binary and triadic action is sometimes evident in Brecht. In *The Caucasian Chalk Circle*, when Grusha arrives at her brother's house, it is her sister-in-law, Aniko, who questions her about the child and her husband. The brother mediates between them. While Grusha's presence exerts a force, demanding help, the brother takes it upon himself to answer his wife's questions for

Grusha. He concocts a story about a husband and a farm, thus seeming to speak for Grusha. He is both allied to her, and therefore redundant in the action, and at the same time his role-playing introduces a third element not completely independent yet somewhat detached from Grusha's presence. Here we have an apparent binary action masking a trio.

Relatively few examples can be found for triadic action. This illustrates the immense difficulty in creating a coherent dramatic action that goes beyond a binary interchange. The reason appears to be located in the nature of presentation itself. Being an offering, it must be directed at the receiver and thus, like other forms of communication, it is essentially binary. Even when the presentation is indirect, as in most of drama, the ability to diffuse the action is restricted by the danger of confusing it. To sustain triadic action, therefore, within a structure of triadic behavior, such as a trial or an observation scene, is extremely difficult. It is far easier to convey the effect of multiplicity by linking together a number of fragmentary duets, as Chekhov sometimes does, than to produce genuine trios.

In *Hamlet*, there are six segments that may be considered proper trios. Three of them fall into the pattern of binary action with commentator. One occurs in the scene in which Hamlet requires Horatio and Marcellus to swear to be secret. The Ghost's below-stage echoes of "swear" might be considered redundant of Hamlet's except for the fact that Hamlet treats the cries as a third voice (I.v.149–82). A second trio occurs in the brief segment in which Polonius admonishes Ophelia to color her loneliness by reading, for as he tells her, "with devotion's visage / And pious action we do sugar o'er / The devil himself" (III.i.46–8). The king's reactive aside is a self-directed commentary about what he heard (49–54). And lastly, as Osric delivers his invitation to the fencing match (V.ii.81–176), Horatio makes satiric remarks about him, possibly as asides, possibly as comments to Hamlet.

Of the other three possible trios, two involve the Ghost. When the Ghost beckons Hamlet to follow him (I.iv.57–78ff.), Horatio and Marcellus, acting redundantly, try to stop him. We thus have the Ghost beckoning Hamlet, and so exerting one force. Horatio and Marcellus exert a counterforce, and Hamlet, caught between the two, tries to break away. In a sense he is aligned with the Ghost, but since his efforts are directed against his friends, one could regard this action as triadic. In effect, this is analogous to the trial structure in which two forces opposed to each other are directed at a third figure caught between the two.

What appears to be a similar instance occurs in Hamlet's scene with his mother when the Ghost appears to chide him for delay (III.iv.103–37). The pattern is different from the first, however. When the Ghost appears, Hamlet speaks to it, while Gertrude looks on in amazement. The Ghost directs Hamlet's attention to his mother. From there, Hamlet tries to point out the Ghost's presence to Gertrude. Thus, the two portions of the segment are made up of binary action with observation followed by a duet with a significant mute.

The final trio (if indeed it is one) is odd. It occurs at the very end of the play when Fortinbras and the Ambassadors from England enter simultaneously (V.ii.350). Both react with astonishment at the display of bodies, though the Ambassadors report the deaths of Rosencrantz and Guildenstern, expecting gratitude for the news. Horatio, however, replies to the prince and Ambassadors jointly, so that in effect they are treated redundantly before Fortinbras assumes the prerogative in his final speech. Thus, although superficially the conclusion has a triadic appearance, it is mostly an extended duet.

In enumerating the trios in *Hamlet*, I have so far omitted larger group scenes. These now have to be considered along with group scenes in general. If the trio has limited forms, what of the many scenes, ceremonial and otherwise, in which numerous people gather onstage? What are their principles of arrangement? Once multiple figures assemble before an audience, their positioning and movements become overtly spectacular as well as potentially chaotic. Their entrances, exits, and dispositions then become pressing matters. Even more pressing becomes the challenge to impart significance to the group.

Assembling many people before an audience is inherently exciting. Whether we call attention to the similarities or the differences between individuals doesn't seem to matter. A crowd begets a crowd. And when the performing crowd assumes any presentational order—the same costumes, for instance, or a processional sequence—the impact is multiplied. I have touched on certain kinds of groups previously, most particularly as they appear in shows of glorification: parades and pageants. But many of the same factors are present when we deal with groups appearing in dramatic shows. In practice, the assemblage of groups in a playing area can take any of dozens of forms, but in effect we can distinguish two main types of organization, sufficiently different in nature, that embrace a host of specific examples. Through the study of their principles we can discern the power and the problems of massing many performers onstage.

One type of group scene has a formal basis of arrangement, fundamentally presentational in nature. That is, in certain periods, a specific principle for relating groups of performers may have evolved and become established as a theatrical convention. The Greek chorus and the *corps de ballet* are two examples of this. Whatever the initial motive may have been that led to the formalization of the Greek chorus into two sub–choruses (both serving under a choral leader), by the classical period this structure was firmly entrenched in theatrical practice. Each Greek playwright could, and to a certain extent did, utilize the chorus in his own way, but no matter how disparate the dramatic uses, the fundamental group structure remained unviolated.

Not all formal group scenes require a presentational basis. The formality of some may stem from a ceremonial source which may be civic, religious, social, or military. The stage show may imitate these schemes either in the order of their observance or in the appearance of the performers. When in 1911 Max Reinhardt first staged his vast pageant, *The Miracle*, he utilized the ritual of the Mass and other church services as the basis for many scenes. Sometimes the strict replication of the ceremony could be appealing (the baptism of the infant Elizabeth in *Henry VIII* [V.v]), though often enough a shorthand version of a ceremony is utilized. This applies to trial scenes as well as ceremonies involving greetings and farewells.

Allied to these formal means of presentation are some instances of staging in which it may be difficult, if not impossible, to separate the presentational from the ceremonial basis of the crowd scene. These cases occur most frequently among peoples for whom the social and religious sources of performance are not entirely divorced from entertainment. The Indian ritual reported by Linda Jenkins is arranged in a highly formal manner for its efficacious purposes.[2] While there is an audience to witness the performance, the motivation of the arrangement seems primarily religious. By contrast, the Okumkpo performance among the Nigerian Igbo has a strict arrangement of two primary performers and a chorus set in an established pattern and oriented toward the male audience which is the recipient of the performers' lampoons.[3] In this instance it is not easy to say to what extent the pattern embodies some extra-presentational intent and to what extent it serves the main purpose of contacting its audience. Probably even in the conventional disposition of the Greek chorus there is a vestigial trace of a religious rite, though by classical times the explicit religious element had disappeared.

Whatever its nature, then, the presentational convention or the ceremonial pattern gives a crowd scene a spatial and temporal order by which the performers can arrange themselves. In most instances the order, whatever it may be, makes considerable use of redundancy and mutes. During the tragic odes the Greek choruses function redundantly as do the choruses in Shakespeare, especially those that were considerably elaborated in the eighteenth and nineteenth centuries, and which utilized many spear-carriers to dress the stage. There is, however, a distinction between a group such as a chorus and a crowd of spear-carriers. In a chorus the performers are images of each other. They speak very much the same lines, if they speak at all; they dance pretty much the same steps; and they operate on a level of equality with each other. In ceremonial processions or assemblages, however, the sort that filled the enormous stages of nineteenth-century England, the crowd is often ordered in a hierarchical manner. A liturgical procession, for instance, may commence with altar boys and conclude with the most eminent prelate. A scene at a monarch's court may have common soldiers ringing officers, knights, high clergy and nobles, all arranged in a spatially hierarchical manner.

A further distinction may be made between the hierarchical and the non-hierarchical schemes. The hierarchical arrangement usually serves to build up the scene for the entrance of the principal performers or it serves as background for them. While occasionally the hierarchy may come to the fore, mainly in processions, normally it remains in the background and often plays the role of living scenery. On the other hand, the equable chorus, while often thrust into the background (in Greek tragedy, opera, or ballet), does have its own performing time when taking the stage. It does so, of course, as a unit, but unlike the hierarchical arrangement, the choral arrangement allows the active performance either of a small group or a moderately large one.

Quite different from the formal type of crowd scene, at least in principle, is the casual crowd scene. A crowd scene is more flexible in numbers and formation than the formal type. It may consist of a handful of characters or an enormous mass. The basis for arranging the activity of the crowd is neither an established theatrical pattern nor a recognized ceremonial action. Therefore, the principles for ordering must derive from the dramatic situation or the way the situation is staged. This does not mean necessarily that the scene will lack presentational order. Rather, the order will appear to arise organically from the act itself no matter how formally or schematically it may be realized.

One illustration of a formal result arising from a casual source is evident in expressionist performance. The manipulation of the crowd in Ernst Toller's *Masse-Mensch* was plastic, the crowd expressing shared emotional and psychical states in a unified manner. Its uniformity in reaching out or shunning persons and objects was carried out in a formal manner. The fact that twenty or thirty people were involved at once made the show more powerful and exciting. Less uniform though nonetheless unified was the kind of standardized rigid movement used by the crowd on Fifth Avenue in Scene V of *The Hairy Ape*. Though some of the actors had individual remarks, they functioned in movement and appearance as a class group with which Yank had to contend. In these cases, although the root idea has no inherently formal expression, the stylistic outlook, which pitted the individual against the mass, led to a formalized staging.

But even where the pattern is less overtly formal, crowd scenes invite some degree of formalization or at the very least considerable redundancy of response in order to maintain presentational focus. When Antony delivers his funeral oration over the body of Caesar, he is the precipitating figure, working on the Roman Plebians, who, in their turn, constitute a single mass (III.ii). Among them there are nearly fifty speeches, yet all are echoes of each other. They fall into six or seven sequences, each with considerable redundancy. Typical of one sequence is the Plebians' response to the unveiling of Caesar's body. One after another, they say in turn: "O piteous spectacle! O noble Caesar! O woeful day! O traitors, villains! O most bloody sight! We will be revenged," and then all join together: "Revenge! About! Seek! Burn! Fire! Kill! Slay! Let not a traitor live!" (III.ii.197–205). This type of mounting response is highly uniform, and constitutes a single mass response for Antony. In this way the scene turns out to be essentially binary in structure.

Contemporary taste may prefer to see the crowd far more

individualized, and productions now do tend to encourage actors to make themselves more distinct. Nevertheless, the action cannot move very far from this essential group response without disrupting the clarity of presentation. Ironically, the ultimate effect of erupting chaos seems best achieved by preserving the unity of a swayed mob rather than by individualizing the figures.

The inclination of more contemporary taste is apparent in another scene centered on an unpopular speaker addressing or attempting to address a crowd. I refer to Dr. Stockmann's speech to his fellow townspeople in the fourth act of *An Enemy of the People*. Having been denied access to the public in order to report his medical findings about pollution in the medicinal baths, he has secured a large house where he calls a meeting. At the meeting are Stockmann, his family, and one supporter, Captain Horster. Also present are his brother, the Mayor, who opposes him, as well as ex-supporters and a crowd of townspeople.

In developing the action, Ibsen avoids the near formal type of redundancy that we find in Shakespeare. Instead, he seeks to give the impression of a group of individuals, all independently attending the meeting. He opens the act by introducing the exchange among four men (Shakespeare also had four Plebians). But Ibsen gives some of them names, though the speech-prefixes indicate First, Second, Third, and Fourth Man. The sentiments they express, however, are fairly uniform. At the end of this brief introductory exchange when a Man in another group asks, "Whose side are we on here, eh?," someone replies, "Just you keep an eye on Aslaksen [the taxpayers' representative], and do what *he* does."[4]

Once the meeting gets under way, Aslaksen takes the lead by calling for a chairman, and by that means assumes control. The Mayor, Hovstad the editor, and others support and echo one another so that the action resolves itself into an essentially binary tussle between Stockmann and the others. Amidst the struggle of Stockmann against the unified group, Ibsen introduces as a subsidiary grace note, a disruptive drunkard. When he interrupts, he is thrown out. Later he returns, and is immediately thrown out again. The action reinforces the unity of outlook, and lends variety and verisimilitude to the performance.

Structurally, the scene has the pattern of the one against the many. It moves forward in two waves: the first wave of action shows Stockmann's futile effort to give his speech about the baths in the face of the concerted opposition of the town leaders supported moderately by the people. The second wave occurs when Stockmann attacks the townspeople as a benighted majority, and builds the intense polarization between himself and the town. In this kind of casual crowd scene, then, there are many minor details that suggest the variety of "real life," but the dramaturgic core consists of Stockmann on the one side and the redundant crowd on the other.

The scripted indications for a crowd suggest only in the most allusive way the full impact of its presentation. Since the nineteenth century, producers and/or directors have used the text as only the pretext for staging a mass scene. Whether or not that staging embodies the core structure of the action depends on the philosophical orientation of the producer. With the rise of antiquarianism early in the nineteenth century and the emergence of naturalism toward the end of the century, the motives in staging often came from outside the script. Both movements shared the assumption that the text should be tied to history, that is, that setting and spectacle should reveal the actual period of a scene. That assumption led to increasing pictorialization at the expense of dramatic development. Or rather, the pictorialization became the means of dramatic development. In particular, group scenes, in court or on the street, supplied the opportunity to amplify the image of modes and manners. All sorts of illustrative business were introduced in order to create a vivid picture of life, whether it be in the Verona of *Romeo and Juliet* or the Senate of Caesar's Rome.

With the emergence of naturalism, authors wrote scripts that stressed the coming and going of daily life at the expense of the development of the action. Elmer Rice's *Street Scene* was notable for depicting tenement life while its central plot told a sordid but conventional story of jealousy and murder. Yet even in those cases where presentation of the hustle and bustle of urban life became the main purpose of a show, the principles of organizing that presentation remained the same. By combining hierarchy, formalization, and fragment sequences, a producer could choreograph a display of life. For the most part, these displays tended to astonish through pictorial means and the deliberate creation of "real" appearances. But in essence they more usually served as a background of action rather than as the action itself.

With the rise of expressionism and its many derivatives, such as Andrei Serban's staging of *The Trojan Women*, the crowd becomes an abstract instrument upon which the director plays. Without resorting to the strict formality of ballet, the director creates expressive patterns to which single individuals are subordinated. These patterns are often so orchestrated that the result is much closer to dance than what is more usually thought of as dramatic movement. Utilizing a dominant image, such as the Tree of Life (*The Serpent*), the performers merge into one another and achieve a presentational focus through the harmonization of their movements and sounds.

In these types of crowd scenes, we have examples, previously discussed, of the vital source of the performance being generated, not by the performers before the audience, but by an external figure who does not appear to be the audience. In *Nicholas Nickleby* one did have the sense that the crowd into which the actors periodically assembled themselves did emerge from the performers' own intentions. When the production shifted from self-generated scenes to jointly-generated crowd scenes or choral statements, the action never seemed to arise from an offstage star—the director or choreographer—but from the common resolution of players.

The crowd scene, then, because of its potential for diffusing attention, utilizes a variety of techniques for concentrating its effects. Formal structures such as choruses have always been and continue to be employed. Organic dramatic arrangements, especially those of a binary nature, also frequently appear. With the explosive experimentation of the twentieth century, performers have made new efforts to utilize large numbers in innovative ways, but in actuality most of the techniques are variants of the conventional means at the disposal of the performer. Given the fact that human beings defying their own limitations provide the foundation of theatrical presentation, neither technological discovery nor sudden illumination is likely to change the basic theatrical conditions. Most of the principles of organization are or have been in operation. We may use them for new purposes, but it is unlikely that we will invent new structures. That is why the binary and triadic exchanges continue to be the basis for most theatrical performance, whether of duets, trios, or crowd scenes.

However true this last point may be, the very aspirations of dramatic form tend to push theatre beyond its presentational limits. Whether to produce a striking show or to create a perfect reflection, theatre constantly seeks to get beyond its own limits of subject and form. Since its very center is self-generating, it is inevitable that the premise of autonomy must be constantly reconfirmed by plays and scenes that do not degenerate into the merely predictable. The predictable is an essential element of performance, but it must be leavened with surprise if a show is to sustain and heighten interest. Consequently, the root binary structure is continuously being modified and disguised so that the hand of the inventor is not evident. Yet, because the binary structure is so necessary to presentational coherence, it cannot be entirely dispensed with.

During the last generation we have seen massive efforts to reject the conventionally structured plays that stem from the Greeks, extend through the French, and come to us by way of Ibsen. In the United States, at least, looser forms, often binary statistically but not dynamically, have appeared. Strongly influenced by the visual media of film and television, writers have attempted to link scenes in allusive rather than self-generated ways. Instead of creating material that can arise assertively from the performer, they have leaned toward tepid kinds of portraiture through which characters reveal passing sensations. With the aid of a camera, such passing sensations can affect us. But as the bases for presentational acts, they lack the vibrant structure the theatre demands. It is no wonder, then, that some of our major dramatists at mid-century have been people like Pinter and Beckett who give us unexpected images often through conventional, in effect, classical patterns.

One kind of multi-personed scene remains to be considered, however. It is probably the most successful attempt by the theatre to escape its simply structured forms. But it is tricky, the kind of scene that can easily lose direction or vibrancy. I am referring to the scene that depicts a sizeable group—a half-dozen to a dozen characters—each of whom it seeks to individualize. Sometimes the characters are individualized separately, that is, in duets and trios, and only later in the play brought together as a group. At other times, the group is together from the beginning, often perpetually together, as in Maxim Gorky's *The Lower Depths* or Eugene O'Neill's *The Iceman Cometh*. In these plays, the individualization has to take place while most of the characters are present.

Plays such as these have a decided spatial orientation. Often, though not always, they occur in a single setting, and the audience follows the action not merely by seeing a sequence of scenes but by observing segments of scenes set next to each other. We think of Chekhov employing this kind of arrangement although he is not necessarily the person who most depends on such spatial organization. While the principal examples of this type of group scene are associated with realistic or naturalistic drama, they do not all come from such plays. Pirandello, for example, frequently has scenes of quasi–philosophical discussion cast into superficially realistic scenes.

It is significant that these group scenes have a novelistic quality. Just as many plays in the last generation show the invasion of film techniques, so did certain plays of the late nineteenth century reflect a fictional ambling. The best among these plays founded the ambling style on a dramaturgic base, however. Chekhov's work, as I mentioned, is usually regarded as having just this sort of ambling or talkative character. Among many of the Russian critics, his work is also regarded as novelistic rather than dramatic. Yet if we look at the apparent drift of conversation in his plays, we see that his action, while not large-scaled, is firm.

He often builds an act on a central form of activity that is repeated by various characters in a sequence of segments. The core action of the third act of *The Three Sisters* is a series of confessions by Tchebutykin, Irina, Olga, Masha, and finally Andrei. Irena's confession is half heard by Olga, but all the rest are delivered as if to thin air since the actual or potential listeners hide or leave rather than hear the deeply personal confession. Some lesser motifs, such as various people's reactions to the fire in the town, also serve to bind the action. Moreover, these motifs and recurrent activities are arranged in a sequence of short duets with the single exception of a group scene that has at varying times from four to seven characters. Each remains individual and does not become redundant in the usual sense. Instead, the coherence is maintained by having them react variously to the same question. In one case the question has to do with aid to the victims of the fire and whether Masha could or should play a concert for their benefit. It is important to note that the shape of action is reactive. No one is pursuing a goal. Instead, a number of people have parallel responses.

In the last act of George Bernard Shaw's *Heartbreak House*, a play that he subtitles "A Fantasia in the Russian Manner on English Themes," hosts and guests at Captain Shotover's house gather on the terrace in the evening. They chat, they dispute, they amble conversationally, and finally when an enemy bomber flies over and drops a bomb nearby, they exult in the excitement. Again, the movement of the act is reflective rather than active. Here and there a character adopts an active stance, but that is momentary and does not have the distinction of making a separate segment. Though claiming ancestry in Chekhov's works, Shaw is doing something quite different. The "extended" conversations in Chekhov are remarkably brief: he tends to write sequences of more or less short fragments so seamlessly stitched together that they appear to be one unbroken action, though they compose a carefully arranged spatial and temporal pattern. It is true that in *Heartbreak House* Shaw comes much closer to stimulating the kind of pervasive mood usually associated with Chekhov. By conjuring this otherworldly nocturnal atmosphere, Shaw allows the characters' thoughts to escape their bodies and to create an awesome premonition of change. But he is in truth much closer to the impressionistic reflectiveness of Maurice Maeterlinck than to the tight mosaic of Chekhov.

In *The Iceman Cometh*, O'Neill seeks to sustain a series of extended group scenes at the same time that he is individualizing his characters. In the main he keeps them from slipping into redundant positions *vis-à-vis* each other. By combining a variety of techniques, he maintains theatrical concentration in tension with apparent verisimilar diffusion.

He does this first by "typing" a number of the secondary characters, that is, giving each a distinctive history and personality. But also a characteristic response. Hugo Kalmar the Anarchist, Cecil Lewis the Limey, Piet Wetjoen the Boer, Willie Oban the Harvard-educated derelict—each has an organic yet highly crystallized response to events and persons. Like musical motifs, these responses are interwoven through the play. In addition, O'Neill has the entire group go through a parallel experience: in the first act they awaken from a drunken sleep; in the second act they react to Hickey's speech; in the third act they attempt to live without their "pipe dreams," and in the fourth they revert to their old illusions. In that way the majority of characters parallel each other's actions.

But the principal lines of action in the play involve Dan Parritt's demands on Larry and Hickey's attempt to change the lives of all the inhabitants of Harry Hope's bar. These two lines are essentially binary in nature and are embodied in binary scenes. Each act has a Larry–Parritt segment, a duet echoed by other duets among characters such as Lewis and Wetjoen. The main action, however, pits Hickey against all the others. Sometimes he has exchanges with the group, sometimes with individuals. While most of the other characters are constantly reacting to events, Hickey's arrival portends an active tone. He tries to change things, and he appears to succeed. By taking the lead, Hickey gives much of the action a simpler dual character than is at first apparent, for on the level of performance, the play invites the creation of a many-peopled setting.

The physical bar as haven for these refugees from life keeps shifting from background to foreground. Sometimes attention moves rapidly from one to another character, creating a mosaic of responses. But then the entire group retreats into the background as a particular exchange comes into focus—between Larry and Parritt or Chuck and Rocky, etc. Thus, by juggling duets with multiple parallel responses, O'Neill achieves an effect of richness and variety. He seems to escape the binary limitations of the drama and to produce the bubbling abundance of the novel.

In this respect, it is interesting to note that the same effect of novelistic richness characterized *Nicholas Nickleby*. However, it was not achieved through the kind of dramatic density found in O'Neill or Chekhov, but through the use of choral background to link an extended sequence of more conventionally structured scenes. It was the unusual length of eight-and-a-half hours, vividly filled of course, which ultimately realized a Dickensian abundance.

The stunning plays that stretch the limits of dramatic presentation emphasize all the more how difficult it is for the drama to get beyond its binary base. The root exchange between performer and audience can be enfolded within other dualities: the exchange of actor and actor becomes an indirect exchange between players and audience. The duet of players can be further extended as an exchange with a chorus that then becomes an exchange with the audience. Or, as play-within-the-play scenes demonstrate, one plane of duets can become the source of another plane of duets.

In the striking conclusion of Kyd's *The Spanish Tragedy*, the inner play has a love segment between Erasto and Perseda that is watched by the Bashaw and the Vizier (also characters in the play). The King of Spain and the Viceroy of Portugal, with others, are spectators of this play. But both the play-within-the-play and the spectators watching the play are watched by the Ghost of Andrea and the figure of Revenge. And finally all of these planes of observance are shown to us, the audience. Thus, spatially we have a series of duets within duets as well as a sequence of fragmentary duets that unfold before us. In the elaboration of action, this is the more common manner in which dramatic presentation has evolved.

The alternate method of creating novelistic multiplicity has produced some extraordinary theatre. But it is limited in scope for two principal reasons: because transforming multiple perspectives into dramatic presentation is so difficult an art, and because the diffusion of presentational energy among too many figures goes against the very nature of the medium.

Chapter 12

Orchestration

One of the keys to successful performing is spontaneity. The actor seeks to create that "illusion of the first time." But is spontaneity wholly an illusion? Insofar as the action to be portrayed is concerned, the actor or actress indeed creates an illusion of experiencing it for the first time. The act of performing that action, however, does have an actual measure of spontaneity which is affected by four factors: the particular circumstances of performance, the people to whom the actor plays, the disposition of the actor at the time, and the professional concern to keep a show fresh. Part of the actor's work is to prevent a performance from becoming routine, and therefore new stimuli that will individualize a performance are welcomed. Thus, spontaneity in dramatic presentation is both an illusion and an actuality, with the actuality often fueling the illusion.

Spontaneity, whether an illusion or an actuality, is the cutting edge of a show's self-generating nature. We expect a performance to address us immediately; we also expect it to arise directly from the performers. One of the most deadly experiences is to hear an actor recite lines as though they have been memorized.

The importance of the show arising—or seeming to arise—from the performer is strikingly evident in animal acts, particularly those involving the display of anthropomorphic skills such as counting or selecting objects. Invariably, the trainer is present while a trick is being performed, yet the appeal of the show lies in the ability of the trainer to create the illusion that a dog, for example, is an independent creature with its own will and judgment. As noted earlier, much of the delight in comic versions of dog tricks grows out of the illusion that the dog does not take the trainer seriously. In short, the illusion of the first time also contains an illusion—or the actuality—of the performer's responsibility for what he or she does.

The central importance of these qualities of self-generation is all the greater in the drama. Words, gestures, lines of action, all should appear to spring immediately from the actor. Whatever the degree of preparation beforehand, the unfolding of a play relies on an organic process that seems located in the people engaged in the action.

The fact that the prevalent type of performance in the drama is the duet, as I have shown, makes self-generation of even greater moment. It makes the illusion of spontaneous exchange between two people a foundation of dramatic presentation. How then to reconcile spontaneity and the self-generating impression with the obvious fact that most plays are carefully rehearsed and planned?

Rehearsal and preplanning can involve the loosest agreement between players about the scenario they will do or the most minute arrangement of movements and intonations. At one extreme is the *commedia dell'arte* with its rough outlines and traditional business. At the other is the Noh theatre with its finely detailed patterns of dance and song handed down from one generation to another. In each case, of course, the actor has a different degree of latitude in varying a performance, the Italian feeling free, perhaps even impelled, to seize upon the momentariness of a performance to run a variation of the scenario, while the Noh actor resists any impulse to alter his design. Nevertheless, despite these wide differences in preplanning, the actor in the midst of performance propels the act both actually and illusionistically.

Self-generation for the actor is thus a paradox. The actor who appears onstage, playing to an audience, is the one responsible for the show. No matter who was involved in the planning, no matter who conducted rehearsals, only the actors actually appearing before the audience can create the play for it. Whatever anyone wishes to communicate theatrically, it has to be done through the performer. Yet to create a convincing illusion of autonomy, the actor draws upon long years of practice and preparation.

This fact does not entirely resolve the question of the nature of performance, however. Between the need for spontaneity and the need for preplanning, a large number of options are possible. In the space between the two needs fall many of the arts that we associate with the theatre: the art of playwriting, the art of stage design, and the art of stage directing. Whatever originality is involved, these are essentially arts of orchestration. They are ways of shaping and refining the potential act of the performer.

Early in my discussion of presentation, I distinguished between self-generating acts and choreographed acts. Obviously, the chorus is a model of the choreographed act, for the performance of the same movements by a group simultaneously points to a joint resolution among them or to the shaping hand of a choreographer. In highly patterned acts, choreography can and often does produce an impression of puppets or stage properties manipulated by an unseen master. The flamboyant dancing in the last scene of *A Chorus Line* is a clear demonstration of this.

In some sense any of the supporting arts of the actor limits and defines the actor's energies and, therefore, imposes some restraint on spontaneity. Yet this is not a necessary consequence of pre-planning. Rehearsal, even the most detailed and careful, can serve to support and encourage the actor's independence onstage. What I am suggesting here is that in regarding the familiar arts of dramatic composition, designing, and directing, we do not consider them as independent arts—indeed, they cannot exist without the performer—but as arts for refining the language of the actor.

From this perspective, writing and designing require further explanation. Undoubtedly, the poet and artist exist independently and nobly outside the theatre. It is when they enter the theatre that their roles become problematic. Before anything else, they surrender autonomy, perhaps the designer less so than the poet. After all, the designer's work appears directly before the audience. But it does so in a subsidiary position, not as the prime focus of attention but as background and support for the player. The poet's work, on the other hand, appears before the public only in a filtered form. It is strained through the art of the actor, and therefore ever so slightly heightened or transformed.

Since the writer is usually the inventor of the fiction that the actor plays, it is tempting to give him or her primacy. From the point of view of actual practice, this is too simple a proposition, for in the shaping of an actor's performance we can discern three distinct planes of form.

The first is the language of forms that the art of presentation can accommodate. It is this plane that is the main concern of this book. It embraces the possible shows that presentation can generate as well as the primary structures into which performance most naturally falls.

The second plane consists of the cultural forms that rise to dominance in any period or among any people. They are governing structures; they often prevail for long periods of time, and they usually drive out competing forms. How such forms crystallize is not easy to say. But it is certainly the case that it is not the writer, so far as we know, who produces this second plane of structures. They appear to evolve, presumably, through the agency of whoever plays them. Tradition has it that Thespis first introduced playing, functioning apparently as player and author, that is, as the completely autonomous player. The origins of Kabuki are traced to Okuni who danced in a dry river bed at the imperial capital of Kyoto in the early seventeenth century. These cases prove nothing because we know so little about them. They do suggest, however, that performing and the planning of performance emanated from a single sensibility. But however the governing forms emerged, by the time we can deal with historical examples, a clearly articulated pattern of performance exists. In effect, the actor's range of possibilities is already defined.

The third plane encompasses the individual expressions of the language of forms. For the most part, for the actors, the governing forms exist prior to any individual shaping of them. If the actors are not creating them themselves, they are working within patterns already established. That does not mean that these patterns are rigid and unchanging. It does mean that their main features are often set before we have fully realized scripts as historical documents. The Athenian tragic contest was in existence at least eighty years before we have the first extant play of Aeschylus, and a hundred years of Tudor drama preceded Shakespeare. In short, a performing process precedes and helps to shape the dramatist's work.

Within the framework, the written script does not merely involve the manipulation of language or gesture, but also provides a preliminary shaping of the art in which others will participate. It involves "predicting" how someone else will handle the material being devised. It is in that sense a matter of orchestration. Depending upon the interaction between the writer and the actor, the written piece can be highly refined or not. That refinement is not merely a matter of making changes in rehearsal. The dramatist can infuse the work beforehand with appropriate material for the actor. We may have another paradox here. In order to realize a personal vision, the playwright may need to take fullest account of the actor's art and allow it maximum expression.

Given the nature of theatrical presentation, it is inevitable that there be struggles for dominance among the various people engaged in theatrical production. History is full of conflicts between dramatists and actors, actors and directors, directors and designers. These conflicts are the natural consequence of the tension inherent in the need for self-generation and planning in theatre. Often that tension, especially as it has existed between dramatist and actor, has proved fruitful, as seems to have been the case between Shakespeare and his fellow actors. But that balance is extremely rare. More frequent are the instances in which one or another of the non-performing artists seeks to make the orchestrating process the prevailing one in performance.

As one might expect, the rise of the stage director at the end of the nineteenth century precipitates the most vigorous effort to turn dramatic performance into a thoroughly orchestrated art. Richard Wagner is the orchestrator *par excellence*. By controlling invention, tone, and image, by attempting to balance all the performing units precisely, he exerted extraordinary control over the shape of presentation. Music itself exerts tremendous restraint on the autonomy of performance. But music allied with control over other facets of the show, as exercised by Wagner, only defined the pattern more clearly. In his aspirations and practice, he was the forerunner of those who work in the looser realms of the spoken drama but who seek a similar kind of orchestration for the entire performance.

Meyerhold's early experiments with Maeterlinck's plays show us directorial orchestration in a highly refined form. Treating his actions as designed properties, he arranged them in flat planes to produce haunting stage pictures. These experiments coincided with Edward Gordon Craig's interest in subjecting the actor to design control. Like Meyerhold, Craig sought to place the performer within a frame in order to function as a visual and sonic element rather than an independent voice. Although these efforts did not become dominant, in large measure they embodied a trend that has prevailed. Orchestration has replaced self-generation as the governing principle of theatrical presentation. Nowhere is this more evident than in the experimental work of Foreman and Grotowski. Usually working through a principal actor who functions as an *alter ego*, they devise and shape the performance precisely, even to the slightest gesture. The quasi-religious tone of performance, especially in Grotowski's work, protects the show from intrusion, either of the audience or of the actor's individuality. In these instances the need for planning—for orchestration—has gone to an extreme. The onstage performer, instead of being an autonomous performer, has become an instrument for an offstage designer. Instead of designing through inanimate matter, however, the designer works through the arrangement of living bodies.

Regarding dramatists, designers, and directors as primarily orchestrators of actors does not diminish their importance, although it does cast their work in a different light. The common notion of theatre as a composite of arts distorts the actual process. So-called closet dramas mutely testify to the dead end to which literary drama is doomed if it is not filtered through the actor's art. That condition, however, (the condition whereby on the phenomenological plane contributory efforts are subordinated to acting) does not mean that the work of orchestration is less significant. In truth, in many cultures it has been the fineness of orchestration that has enabled acting and through it writing to reach the most sophisticated levels. But the ultimate quality of any contribution depends upon the degree to which it aids actability, that is, presentation.

Each of the three principal orchestrators works through a major facet of the actor's art. While the playwright does invent the fiction in large measure, and arranges its parts in an effective sequence, we usually think of the writer as providing the words that the actor speaks. And with few exceptions that is indeed the case. The words, however, not only carry the sentiments and thoughts of the separate characters; they also have to embody the potentialities for different kinds of interchange between actor and audience, actor and actor. Much of playwriting is rudimentary, providing an outline of events and rough expression of relations which the actor has to particularize. The text of a melodrama often illustrates this kind of rough orchestration. In effect, here the writer does not go much beyond creating a primary structure of acting, while infusing that action with details and sentiments appropriate for the audience of the time.

Even in the most vital of theatrical periods, it is this sort of material with which the actor has to work, and it is remarkable—as is so evident in commercial as well as institutional production—how much an actor can do with limited material. But it is with the work of the handful of exceptional writers that we usually associate the art of playwriting. The major playwrights may utilize the same primary structures that are available to the hacks, but they alter and refine them into plays of extraordinary resonance. That is where the role of orchestrator achieves highest fulfillment. No matter how versatile and resourceful a performer may be when working alone, seldom is that subtlety achieved that comes about in partnership with a great writer.

Orchestration in this sense takes account of the special art of the actor and the special nature of presentation. It provides material with which the actor can fuse so that what emerges onstage is a single, autonomous performance. Where the actors recognize and respect that kind of refinement, they come closer to realizing their art.

Unquestionably, the English Renaissance offers the best example of rich exchange between actors and writers, and within the period, the company in which Shakespeare was a partner was the prime example. Certainly, the actors did not make Shakespeare the genius he was, yet without them and the conditions that the age afforded, he hardly could have produced his masterpieces. Although the actors were the operators and prime movers of the professional acting companies, they ceded to writers the job of supplying them with texts. They commissioned writers, approved the final copy, and ordered revisions, as they wished. On the other hand, there is little evidence of interference with scripts. Rather, it appears that once the subject was agreed upon, the carrying out of the work was left in the hands of the writers. Yet since the plays always had to go back to the actors for approval and were immediately put into production, the relationship between literature and stage was unusually close.

Unfortunately, we know very little about how Shakespeare worked with his partners. We have only the evidence of the results. We do know that he and the other actors worked closely for nearly twenty-five years. After an initial start, he wrote for the same people. And they sufficiently respected his work to see that at last it got into print. To the extent that they shared in his growth as an artist, he and they jointly orchestrated four to five thousand performances of all kinds of plays that they gave in his working lifetime.

Shakespeare's power as a writer for actors arises from his firm command of binary action. From the very beginning he had some measure of control in this direction, but as he developed as a dramatist, his artistry in evoking action became astonishing. In his

greatest works, he infuses almost every line with its implicit
counterforce. Most obvious are those instances where an opening
line tells a history of dispute. "Tush! never tell me," opens *Othello*
in the midst of Roderigo's argument with Iago (I.i.1). Such focused
and vivid energy is easy for the actor to incorporate and make his
own. But Shakespeare supplies such movements in far more subtle
ways. As the Venetian nobles sift through reports about Turkish
naval action, one of the Senators, who lacks even a name, rejects
the apparent Turkish feint at Rhodes. "'Tis a pageant / To keep us
in false gaze" (I.ii. 18–19). Even this direct statement is filled with
its counter-action, for in its use of the image of a pageant or show
to distract us, the line urges us to look elsewhere. That capacity to
suggest and promote dialectic action is the very thing that enables
actors to shape their performance finely without surrendering their
own generating impulse. In fact, the playwright, by infusing the
language with its own resonant response, makes it absolutely
necessary that an independent-spirited acting group realize the
work. Shakespeare's early formal rhetoric might be orchestrated
artificially, but only the organic exercise of acting can lead us to
realize his major plays.

The designer too affects the actor's work, not simply by
controlling the visual presentation but by shaping the context
within which the actors present themselves. Obviously, the more
they are embedded in that context, the greater the role played by
the designer. In this sense the designer is not merely the person
who plans the setting, but any of the persons engaged in creating
the visual and auditory environment as well as in determining the
garments and make-up worn by the actors. Although in the
contemporary theatre, practical exigencies of production have
encouraged specialization in various aspects of design, the designer's
field of operation is that of connecting in some way the performer
with the environment. In essence, the designer has a framing
responsibility, although it is not uncommon for the design to
swallow or attempt to swallow the performer.

Theatre which relies on found space—a street or a square—
does not offer the designer much room to shape the physical
environment. The design of pageants, for example, involves
discrete theatrical pieces: floats and street structures such as arches
of triumph. The performers can be incorporated within them,
although the plan often serves to celebrate the individual. Similarly,
theatres with traditional stages, such as the Greek, Elizabethan, or

Noh, because of the generalized space and the familiar costumes, tend to recede from the actor. That is, the actor usually plays before such a stage, not within it, and maintains a certain degree of independence from it.

In the western theatre, however, the Italian Renaissance introduced control over the actor's space, and, therefore, control over the actor's presentation. This absorption of the actor into an idiosyncratic environment was not complete until the advent of naturalism. It is thus easy to underestimate the long gestation of such control. Nor was the absorption of the actor immediate. Beginning early in the seventeenth century and until the mid-nineteenth, the process was underway. For many years, despite the visual attraction that the designer could provide, the players and their audiences remained in front of the stage picture. It was not until the nineteenth century, when the theatricalized composition of the tableau caught people's fancy, that the embedding of the actor in space was brought to completion. It is not surprising that the process first began in operatic and balletic theatre where the orchestration of voice and movement could be assisted by the orchestration of space and light.

We cannot gainsay the wonders that designers produced. Once they took command of the highly defined space of the proscenium stage, they were able to create astonishing effects within which the performer had a subsidiary place. The subordination of the actor to the effect was a necessary part of the design. It is no wonder that the first English stage artist, Inigo Jones, flourished in a theatre with amateur actors while the professional actors of the day continued to use a fixed stage. Ultimately, however, the professional actors had to come to terms with the designer: to use him or be used by him.

Like the playwright, the designer refines one aspect of the performer's art in order to enrich it. But if designers are to do that without absorbing the actor, then they must accept the inevitable incompleteness of their work, leaving the actor to complete it. So much seems obvious. Yet in practice, this is extraordinarily hard to accomplish, as is evident in the most intimate interaction between actor and designer, that of costuming. Costume design operates at the intersection between the setting and the actor.

It was the last phase of design to pass from the actor to a specialist, for until the end of the nineteenth and even into the twentieth century, actors were largely responsible for what they wore. With the growing use of the design plate as the point where costuming begins, the costume emerges as an autonomous piece of art into which the actor fits.

In practice, naturally, there are varying degrees of accommodation between actors and designers. One assists the other, or one makes use of the other. But in principle and in the historic process guided by that principle, the actor is drawn into the design frame to realize the designer's conception. When the actor seizes design, as Henry Irving did with sets and lights, he can turn it to his own use. He can determine the frame within which he chooses to appear. In that respect, he accedes to the dominance of design. The essential task, however, is to utilize design to support and enhance the autonomous action of the performer.

The director is the person whose involvement in presentation is both the most ephemeral and the most pervasive. By director we must understand not only the figure who works with the actors in a production but also the producer insofar as he or she conceives of a show or determines the form it is to take. Diaghilev, though more producer than choreographer, did determine the style and repertoire of the Ballets Russes so that he cannot be ignored in any consideration of stage direction. Unlike the playwright and the designer, the director tends to work through the sensibilities of others. While the lines written by the writer are those actually uttered by the actor, nothing tangible emanating from the performer belongs to the director. The consequence is that the director is doubly unseen, and ultimately operates indirectly.

Until the nineteenth century, the various functions that are now the privilege of the director were in the hands of actor, playwright, or designer. Much of the time the principal actor of a company served as producer-director. Occasionally, the writer assumed some of the functions, as the Greek poets seem to have done and as Goethe did at Weimar. Commencing with the Renaissance, as design came into prominence, designers such as Inigo Jones and Giacomo Torelli began to determine the shape of performances.

At certain times, and increasingly with the rise of commercial theatre after the Renaissance, a manager or a patentee lurked in the background. Men like John Rich in England and Jean-Baptiste Nicolet in France during the eighteenth century exercised effective control over the content and form of presentation at their theatres.

The emergence of a director who was not primarily an owner belongs to the nineteenth century, however. It is appropriate that his emergence in the late nineteenth century is linked with the choreographing of crowd scenes in the company of the Duke of Saxe-Meiningen. The German Duke, working directly with the actors and through the person of his stage manager, Ludwig Chronegk, sought to harmonize the physical expressiveness of the stage with correct and appropriate dress. Their work is paralleled by the care with which Boucicault staged the melodramas of his own composition. They too included action that required the careful adjustment of performance to setting and scenic transformations.

In the nineteenth and early twentieth century, the director worked through groups of actors and stage decor, usually in association with a designer. Gradually, however, the director could not ignore the fact that the principal art of presentation lay in the body and sensibility of the actor. Guiding the physical expression of the performer did not enable one to affect that psychic center from which performance stems: the imagination and its energy. While director-producers have always influenced the minds of performers, as Augustin Daly certainly did the mind of Ada Rehan, it remained for men like Stanislavsky and even more for Strasberg and Grotowski to enter the performer's psyche. Their aim was not only to determine the form of the actor's expression but to calibrate the very resonance that it evoked. In its most extreme form, such directorial invasion required the actor and actress to surrender their awareness that what they are doing is performing, and leave the entire responsibility for presentation in the hands of the director. For certain actors such actions, such childlike surrender, opened the way to exquisite nuances of sensation. The actor became a sensory machine upon which the director could play. With surrender, though, went the peculiar strength of the performer, the doubleness of playing: one plane of performance reverberating with and transcending the other.

In practice few directors so absorb the actor that the actor becomes an *alter ego*. But in principle, such potentiality for absorption always exists. The director's power lies in orchestration. Not producing anything tangible to place before an audience, the director can only influence and control others. The actor, however, can escape the director. By going onstage, and leaving the director behind, the actor is above control unless the director has achieved a psychological mastery over the performer. The more the director conceives of himself or herself as the creator of the total effect of production, the more he or she has to exert mental control over the presentation.

Of course, the advantages of directorial supervision are apparent, manifesting themselves in two main ways: through the control of proportion and of timing. However he or she may work with actors, the director seeks to place one player in relation to another in an appropriate balance, determining degrees of emphasis. The director also places the performers within a spatial frame, again deciding the arrangement of the composition. From a number of points of view, the advantages of such supervision are obvious. The performance as a whole rather than any one part receives attention, and the exhibitionist tendencies that some actors have are kept under control. Above all, it is easier to convey a single, coherent idea, a factor that is one of the irresistible attractions of directing. Through determining the portions of the play world, the director can play God in a stage universe. In this way, the director replaces the God who assigns men their parts in Calderon de la Barca's *The Great Theatre of the World*.

Influencing timing is one of the specific ways of maintaining proportion. No wonder directors such as George Abbott and George S. Kaufman were known for the pacing of their shows. Timing is one of the most important yet subtle features of performance. To the degree that a director can maintain management of the timing of a performance, to that degree he or she truly controls it. Yet timing is almost wholly in the hands of the performers. With the exception of musical performance in which the conductor plays a role, the solo performer or the performers in their various duets and trios set the rhythm of a show. Since timing and rhythm reflect the natural breathing of the action, the director uses a wide variety of methods to influence them and to assure that the rhythm evolved in rehearsal is retained in performance.

Ideally, an orchestrated performance should be a joint venture which allows a balance between spontaneity and self-generation on the one hand, and programming on the other. In such a venture the performer participates both independently and yet as a social member. How difficult it is to achieve such a balance is evident in a spectrum of theatres during the latter half of the twentieth century. Beginning in the 1950s a number of collectives appeared whose aims were to allow co-operative creation of performance. Later that co-operation went to the heart of performance in the Open Theatre where works were jointly conceived and executed. One of that theatre's last major efforts, *The Mutation Show*, was an attempt to allow each actor independent authority to shape his or her performance and yet to retain for the group the responsibility of coordinating the entire piece. The director, Joseph Chaikin, was a catalyst and yet seemed to reserve some measure of guidance, if only as a result of his previous leadership. In effect, the work sought to defy the tendency of performance to resolve itself into solos, duets, and trios by transforming redundancy into primacy. The effort failed, perhaps because performance became confused and swamped by other functions. In using themselves to dramatize themselves, the actors abandoned the doubleness of performance and only made a feint at self-generation.

One production, however, the heir of the experiments of the 1960s and 1970s, did strike a balance between self-generation and orchestration. That production was the Royal Shakespeare Company's *Nicholas Nickleby*, a work to which I have referred extensively. While it was developed by the actors and directors, it was finally shaped in its main features by a playwright, David Edgar. The directors, Trevor Nunn and John Caird, refined the work of others, and contributed to the content and scene work too. Involved in the planning from the very beginning, the actors in many cases evolved their characters from Dickens' novel directly, thus contributing independently to the final production in unusual ways. The result of this joint work was that the production combined highly coordinated segments, such as the chorus' review of the narrative at the beginning of parts two, three, and four, with vivid individual performances. Using a succession of solos, duets, and group scenes, playing sometimes directly, sometimes indirectly, *Nicholas Nickleby* exploited an immense range of performing possibilities.

The influence of years of playing Shakespeare was perhaps most visible in the production's juxtaposition of binary scenes within a performance frame that was essentially iconic. The group narration, together with the periodic stress on a narrative voice, gave the work a moral and social orientation that reaffirmed traditional values in an apparently modern style. The iconism operated on two levels. First, it worked through the exemplary story from a past world, yet a world not so past that we do not inherit its values. Secondly, in giving us Dickens' world and story, the production celebrated the author's point of view. Among its most successful features was the production's insistence on the double world of the actual and the implied, the mundane and the wondrous, presentation and representation. It gave full scope to the director's influence without inhibiting the actor's independence. In that respect, if for no other, it is a show of immense exemplary importance.

What effect this production will have on theatrical production in the future we do not know. Its elements reveal the contemporary unity of actor, actor–actor, actor–audience—a total orchestration of the elements.

Notes

Prologue

1 Leone Battista Alberti, *Ten Books on Architecture*, translated into Italian by Cosimo Bartoli, and into English by James Leoni, edited by Joseph Rykwert, London, Alec Tiranti Ltd., 1955, p. 175.
2 ibid., p. 176.
3 ibid., p. 175.

1 The idea of presentation

1 Susanne K. Langer, *Feeling and Form: A Theory of Art*, New York, Charles Scribner's Sons, 1953, pp. 45–68.
2 Kenneth Burke, *A Grammar of Motives*, New York, Prentice-Hall, 1945, p. 283.
3 Paul Zimmerman and Burt Goldblatt, *The Marx Brothers at the Movies*, New York, G. P. Putnam's Sons, 1968, pp. 103, 124.
4 David Cole, *The Theatrical Event*, Middletown, Ct., Wesleyan University Press, 1975. See Chapter 2, "The Actor," pp. 12–57, for his discussion of the "actor-as-shaman."
5 Michael Goldman, *The Actor's Freedom: Toward a Theory of Drama*, New York, Viking Press, 1975, p. 7ff.
6 See William Hooker Gillette, "The Illusion of the First Time in Acting," in Toby Cole and Helen Krich Chinoy (eds), *Actors on Acting*, New Revised Edition, New York, Crown Publishers, 1970, pp. 564–7.
7 Lee Johnson, "The 'Raft of the Medusa' in Great Britain," *Burlington Magazine*, 6 August 1954, p. 251.
8 David C. Huntington, *The Landscapes of Frederick E. Church*, New York, George Braziller, 1966, p. 5.
9 Osmond Ouua Enekwe, "Igbo Masks: The Oneness of Ritual and Theatre," unpublished Ph.D. dissertation, Columbia University, 1982, Chapter 4.
10 Charles and Louise Samuels, *Once Upon a Stage*, New York, Dodd, Mead and Company, 1974, pp. 243–5.
11 Arthur R. Blumenthal, *Theatre Art of the Medici*, Catalog of Dartmouth

College Museum and Galleries, Hanover, N.H., University Press of New England, 1980, p. 57.

12 Spencer Golub, *Evreinov: The Theatre of Paradox and Transformation*, Ann Arbor, Mich., UMI Research Press, 1984, pp. 191–202.

13 Victor Shlovsky, "Art as Technique," in *Russian Formalist Criticism: Four Essays*, translated and introduced by Lee T. Lemon and Marion J. Reis, Lincoln, Nebr., University of Nebraska Press, 1965, pp. 12–13.

14 Tennessee Williams, *The Glass Menagerie*, New York, New Directions, 1970, p. 22.

2 Imitation and presentation

1 See "The Life and Death of Vaudeville," Chapter 14 in Fred Allen's stage autobiography *Much Ado About Me*, Boston, Mass., and Toronto, Little, Brown, 1956, pp. 236–57.

2 Joseph Laurie, *Vaudeville: From the Honky-Tonks to the Palace*, New York, Henry Holt and Company, 1953, pp. 29–31.

3 Theatre Collection, New York Public Library at Lincoln Center, Vaudeville, U.S. Clippings 1911–1920, B. F. Keith's Palace Theatre program, 8 December 1913.

4 Richard D. Altick, *The Shows of London*, Cambridge, Mass., and London, The Belknap Press of Harvard University Press, 1978, Chapters 3 to 34.

5 Harry Blackstone, Jr., with Charles and Regina Reynolds, *The Blackstone Book of Magic and Illusion*, New York, Newmarket Press, 1985, p. 47.

6 Milbourne Christopher, *The Illustrated History of Magic*, New York, Thomas Y. Crowell Company, 1973, p. 268.

7 ibid.

8 Theatre Collection, New York Public Library at Lincoln Center, Vaudeville, U.S. Programs 1900–1910. For *The Orpheum* [Brooklyn], week beginning Monday matinee, 19 February 1906.

9 *The Christian Science Monitor*, 14 January 1961.

10 *The New York Herald Tribune*, 10 January 1961.

11 Thomas R. Dash, *Women's Wear Daily*, 10 January 1961.

12 *The New York Herald Tribune*, 15 January 1961.

13 Pierre Louis Ducharte, *The Italian Comedy*, translated by Randolph T. Weaver, New York, Dover Publishers, 1966, p. 55.

14 The full title of this play by Peter Weiss is: *The Persecution and Assassination of Jean-Paul Marat As Performed by the Inmates of the Asylum of Charenton Under the Direction of the Marquis de Sade.*

3 Iconic presentation

1 See David M. Bergeron, *English Civic Pageantry, 1558–1642*, Columbia, S.C., University of South Carolina Press, 1971, pp. 75–83; G. P. V. Akrigg, *Jacobean Pageant*, Cambridge, Mass., Harvard University Press, 1962, pp. 30–3; and Robert Withington, *English*

Pageantry, Volume One, Cambridge, Mass., Harvard University Press, 1918, pp. 224–5.

2 See E. K. Chambers, *The Medieval Stage*, II, England, Oxford University Press, 1903, pp. 12–14; Joseph Quincey Adams (ed.), *Chief Pre-Shakespearean Drama*, Boston, Mass., Houghton Mifflin, 1924, pp. 9–10; and V. A. Kolve, *The Play Called Corpus Christi*, Stanford, Ca., Stanford University Press, 1966, pp. 5–6.

3 Jean Genet, "The Strange Word *Urb* . . .," in *Reflections on the Theatre and Other Writings*, London, Faber and Faber, 1972, pp. 63–74.

4 Dialectic presentation

1 Mae Noell, "Recollections of Medicine Show Life," in Myron Matlaw (ed.), *American Popular Entertainment*, Westport, Ct., and London, Greenwood Press, 1979, pp. 215–25.

2 Susanne K. Langer, *Feeling and Form: A Theory of Art*, New York, Charles Scribner's Sons, 1953, pp. 306–25.

3 Richard J. Quinones, *The Renaissance Discovery of Time*, Cambridge, Mass., Harvard University Press, 1972, p. 3.

4 For the principal documents concerning this controversy see Bernard F. Dukore, *Dramatic Theory and Criticism: Greeks to Grotowski*, New York, Holt, Rinehart and Winston, 1974, pp. 211–26.

5 The most easily accessible French edition of Diderot's writings on theatre is *Oeuvres Esthétiques*, edited by Paul Vernière, Paris, Editions Garnier Frères, 1968. In English there is Diderot's "The Paradox of Acting," translated by Walter Herries Pollock, published together with "Masks or Faces?" by William Archer, New York, Hill and Wang, 1957.

6 Richard Southern, *The Seven Ages of the Theatre*, New York, Hill and Wang, 1961, pp. 35–82.

7 Richard Fawkes, *Dion Boucicault: A Biography*, London, Melbourne, and New York, Quartet Books, 1979, pp. 263–4.

8 See *London Times*, 12 November 1889, and Raymond Fitzsimmons, *Barnum in London*, New York, St. Martin's Press, 1970, p. 168.

5 Act and audience

1 Northrop Frye, *Anatomy of Criticism: Four Essays*, Princeton, Princeton University Press, 1957, pp. 163–86.

6 Act and show

1 David M. Bergeron, *English Civic Pageantry, 1558–1642*, Columbia, S.C., University of South Carolina Press, 1971, pp. 30–5.

7 The act-scheme and the act-image

1 Gerald Else, *Aristotle's Poetics: The Argument*, Cambridge, Mass., Harvard University Press, 1957, p. 322.

2 Richard Southern, *The Seven Ages of the Theatre*, New York, Hill and Wang, 1961, pp. 19–82.
3 V. A. Kolve, *The Play Called Corpus Christi*, Stanford, Ca., Stanford University Press, 1966.

8 Actor to audience

1 All quotations from Shakespeare in this book are taken from Alfred Harbage (ed.), *The Complete Pelican Shakespeare*, Baltimore, Md., Penguin, 1969. This edition also contains an essay on "Shakespeare's Theatre" by Bernard Beckerman, pp. 21–9.
2 Sam Shepard, *Angel City*, in *Fool For Love and Other Plays*, New York, Bantam Books, 1984, p. 77.

9 Actor to actor

1 Susanne K. Langer, *Feeling and Form: A Theory of Art*, New York, Charles Scribner's Sons, 1953, pp. 306–25.
2 Charles Kean, F.S.A., [Boucicault] *The Corsican Brothers*, first performed 24 February 1852, and privately printed, London, John K. Chapman and Co., p. 27.
3 Bert O. States, *Irony and Drama: A Poetics*, Ithaca, N.Y., and London, Cornell University Press, 1971, pp. 17–35 and 195–221.
4 Lehman Engel, *The Making of a Musical*, New York, Macmillan, 1977, pp. 68–9.
5 Bernard Beckerman, *Dynamics of Drama: Theory and Method of Analysis*, New York, Alfred A. Knopf, 1970, pp. 210–21.

10 Actor and actors

1 V. Propp, *Morphology of the Folktale*, translated by Laurence Scott, Austin, Tex., and London, University of Texas Press, 1968, pp. 3–24.
2 Niccolò Machiavelli, *The Comedies of Machiavelli*, edited and translated by David Sices and James B. Atkinson, Hanover, N.H., and London, University Press of New England, 1985, pp. 173–5.
3 "Shakespeare's Dramaturgy and Binary Form," *Theatre Journal*, vol. 33 (March 1981), pp. 5–17.
4 Mark Rose, *Shakespearean Design*, Cambridge, Mass., The Belknap Press of Harvard University Press, 1972, p. 37.
5 Curtis Bill Pepper, "Talking with Olivier," *The New York Times Magazine*, 25 March 1979, p. 60.
6 Bertolt Brecht, *Collected Plays*, Volume Seven, edited by Ralph Manheim and John Willett, New York, Random House, 1974, p. 316.

11 Beyond binary action

1 Whitney J. Oates and Eugene O'Neill, Jr. (eds), *The Complete Greek Tragedies*, Volume One, New York, Random House, 1938, p. 734.
2 "Sex Roles and Shamans," in Helen Krich Chinoy and Linda Walsh

Jenkins (eds), *Women in American Theatre*, New York, Crown, 1981, pp. 12–18.
3 Osmond Ouua Enekwe, "Igbo Masks: The Oneness of Ritual and Theatre," unpublished Ph.D. dissertation, Columbia University, 1982, Chapter 4.
4 *An Enemy of the People*, in *Ibsen*, Volume Six, translated and edited by James Walter McFarlane, London, New York, Toronto, Oxford University Press, 1960, p. 88.

Index

Abbott, George 195
Abe Lincoln in Illinois (Sherwood)
    143
acrobatics 30–1, 56, 64
act: audience and *see* audience and
    act; length of show 88–90;
    performance and 11–20;
    -performer autonomy 4–11;
    show and *see* show and act;
    vaudevillian 23–5
act-image 31, 36; act-scheme
    relation 101–9; double display
    38–42
act-scheme 6; act-image
    relationship 101–9; acts of
    glorification 28–30; acts of
    illusion 31–8; acts of skill 28,
    30–1; double display 38–42
action (structures): active structure
    137–45; balanced structure
    142–5; non-active structure
    141–2, 143–5
action-time 132
active and reflective songs 141–2
active structure 137–45
actor 6–7, 10–11; as character
    110–12, 125–7; *see also* audience,
    actor to
actor to actor: active structure
    137–45; allow for control
    130–31; central to drama 128–9;
    dramatist-actor relationship 131;
    energy to control 132–5; energy

projection 129–30; persuasion
    model 135–8
actor and actors: binary mode
    146–56; duets 156–66; context
    160–2
Aeschylus 147, 187; *Agamemnon*
    123, 148; *Choephori* 148, 149;
    Prometheus Bound 148; *The
    Suppliants* 108
agency, performer and 4–5
agit-prop drama 50, 81
agon 129
Albee, Edward 153
Alberti, L. B., xii–xiii, 137
alienation 52, 125
Allen, Fred 23
alter ego 21, 188, 194
Altick, Richard D. 24
Amadeus 115, 116, 127
American Society for Theatre
    Research 60
analogue 8, 9–10
animal acts 24–5
anti-masque 95
antiquarianism 177
appearance 33–4, 107
architecture (role) 19, 68
Aristophanes: *The Birds* 116; *Peace*
    148, 149; *The Wasps* 149
Aristotle 51, 66, 86, 88, 91, 92, 96,
    98, 109, 136; *Poetics* 92, 147
art: notable triumph of 51;
    socialization of 12–13